THE PRESBYTERIAN MINISTRY
IN AMERICAN CULTURE

PRESBYTERIAN HISTORICAL SOCIETY

STUDIES IN PRESBYTERIAN HISTORY

Published by The Westminster Press

The Presbyterian Enterprise: Sources of American Presbyterian History, edited by Maurice W. Armstrong, Lefferts A. Loetscher, and Charles A. Anderson

The Presbyterian Ministry in American Culture: A Study in Changing Concepts, 1700–1900, by Elwyn A. Smith

Published by Pennsylvania State University Press

The Journals of the Reverend Charles Beatty, 1762–1769, edited by Guy S. Klett

To Be Published by The Yale University Press

Hoosier Zion: A Study of Presbyterians in Indiana to 1850, by L. C. Rudolph

The
PRESBYTERIAN MINISTRY
in
AMERICAN CULTURE

A Study in Changing Concepts, 1700–1900

ELWYN ALLEN SMITH

Published for the Presbyterian Historical Society
by
THE WESTMINSTER PRESS
Philadelphia

LIBRARY OF CONGRESS CATALOG CARD NO. 62–16251

PRINTED IN THE UNITED STATES OF AMERICA

IN MEMORIAM

H. FRAMER SMITH

CONTENTS

PREFACE

WE ACKNOWLEDGE with gratitude the assistance of a number of persons who have submitted to close questioning or given time to criticism of this manuscript: Rev. Hermann N. Morse, former General Secretary of the Board of National Missions of the Presbyterian Church in the United States of America; Rev. Thomas Goslin, of Doylestown, Pennsylvania; Profs. Maurice Armstrong and Lefferts Loetscher, respectively of Ursinus College and Princeton Theological Seminary.

Dr. Clifford E. Barbour, President of the Pittsburgh Theological Seminary, has proved himself a good friend of his writing scholars. The tedium of the typewriter has been cheerfully endured by Mrs. Warren Eakin. The wives of men whose writing efforts preempt their minds will be the first to understand my debt to my wife, Malvine.

E. A. S.

ABBREVIATIONS

BRPR   *The Biblical Repertory and Princeton Review.* Called first the *Biblical Repertory* (1825), then *The Biblical Repertory and Princeton Review* until 1872, when it was titled *The Presbyterian Quarterly and Princeton Review* (1872–1877), *The Princeton Review* (1878–1884), and *The New Princeton Review* (1886–1888).

CH   *Church History,* published by the American Society of Church History.

E   *American Bibliography,* by Charles Evans.

HSP   The Historical Society of Pennsylvania.

JPHS   *The Journal of the Presbyterian Historical Society.*

LCP   The Library Company of Philadelphia.

LW   *Luther's Works,* 55 vols., edited by J. Pelikan and H. T. Lehmann. Muhlenberg Press and Concordia Publishing House.

MGA   *The Minutes of the General Assembly of the Presbyterian Church in the United States of America,* unless otherwise specified.

PHS   Library of the Presbyterian Historical Society.

PR   *Princeton Review.*   See above, *BRPR.*

PSL   Princeton Theological Seminary Library, Princeton, N. J.

Spr.   Sprague Collection.

SPR   *The Southern Presbyterian Review.*   Published at Columbia, S. C., 1847–1888.

ST   *Systematic Theology,* by Charles Hodge, 3 vols.   (New York, 1872–1873).

I

THE MINISTRY OF THE CHURCH

THE CONTEMPORARY CHURCH is confused about the nature of the ministry," wrote Prof. H. Richard Niebuhr. "Neither ministers nor the schools that nurture them are guided today by a clear-cut, generally accepted conception of the office of the ministry." [1]

There have been eras in church history when there existed a general consensus about the nature and work of the ministry, but it is the peculiarity of modern times that the decision as to what belongs at the center of a minister's work and what is marginal is increasingly difficult to make. " The average minister actually does so many different things varying widely in conscious spiritual meaning and is subject to so many different pressures that it is all but impossible to develop a feeling of his total ministry as a unified spiritual experience," observes a recent report of the United Presbyterian Council on Theological Education. " This simply means that both minister and church are burdened with the necessity of maintaining an institution and operating a program the deeper spiritual meaning of which may be easily obscured." [2]

[1] H. Richard Niebuhr, *The Purpose of the Church and Its Ministry* (Harper & Brothers, 1956), 50.
[2] *The United Presbyterian Enterprise of Theological Education* (a report prepared for the Council on Theological Education of The United Presbyterian Church in the United States of America by its General Survey Committee, 1959–1960), 1.

The problem is not that the demands of the American parish are vague. Prof. Samuel Blizzard's study of the use of time by the ministers of 690 churches showed that quite definite patterns of work impose themselves. "Almost two-fifths of their total workday was spent on administration," reports Blizzard. "Slightly more than one-fourth was devoted to the pastor role. . . . Preaching and priestly activities took up almost one-fifth of the workday. Organizing consumed more than one-tenth of the workday. The residual time (about one-twentieth) was devoted to teaching." [3] The problem is whether the work that clergymen are doing is the ministry.

The Relation of Church and Ministry

The vexation of the modern minister rises out of a prolonged movement from the reasonably specific views of the ministry that existed at the Reformation through an era of rapid change in both church and society until at the present time American Protestants find that they lack a consensus not only on the nature of the ministry but on the nature of the church itself.

Of cardinal importance for understanding this evolution is the fundamental point on which the Reformation, both Lutheran and Calvinist, agreed: God called the church into existence in order to perform his own service. The church's existence is inseparable from its function. God has appointed other services: that of civil government, for example, whose rulers "have been ordained ministers of divine justice," as John Calvin put it. [4] But the ministry of the Word, the announcement of the gospel of forgiveness, is peculiar to the church.

[3] Samuel Blizzard, " The Minister's Dilemma," The Christian Century, April 25, 1956.

[4] John Calvin, Calvin: Institutes of the Christian Religion (Library of Christian Classics, Vols. 20 and 21), edited by John T. McNeill; translated and indexed by Ford Lewis Battles (The Westminster Press, 1960), IV. xx. 6. Cf. LW, Vol. 35, " Preface to the Prophet Daniel," Word and Sacrament I, edited by E. T. Bachman and H. T. Lehmann (The Muhlenberg Press, 1960), 298.

So intimately united are church and ministry that it is impossible to speak of the ministry in the Reformation tradition without understanding the character of the church. The church, wrote Martin Luther, " was born by the word of promise through faith and by this same word is nourished and preserved." [5] The Word is not only the work of the church but its source as well. " The church comes into being because God's Word is spoken," stated Luther. " The church does not constitute the Word but is constituted by the Word. A sure sign, by which we may know where the church is, is the Word of God." [6] Calvin's summary statement of the matter is the most familiar. " Wherever we see the Word of God purely preached and heard, and the sacraments administered according to Christ's institution," he wrote in the *Institutes*, " there, it is not to be doubted, a church of God exists." [7]

The Word, however, is not a " living voice " until it is preached: that is, until the church becomes the minister of the Word. It must also be said, therefore, that we do not know the church until we encounter the ministry. For the Reformers, preaching articulated the Word; and preaching is a function of duly authorized officers of the church. Word, church, and ministry are one; none is found apart from the other. " It is by the faith in the gospel that Christ becomes ours . . . ," wrote Calvin. " In order that the preaching of the gospel might flourish, he deposited this treasure in the church. He instituted ' pastors and teachers ' through whose lips he might teach his own; he furnished them with authority; finally, he omitted nothing that might make for holy agreement of faith and for right order." [8] In the order of human experience, a man knows he is in Christ's church when he hears the Word from a faithful preacher.

Nevertheless, the ministry is not first of all a task of clergy-

[5] Martin Luther, " The Babylonian Captivity of the Church," *Word and Sacrament II*, edited by Abdel Ross Wentz (The Muhlenberg Press, 1959), 107.
[6] Luther, " The Misuse of the Mass," *Word and Sacrament II*, 145.
[7] Calvin, *Institutes*, IV. i. 9.
[8] *Ibid.*, IV. i. 1.

men but of all Christians alike. " The ministry of the Word is the highest office in the church," affirmed Luther. " It is unique and belongs to all who are Christians, not only by right but by command." [9] To be a Christian is to be a minister: " All of us that have been baptized are equally priests." [10] Calvin accepted Luther's teaching on the priesthood of Christian individuals but applied it primarily to the priestly character of the church itself. Of the communion of the saints, for example, he said: " This clause . . . very well expresses what the church is. It is as if one said that the saints are gathered into the society of Christ on the principle that whatever benefits God confers upon them, they should in turn share with one another." [11] As minister of the gospel, the visible church is the " mother of believers."

We do the Reformed conception of the relation of church and ministry no injustice to assert that as God is made known in his Word, so the truth of the church appears in its ministry. The ministry voices the very being of the church. It follows that the actual ministry of the church in a historical period reveals what the church is in that era. To Reformed thought as to the historian, it is artificial and misleading to argue that the church " is " something which is distinct from its actual practice of ministry. What the church *is* may be seen in what it does. The acid test of performance was imposed by the Reformers.

The Work of Ministers

What, then, is the ministry of the church?

Most conspicuously, it is what ministers do. To be sure, the ministry of the church belongs to all Christians; but the whole body of believers customarily appoints special officers to per-

[9] Luther, " Concerning the Ministry," *LW*, Vol. 40, 23.
[10] Luther, " Babylonian Captivity," *loc. cit.*, 112. " A Christian, thus is born to the ministry of the Word in baptism." " Concerning the Ministry," *LW*, Vol. 40, 37.
[11] Calvin, *Institutes*, IV. i. 3.

form some of its ministerial duties on its behalf.

"Priests, as we call them," wrote Luther, "are ministers chosen from among us. All that they do is done in our name; the priesthood is nothing but a ministry. From this it follows that whoever does not preach the Word . . . is no priest at all and that the sacrament of ordination can be nothing else than a certain rite by which the church chooses its preachers." [12] If the history of the ministry of the Reformation churches is largely written in the work and thought of its ministerial officers, they did not at the outset comprise a professional fraternity distinct from the church, even though within it.

Among Calvinists, the ministry has always demanded that clergymen preach, administer the sacraments, teach the young, visit the sick, and share in the government and discipline of the church. But what ministers have intended to accomplish as they carried out the traditional duties of their profession, what they have believed to be true of their work in the whole pattern of church ministry that includes all particular functions, is not always apparent from a scrutiny of their daily work. Often it is not what they have done or even what they have been able to articulate in sermons and tracts that reveals the " deeper spiritual meaning " of their activity, but rather the assumptions they made about the character of the church and the means by which men know and describe and serve God. Ministry is a function; but until function is illuminated by the conviction that the church itself injects into the daily work of its ministers, it is all but impossible to answer the question: What is church ministry?

PURPOSE OF THIS STUDY

It is the purpose of this book to show how American Presbyterians, themselves only a part of a larger Calvinist community, have understood and performed their churchly duty of ministry. Throughout this inquiry, ministerial work is interpreted

[12] Luther, " Babylonian Captivity," *loc. cit.*, 113.

as an expression of the church's understanding of its service to God in the American environment.

Contemporary thought has reminded us that there is also a definable relationship of church and ministry to culture. The church does not live apart from culture but within it. The church does not create a special law to itself; its ministers in one way or another come to terms with culture. Early in their history, American Presbyterians recognized that culture penetrates church life and thought. Just as God's gifts of Word and Spirit to the church grant it a kinship with the divine, involvement with culture gives content to the humanity of the church. This study, therefore, attempts to describe the impact on Presbyterian and other Reformed ministerial personnel of cultural forces that clearly affected them.

Beyond and beneath both the daily work and the professed or inherent theology of ministerial officers lies the difficult question of the mentality of the church that produces them, what H. Richard Niebuhr termed "those strange tides in history called 'climates of opinion.'"[13] The emotional structure of any group determines *how* it believes what it professes. Climate, whether the revolutionary spirit of 1776 or the optimism of industrial expansion a century later, deeply affects a church and its ministry. So far as this elusive question can be brought to light, this study attempts to take account of cultural and ecclesiastical moods that formed the ways in which Presbyterian ministerial officers believed and behaved.

While the formal education of ministers is the product of the doctrine, conduct, and attitudes of a church body, theological seminaries also shape a church by their selection of professors and the mentality that campus life fosters in students. Although this study includes a summary history of the permanent Presbyterian seminaries, its primary interest in theological ed-

[13] H. Richard Niebuhr, "The Protestant Movement and Democracy in the United States," *The Shaping of American Religion*, Vol. I of *Religion in American Life*, edited by James Ward Smith and A. Leland Jamison (Princeton University Press, 1961), 21.

ucation is to discover the effect of its curriculum and piety on the clergy.

The center of these widening circles of investigation nevertheless remains constant: How have Presbyterians conceived and performed their duty of ministry? All discussion presented here, whether theological or philosophical, functional or demographic, is designed to explain the professional conduct and the rooted assumptions of those who undertook to fulfill American Presbyterianism's responsibility of ministry. This book is aimed at the persistent problem of Christian ministry in our times: the need to grasp more clearly the inner spiritual meaning of what churches and ministers do.

II

THE MINISTRY
OF THE FIRST PRESBYTERIANS

PRESBYTERIANISM was implanted in North America in pieces and parts as English Presbyterians took to the sea in hope of realizing in the New World a religious society that England apparently would not countenance. Scattered churches in New England and on Long Island, for example, were governed by elders and ordained their ministers in the Presbyterian manner,[1] and the men who formed the first continuing presbytery in 1706 were not the only ministers to associate themselves for mutual aid in the first generation of the eighteenth century. In South Carolina a presbytery was formed about 1722 and at least four Presbyterian ministers left writings concerned with the most troubled issue of the era — mandatory subscription by the clergy to the Westminster Confession of Faith.[2] Between 1714 and 1720 fifty-four ships bearing Irish immigrants landed at Boston. Scattered in the hinterland of New England, these Presbyterians also established the presbyteries of Londonderry, Grafton, and Boston.[3]

[1] Leonard J. Trinterud, *The Forming of an American Tradition* (The Westminster Press, 1949), 21 ff.
[2] Presbyterian clergymen from South Carolina whose writings may be found listed in the Evans *Bibliography* and in microtext reproduction in the American Antiquarian Society series are as follows: Hugh Fisher (E3279), Josiah Smith (E2813, E4076, E4600, E8039), and Hugh Alison (E15233). From the Presbytery of Grafton, New Hampshire: Asa Burton (E23243), Peter Powers (E16019), Thomas Fessenden (E17533), and Eleazer Wheelock (E15220).
[3] Henry J. Ford, *The Scotch-Irish in America* (Princeton, 1915), 221.

None of the beginnings outside the middle colonies had the tenacity to survive. The Presbytery of South Carolina disappeared after the Revolution; the members of the Presbytery of Londonderry were scattered by emigration from New England; and the Presbytery of Grafton was remote from any other concentration of Presbyterian churches, and its members drifted into the surrounding Congregational churches.[4] The significance of the association of ministers in Philadelphia lay in its power of survival and its steady progress toward specifically Presbyterian church government. It was the pastoral work, preaching, and writing of the men of the middle colonies that formed the theory and practice of the ministry of colonial Presbyterianism.

Who were the principal figures whose debates, writings, and activity first gave expression to the ministry of Presbyterians?

Francis Makemie, a member of the Presbytery of Laggan, Ireland, arrived in 1683 in response to an appeal from Irish settlers in Maryland, Virginia, and the Barbados.[5] He was licensed to preach in the latter islands but did not settle there, preferring to combine business activity with travel on the Atlantic coast. Makemie was an energetic man of sound practical judgment. He enjoyed the respect and support of Puritans in both England and New England, notably Increase Mather of Boston. In 1692, Makemie fell into controversy with George Keith, a Presbyterian turned Quaker who later joined the Church of England. From their writings we may obtain a view of some of the earliest concerns of American Presbyterians.

Jonathan Dickinson, pastor of the church at Elizabethtown, New Jersey, was the senior statesman of American Presbyterianism. In all his thought he was orderly and thorough, the best-structured mind of the first generation of Presbyterian clergy. He reflected much upon events and introduced a

---

[4] Charles A. Briggs, *American Presbyterianism, Its Origin and Early History* (Scribner, 1885), 337, 359.
[5] Trinterud, *op. cit.*, 29.

broad spectrum of theological and practical considerations in writing about them.

Gilbert Tennent, the key figure of the revival that began about 1729, was a man of fire who singed his friends while consuming his foes. He preached like a " Boatswain of a ship, calling the Sailors to come to Prayers and be damned," as a New Englander once described him; [6] but he handled the common heads of orthodoxy competently. Beyond these personalities, a number of others also contributed to the forming of the ministry of Presbyterianism's earliest generation.

What occupied the minds of these men? What did "ministry" mean to them?

THE AUTHORITY AND PARITY OF THE MINISTRY

The writings of the early presbyters were almost wholly controversial; the defense of their positions reveals as well as conceals their understanding of the ministry. In the course of defending the parity of the clergy against episcopacy, a dispute that has arisen persistently in Presbyterian history from its very outset, both Francis Makemie and Jonathan Dickinson enunciated views that closely corresponded to the thought of John Calvin.

Makemie, pastor of the church at Rehoboth, Maryland, replied to the attack of the Quaker, George Keith, in a treatise published at Boston in 1694–1695: *An Answer to George Keith's Libel Against a Catechism* of his own composition. Keith's pamphlet had contained two points particularly significant for a Reformed ministry: his doctrine of the Holy Spirit and the charge that the Presbyterian clergy " go to the Church and Pope of Rome by that dirty channel and conduit to have their call conveyed to them." [7] The first of these touched broadly on the fundamental theological question of man's

---

[6] Perry Miller, *Jonathan Edwards* (William Sloane Associates, Inc., 1949), 116.

[7] Francis Makemie, *An Answer to George Keith's Libel* (Boston, 1694), E693, 17.

knowledge of God. There was, in Keith's view, a "word of God in people"; the divine Word is by no means limited to the Scriptures alone. The content of preaching, therefore, is not wooden doctrinal exposition but an account of the minister's own "spiritual experiences." The call is an assertion of the divine Word within the minister, qualifying him to instruct others out of his immediate grasp of the divine. Makemie erred, argued Keith, in that "he doth not inform people that none are true ministers of Christ but such as are really Holy and Godly men and have a living experience of the work and dealings of God's Spirit in their hearts." These alone are called and "furnished by the Spirit of Christ in the work of their ministry to preach and pray." [8] In such a perspective, the ministry could only be impoverished by narrow confinement to the Bible.

The practical mentality of Makemie appears in his selection of a line of defense. He did not hold up to view the mischievous consequences for theology and church order of abandoning all contact with the Bible in favor of mystical individualism, as the sixteenth-century Reformers had done. Instead, he denied that he lacked spiritual experiences and described "a work of grace and conversion wrought on my heart at fifteen years of age by and from the principles of a godly schoolmaster." He cited the sufferings of the Scottish clergy, much in the minds of Scottish Americans at that date, to vindicate the spirituality of the clergy. But the Calvinist sense for church order was there: to his inward experience of grace was added a "Scriptural and orderly separation unto my Holy and ministerial calling" by the hands of presbyters. Because Keith's criticism was directed at a catechism, Makemie was at pains to vindicate education. "I am persuaded Quakers should not have so great success in drawing aside silly souls from the truth and ways of God if it were not for the abounding ignorance of Virginia and other dark corners of the world." [9]

In response to the charge that Presbyterian ordination goes

[8] *Ibid.*, 16.   [9] *Ibid.*, 24.

back to the Roman succession, he remarked that his calling and commission came from " Jesus Christ and [was] warranted from the Scripture," [10] not the pope. He introduced the familiar distinction between the extraordinary spiritual manifestations of the apostolic age and the ordinary forms, such as the laying on of hands for ordination, required for a valid ministry. After attacking Keith for teaching Quakerism in publicly supported schools, a complaint of the Scotch-Irish of Pennsylvania, he concluded with a general indictment of antisacramentalism.

At the other extreme of the debate, Jonathan Dickinson of Elizabethtown, New Jersey, advanced the principal argument of the American Reformed community against episcopacy: the parity of the ministry. The mooted point was the meaning of the predicate " apostolic." The apostles exercised ordinary offices with extraordinary gifts, said Dickinson. They alone could testify to personal encounter with Jesus and they did miraculous works by direct Christly authority. By their very nature, these functions cannot be performed by an ecclesiastical succession. " Ordinary " functions may be performed by any ordained person: " preaching the gospel, dispensing the sacraments, ordaining others to the work of the ministry; and governing the church." [11] Christ's command to the apostles, as regarded these offices, was no different from his command to all who perform them. " All ministers of the Gospel are authorized by the same commission. . . . It necessarily follows that they have all the same office and authority."

Anglicanism's claim to the priestly function, in Dickinson's view, was groundless. Christ totally fulfilled the office of the High Priest by offering final sacrifice. The perpetual apostolate could be nothing but a false claim to possession of the gifts of the apostles themselves. " The plain truth of the business is that the apostolate was a temporary office calculated only for the infant state of the church. . . . The ordinary office of pastor and teacher [is] only to continue until we all come

[10] *Ibid.*, 26.   [11] *Ibid.*, 72.

into the unity of the faith. . . . The apostolic office was extraordinary and admitted no succession." [12] A bishop was not superior to a presbyter; these were two names for one office and authority in the church.

The extraordinary gifts of the Spirit of the earliest age of the church came upon laymen as well as the preachers.[13] They gave no one authority over his brother but, rather, "power and authority over devils; by this we are excited to love God; . . . by this our minds are led, with the most rational conviction, to embrace the gospel." Bishops (presbyters) acting together perpetuated the ministry after the apostles died, and this right and commission to ordain survives in presbyteries. All this, Dickinson set over against "prelatical government." Although Dickinson believed that the apostolic charism was given to "laymen," the general view of New England reformed thought was that in some sense the minister's status was special. This was usually attributed to his particular call, education, and the sacredness of the Word and sacraments. Dickinson's thought virtually reproduced Calvin's.

LOCAL CHURCH ORDER

In its riposte to the Church of England, Reformed America was substantially agreed; but this did not mean that Presbyterians had defined their views of ordination and church order in a distinctive or even altogether clear way. The actualities of the period are exhibited in the history of the First Presbyterian Church in New York.

This congregation was founded by a nucleus of Presbyterians

12 Jonathan Dickinson, A Defense of Presbyterian Ordination, 15.
13 Ibid., 25. Cf. the controversy with episcopal church government continued into the nineteenth century. Jonathan Dickinson wrote several substantial essays after the revival began: The Scripture Bishop; The Reasonableness of Non-Conformity; A Defense of Presbyterian Ordination (Boston, 1724), E2525; The Vanity of Human Institutions in the Worship of God (Newark, 1736), E4010. Samuel Miller, professor of church history at Princeton Theological Seminary, engaged in a voluminous exchange of essays and letters with episcopal apologists.

to whom Francis Makemie first preached on the notable occasion of his detention by Lord Cornbury in 1707. In 1716 a congregation formed, and a church was built on Wall Street in 1718. In 1722 there was dispute between those who favored the " Scottish model " and others who had " been accustomed to the less rigid habits of the Presbyterian and Congregational churches of South Britain [and] were not pleased with the strict Presbyterianism " of their first pastor, James Anderson.[14] The Puritan-minded minority was briefly supplied by Jonathan Edwards but was financially unable to continue and rejoined the Scots. In 1727 a young licentiate, Ebenezer Pemberton, was called. He returned to Boston to be ordained " with a special view to his taking charge of the church in New York, by the association which had licensed him." Congregational ordination was accepted without protest by the Scots. In the troubles that led up to Pemberton's departure in 1753, the propriety of his ordination was apparently never questioned, although the quarrel hinged on differences between Scottish practice and the New English manners of Pemberton and his associate. Similarly, the enthusiasm of the Scottish members of the congregation for Joseph Bellamy, a Congregationalist who refused an invitation to succeed Pemberton, was not diluted by any doubts about his ordination or churchmanship.[15]

Anglican political pressure prevented the church from obtaining a charter, so the congregation affiliated with the Church of Scotland and elected trustees to take responsibility for the property. Pemberton welcomed Whitefield in 1740 — the only pulpit open to him in New York — and Whitefield returned twice during Pemberton's tenure. The Scots and Irish were as pleased as any with the effects of the Awakening upon their church.

[14] Samuel Miller, *Memoir of the Rev. John Rodgers* (New York, 1813), 136.
[15] Richard Webster, *A History of the Presbyterian Church in America . . . until 1760* (Philadelphia, 1857), 631. Cf. Letter of Jos. Bellamy to the Presbytery of New York. HSP, Gratz, New England Clergy. Cf. Ford, *op. cit.*, 363 ff.

The congregation had elected deacons but not ruling elders in the Presbyterian pattern and was governed rather by the trustees and deacons jointly. Scottish members now charged undue interference in the spiritual affairs of the church by trustees, and the problem was compounded by rising sentiment for relief from the "old Scotch version" of Rouse's psalmody. Watts's version was introduced despite opposition from the Scottish minority, which appealed to the Presbytery of New York in 1752. In reference to this situation the Synod issued a directive: the church was promptly to elect ruling elders to assume governmental and disciplinary powers but the use of Watts was granted as the preference of the majority. The Scots, now a minority, continued their campaign by attacking the ministers, who had concurred with the majority and the two superior judicatories. Cummings, the assistant, pleaded poor health and was released. Pemberton positively refused to continue despite Presbytery's urgings, and the church got nothing but refusals from men who knew only too well the reputation of the dissident handful. When the Synod stood firm, the Scottish-minded group withdrew and five years later obtained the services of the very able John Mitchell Mason.

The incident illustrates the fluid condition of Presbyterian order at mid-eighteenth century in such essentials as ordination, congregational organization, and even the rights and functions of higher judicatories. The precise terms of American Presbyterian churchmanship were hammered out through debate; they were not modeled on an ideal, either Biblical or Scottish. It was the misfortune of American Presbyterians that this discussion had to be conducted at a time when other provocations were exciting and dividing the church.

PREACHING AND PIETY

Before the outbreak of the Awakening in New Jersey, Jonathan Dickinson was troubled by the apparent ineffectiveness of the colonial clergy and was becoming increasingly concerned with the general state of religion. It was a long journey, however, from the frame of mind of the church at the time he was ordained in 1709 to his decision in 1745 to make common cause with the revival. The conventional view of the ministry at the earlier date was described at Dickinson's own ordination by Joseph Morgan.

For Morgan, faith was the end product of preaching, and "faith according to truth operates upon the will and works a change in the person in whom it is." Thus the preaching task overshadowed all others. Not that preaching was made effective by being "varnished with excellent words": "the outward means is to be used only because of [God's] appointment and institution" and derives power only from "the blessing of God." Preaching was also teaching, for "wholesome doctrine" furnishes man "food or physic, according to the need." [16]

Morgan's New England training had taught him that a preacher must subordinate both self and style to the message. "The ears of the hearer being tickled with fine words has a tendency to divert their mind from the sense of the weight of the truth. Let plain, intelligible, significant words be used in religion." [17] To hear the gospel, a listener must digest a sermon; and to that end, the Sabbath should not be cluttered with discourses on other subjects, conversations, or "frolicks." The habit of visiting relatives on Sunday afternoon drowned reflection on the sermon in a flood of neighborly chatter.[18] The proper business of a Sunday afternoon was to instruct children at home so they might learn to repent through application of the sermon to their own lives.

Dickinson himself characterized the task of the Christian preacher-theologian innumerable times but never more clearly than in his *Familiar Letters* to "a Gentleman" troubled by

[16] Joseph Morgan, *Sermon Preached at the Ordination of Jonathan Dickinson*, September 29, 1709 (New York, 1712), 4.
[17] *Ibid.*, 15.
[18] *Ibid.*, 33.

many questions about revival, rationalist criticism, and Christian doctrine. The whole purpose of the ministry, affirmed Dickinson, is to produce a " true and saving faith " instead of a " dead faith." " A true and saving faith, is a realizing and sensible impression of the truth of the gospel: whereas a dead faith is but a mere notional and speculative belief of it. Faith is by the apostle described, the substance of things hoped for, and the evidence of things not seen: that which brings eternal things into a near view; and represents them unto the soul as undoubted realities. Whence it is, that the true believer, when he has experienced the defect of his own purposes and endeavours, when he is wearied out of all his false refuges, emptied of all hope in himself, and is brought to see and feel the danger and misery of his state by nature, he is then brought in earnest to look to Jesus, as the only refuge and safety of his soul. He then sees the incomparable excellency of a precious Saviour, breathes with ardent desire after him, repairs to him as the only foundation of his hope; and proportionably to the evidence of his interest in him, rejoices in Christ Jesus, having no confidence in the flesh. Now, the blessed Saviour and his glorious salvation is the subject of his serious, frequent, and delightful contemplation. . . .

" But now, on the other hand, if we take a view of the influence which a dead faith has upon the soul, it is visible that this usually leaves the subjects of it secure and careless, trifling and indifferent, in the concerns of the eternal world. These appear to such a person but distant futurities, which does not engage his solemn attention, and make him in earnest solicitous about the event; nor give any effectual check to his inordinate appetites and passions. Or if (as it sometimes happens) any awakening dispensation alarms the conscience of such a person, to a distressing apprehension of his guilt and danger, drives him to duties and external reformations, and makes him more careful and watchful in his conduct, he has yet no sensible impressive view of the way of salvation by Jesus Christ. . . .

"Here then you see an apparent difference between a true and a false faith. The one realizes the great truths of the gospel, by a lively and feeling discovery of them; giving the light of the knowledge of the glory of God in the face of Jesus Christ. The other gives but a lifeless and unactive assent to these important truths. The one influences the heart and affections, and by beholding with open face, as in a glass, the glory of the Lord, changes the soul into the same image, from glory to glory: the other only swims in the head, and leaves the heart in a state either of security or despondency. The one is an abiding principle of divine life, from which there flow rivers of living water: the other is transient and unsteady, and leaves the soul short of any spiritual principle of life and activity." [19]

Dickinson's description of the awakening of true faith, the central responsibility of the minister, reflects the burden of the Puritan mind. He is also at one with Luther. "There are two kinds of believing," wrote the German Reformer. "First, a believing about God, which means that I believe that what is said of God is true. This faith is rather a form of knowledge or observation than a faith. There is, secondly, a believing in God, which means that I put my trust in Him, give myself up to thinking that I transact with Him and believe without any doubt that He will be and do to me according to the things said of Him. Such faith, which throws itself on God, whether in life or in death, alone makes a Christian man." [20]

PRESBYTERIAN PIETY IN THE FIRST GENERATION

The concern of Dickinson for a faith of affection as well as assent was not unique to him. A great weight of colonial thought hung on the proposition that "heaven and hell are . . . in a strife about the souls of men." The long-standing distur-

---

[19] Jonathan Dickinson, *Familiar Letters to a Gentleman upon a Variety of Subjects in Religion* (Dundee, 1722), 80 f.

[20] Luther's exposition of the Second Main Article of the *Kurze Form.* Cf. Adolf Harnack, *Dogmengeschichte*, Part II, Book 3, "The Christianity of Luther."

bance of the colonial Calvinist clergy over the state of man and society was the power behind the coming Awakening. Satan was winning the battle. It was not only that the ministers most specifically affected by English Puritanism were sensitive moralists. Their fundamental interpretation of the meaning of life in America and the very structure of their theology rang the alarm. If we are to understand the profound transformation which the Great Awakening worked in the American Presbyterian ministry, it is essential to grasp its intellectual undergirding and recognize its power to produce a fresh understanding of the function of preaching and pastoral service.

All English-speaking Calvinism had long since been committed to a structure of theological thought that hinged on the " covenant ": a view that God had engaged to perform deeds indispensable to human welfare and that man owed reciprocal duty. There were important variations within this theology, most notably around the question of whether or not man must fulfill his part before God will consummate his own commitments.[21] But in all covenant thought, man is born into an identity of destiny with his first parent, Adam. The effect of this is catastrophic, since the sin of Adam has passed both sin and guilt to all newborn men. But God has offered another covenant established in Jesus Christ that creates the possibility of a saving identification of man with the " Second Adam " through faith.

The first critical point for a covenant ministry was this: in order to serve men, the preacher must expound the precise character and effects of man's bond with Adam. Sin flowing from that source must be surmounted if the purpose of the ministry, the salvation of man's soul, was to be accomplished. Second, the terms and nature of the new identity with Christ must be clearly grasped so that men may be correctly instructed in the way to engage themselves in the new covenant in Christ. Numerous intermediate issues are also very impor-

---

[21] The development of the conditional covenant is discussed by Leonard J. Trinterud, " The Origins of Puritanism," CH, XX, 37 ff.

tant to the working minister. By what precise method do men move from hardened neglect of the gospel to that state of mind and heart in which they are able and ready to act on God's invitation? What is the situation of the churchman who exhibits little evidence of the divine life within?

Preachers before the Awakening had clearly discerned the prevalent coldness and formality in church life but they had not yet found practical ways of breaking down the obstacles to a more significant religion. Yale, which trained seventeen of the first seventy-eight clergymen to serve the new Presbyterianism, was founded for the explicit purpose of renewing the obedience of New England to God. The full duty of the ancient covenant had been betrayed at Harvard. In 1723, Moses Noyes recalled to Judge Samuel Sewall, the moving spirit in the founding of Yale and an ever-faithful friend of Increase Mather, the motive for establishing the new school. "The first Movers for a College in Connecticut alledged this as a Reason, because the College at Cambridge was under the Tutorage of Latitudinarians." [22] In 1701, Sewall had provided that Yale students were to be instructed "as the late Reverend and Godly Learned Mr. Charles Chauncey was wont to do at Cambridge." [23]

The choice of Chauncey's administration as model for Yale was significant. At his death in 1672, both the practical fortunes of Harvard and the general social and intellectual life of New England were hastening toward change — mostly, in the view of the Yale founders, for the worse. By 1675, at the death of Leonard Hoard, successor to Chauncey, there remained but one student, and he no credit to it.[24] The decline of Harvard was partly the fault of the president; but the problems of the college reflected a drastic alteration in the self-consciousness of New England society. The old Puritan sense of duty to the

[22] F. B. Dexter, *Documentary History of Yale University* (New Haven, 1916), 242.

[23] *Ibid.*, 8.

[24] Samuel Eliot Morison, *Harvard College in the Seventeenth Century* (Harvard University Press, 1936), II, 408.

covenant was failing, and there was suffering in the souls of those who remembered God's blessings on the faithful founders whom he had spared from the sea and the savages. What had God's people done in return? They had surrendered to wealth and pleasure. Unless a new power of God were to break forth in a faithless land, judgment would surely come. Both history and theology testified to New England's ministers that it was a choice between a living faith and disaster. Cold consent would not do.

A MINISTRY OF NEW CONCERN

Dickinson's declaration that the purpose of the ministry was to "bring [man] in earnest to look to Jesus" was an enunciation of the Puritan tradition he had learned in New England. Presbyterianism was by no means strange to "awakening" preaching before the Great Awakening of the 1730's. Neither was there any sudden loss of interest in defending Calvinist doctrine and churchmanship against assailants like George Keith and the Church of England. But there was a shift of balance. The principal problem in the minds of Presbyterians ceased to be the danger of ideological defeat by Quakers and their ilk or Anglican-inspired repression.

The critical problem of the ministry was increasingly understood to be internal to the church. "The ordinance of the Gospel, and especially the preaching of it," said Joseph Morgan in 1709, "is that wherein men's salvation and damnation is concerned." [25] Either the clergy would press relentlessly for the decisive enlistment of their people on the side of Jesus Christ or they would surrender to other concerns, which could only create a serious risk of failure. This orienting conviction never disappeared from the revival movement. In 1752, Samuel Davies, a second-generation revivalist, put it bluntly to the Presbytery of Newcastle: "These are the great and noble and

[25] Preached at Elizabethtown, N. Y., September 29, 1709. Published at New York, 1712.

beneficent ends of our office: . . . To save perishing immortals from intolerable, irrecoverable, eternal ruin and misery and to bring them to a happy immortality." [26]

It is along these lines that the emerging difference between Old Side and New Side views of the ministry must be defined. Before the quarrel matured, men who later opposed one another joined in supporting strong measures of discipline for immoral clergymen, a manifest need of the time. As late as 1742, when the church lay broken, George Gillespie, an Old Side stalwart, granted that "the causes of this foresaid decay among many others I conceive to be . . . our admission of young men to the ministry without examination of them in soul experiences and a strict search into their actions, if holy and exemplary." [27]   Gillespie deplored the prevalent professionalism of the clergy and "our church rulers passing over the faults of one another without due and suitable censures." Such words might have been written by Gilbert Tennent himself. But as the Old Side fought its own dissolution, concern for moral standards diminished. The New Side men did not dispute the gravity of the threat to orthodox doctrine which so concerned the Old Side; but they believed that only an overwhelming show of strength in winning men from eternal fire could prevail against the Arminians. To awaken a moribund church would win the day. For this, a morally vigorous ministry was essential; so in the end, the New Side proved to be the more rigorous in discipline.

[26] *Literary and Evangelical Magazine,* John H. Rice, ed., IX (1826), 516 f.
[27] George Gillespie, *A Letter to the Reverend Brethren of the Presbytery of New York* (Philadelphia, 1742), 5.

III

THE AWAKENING OF THE MINISTRY

THE UNVARNISHED TRUTH in the second and third decades of the eighteenth century was that preaching, for all Morgan's earnestness and Dickinson's insight, was not getting results. Gilbert Tennent saw fault both in himself and in his congregation at New Brunswick, New Jersey. As with other historic personalities of the evangelical tradition, Tennent's personal experience was intrinsic to the development of the awakening of the Presbyterian ministry in the era of revival. To Thomas Prince, Jr., he wrote: " I began to be very much distressed about my want of success; for I knew not for half a year or more after I came to New Brunswick, that any one was converted by my labors, although several persons were at times affected transiently." During serious illness, continued Tennent, " I was then exceedingly grieved that I had done so little for God, and was very desirous to live one half year more . . . that I might . . . plead more faithfully for his cause, and take more earnest pains for the conversion of souls. . . ."[1]

Gilbert Tennent was no theorist and he was certainly not an eighteenth-century " organization man." He was sensitive, passionate, and individualistic. He was unusually objective in self-appraisal and candidly recognized failure in himself and others. He was aware that his commitment to the gospel and the ministry had larger implications than he had ever

[1] Trinterud, *The Forming of an American Tradition,* 56.

35

realized. Tennent had read the English Puritans who had taught five generations of English-speaking Calvinists the truth about the human soul and how to expose it. He seriously believed that God and Satan were locked in combat for the souls of men, and the smugness of the Presbyterians of New Jersey overwhelmed him. Tennent was deeply frustrated by his inability to excite in Presbyterians a livelier apprehension of their true state.

Gilbert Tennent's radicalism is incomprehensible apart from his familiarity with the mood of Puritan preaching. The Puritan talent for projecting vivid pictures of the soul appeared in the preaching of Henry Smyth (1554–1612). "If there be any hell in this world, they which feel the Worme of conscience gnaw upon their hearts, may truly say, that they have felt the torments of hell. Who can expresse that man's horror but himselfe? Sorrowes are met in his soule at a feast: and fear, thought, and anguish divide his soule between them. All the furies of hell leaps upon his heart like a stage. Thought calleth to Fear; Fear whistleth to Horrour; Horrour beckoneth to Despair, and saith Come and help me to torment the sinner; One saith, that she cometh from this sinne, and another saith, that she cometh from that sinne: so he goeth thorow a thousand deaths, and cannot die. Irons are laid upon his body like a prisoner. All his lights are put out at once: he hath no soul fit to be comforted. Thus he lies upon the racke, and saith that he beares the world upon his shoulders, and that no man suffereth that which he suffereth. So let him lye (saith God) without ease, untill he confesse and repent, and call for mercie. This is the godly way which the Serpent said would make you Gods, and made him a Devill." [2]

Such a troubled state of mind was remote from the experience of the solid Presbyterians of New Jersey. Encouraged by the " spiritual preaching " of the more mature Theodorus

---

[2] *Sermons*, 396. Quoted in William Haller, *Rise of Puritanism* (Columbia University Press, 1938), 33 f.

Frelinghuysen, a Dutch minister at New Brunswick, Tennent began to speak publicly and privately of the need for a far richer harvest of godliness among his people.

Tennent preached pointedly and personally. The conventional method, illustrated by Joseph Morgan, was to announce the Christian doctrine, explain it, and insist that it be pondered. Discipline awaited the inattentive and unresponsive. With all its rigidity, this preaching still expected Christian ideas to penetrate the soul of the hearer. But it was failing.

Tennent realized that the problem lay in the impersonality of preaching. Tennent began, in his own words, to go "among my people dealing with them plainly about their souls' state in their houses; examining them one by one as to their experiences, and telling natural people the danger of their state; and exhorting them that were totally secure, to seek convictions; and those that were convinced, to seek Jesus; and reproved pious people for their faults; and blessed be God, I have seen hopeful appearances of concern amongst a pretty many in the places I belong to." [3]

Pulpit dissertations against Anglican errors and expositions of the common heads of Calvinist theology seemed to Tennent precisely at fault. Men could agree and yet lack "convictions": that is, earnest personal persuasion that they themselves were affected by the work of Christ, capable of then leading them to testify to its significance for their own existence. "A minister may live long, may preach Truth, and nothing but Truth, as long as he Lives," wrote Samuel Finley, a later revivalist, "and yet do no real Service to the Souls of men; because he Preaches not those Truths which have a Tendency to answer the End of God's Glory, and Sinners Salvation." [4]

The enemy, for Tennent, lay within the Presbyterian Church, not in the Church of England or among the Quakers or even the Arminian meddlers with orthodoxy. It was the lukewarmness of baptized members whose profession of faith amounted

[3] Trinterud, *op. cit.*, 59 f.   [4] *Ibid.*, 60.

to little more than a formal adoption of correct Calvinism. Tennent saw that it amounted to nothing but works salvation to adhere dutifully to ideas which, like all good habits, men can be taught. For him the goal of the ministry was "the great necessity of a work of humiliation, or conviction, in order to a sound conversion." Failure to grasp this had led to a "presumptuous Security fatally introduc'd . . . for hereby they are induc'd to content themselves with a dead . . . Faith; instead of seeking after the Power and Life of Christianity."[5]

THE DOCTRINAL GROUNDWORK OF REVIVAL MINISTRY

Revival preaching and pastoral work were supported by a body of practical doctrine, and the Tennents were now accused of introducing novelties in theology as well as churchmanship. Later reflection was to assure even the Old Side that the quarrel did not involve material differences over Westminster doctrine; but at three points, there were distinguishable emphases in the doctrinal teaching of the two branches. All arose directly from practical questions: first, the New Side insistence on examination of the "spiritual experiences" of candidates for the ministry; second, the "call" to the ministry; third, in the words of John Thomson, an embittered opponent of Gilbert Tennent after 1740, the doctrine of "conversion and regeneration." Each of these is a facet of the theological problem of the knowledge of God; all converged upon the revival and its complex political undertones. Discussion of them was to determine the character of the ministry of American Presbyterianism in the eighteenth century.

All through the 1730's, the Old Side had been maneuvering for control of the Synod of Philadelphia. An action in 1736, taken in the absence of the New York (Dickinson) and New Brunswick (Tennent) groups, affirmed categorial subscription in place of the moderatism that had been agreed upon by the whole Synod in 1729. Hostility to the revival developed

[5] *Ibid.*, 57.

around a number of private or official conflicts in the presbyteries and in 1738 the Synod, again in the absence of the New York men, passed two acts aimed at the heart of the revival. One of them provided that the Synod should discountenance all preaching outside the bounds of the parish in which a minister might be serving. This would have put an end to the extension of the revival into parishes where Old Side ministers presided. Had these partisan acts prevailed, revival would have been quenched in Presbyterianism. Thus provoked, Gilbert Tennent brought his heaviest artillery to bear on the men and the views opposing him.

The most provocative document of the entire period of dispute now issued from Tennent's mouth and hand: *The Danger of an Unconverted Ministry*. He was brutal. He flatly ruled his opponents out of the Kingdom. Beyond the offense of his language was his assertion of the "new" doctrines that define the contribution of this troubled period to the developing Presbyterian conception of the ministry.

The enemies of the revival were "Pharisee-teachers" — and Tennent elaborated their shortcomings not only here but in other sermons. Their worst failing was that, quite simply, they were "unconverted." This word had the largest significance for Tennent. In his view there were two kinds of persons: "natural men," who have not received any gift of grace and in whom, therefore, no spiritual experience can be detected; and "gracious men," whose reception of grace is apparent because it has affected their actual experiences.

When Tennent spoke of "spiritual experience" he did not mean that a candidate or minister should adhere to the Westminster doctrine of the work of the Holy Spirit in the heart; he expected that, in any case. He meant that a minister was qualified in part by experiencing divine grace so concretely that it could be described, frequently by date and place. His antagonist, John Thomson, also deplored the moribund state of the church and favored a sanctified ministry: but all that was necessary, he contended, was that the candidate should sincerely hold the doctrine of the Spirit's work in the church. He need not be required to recount the effects of that work in himself.

Tennent was adamant on this point. The Puritan assumption that no work of grace, however secretly wrought, could fail of visible effects in the life of man was strong in him. Thomson's claim that all this was much too private for public investigation Tennent considered merely a screen for the introduction of "natural men" into the ministry. In his inflammatory sermon at Nottingham, he stated flatly that "natural men have no call of God to the ministerial work under the gospel dispensations." [6] Such are necessarily wicked. There is no halfway house between the grace and calling of conversion and the law-mindedness and evil of the natural state. Pharisee-teachers are "very proud and conceity . . . and ignorant of the new birth." The ministry of natural men is "uncomfortable to gracious souls, . . . their discourses are cold and sapless and, as it were, freeze between their lips." Lacking a work of grace, "they are neither inclined nor fitted for discoursing . . . pathetically." Applications of their sermons are "short, or indistinct and general; they difference not the precious from the vile." In confrontation with the carnal security of the people, they refuse to "thrust the nail of terror into sleeping souls" but rather "comfort people before they convince them" of sin. In the end they only "strengthen men's carnal security."

Several important theological points undergird these polemic assertions. Tennent himself was well aware of the relevance of the doctrines of law and grace to the problem of the ministry. Old Side preachers "do not distinguish between law and gospel," he charged. "They keep driving driving to duty, duty under this notion that it will recommend natural men to the favor of God." Such preaching did nothing to cause men to seek the "divine glory." Natural man abhors the "nature humbling doctrines" of original sin and justification by faith

[6] Gilbert Tennent, *The Danger of an Unconverted Ministry* (Boston, 1742), 2d ed., E5070, 5.

alone and will never cease striving to explain them away or
deny their truth. For this reason, the ministry of the Pharisee-
teachers was dangerous to orthodoxy.

"Is not the carnality of the ministry one great cause of the
general spread of Arminianism, Socinianism, Arianism, and
Deism?" demanded Tennent. It was particularly exasperat-
ing to Old Siders that Tennent should question their soundness.
True, they "prate a little more orthodoxly about the new birth"
than Nicodemus, said Tennent, but they know no more of it.

Any distinction between conversion and regeneration Tennent considered an empty rationalization. Only enemies of the
revival would argue that men could be regenerated *without*
being converted. To Tennent, conversion was simply the
visible face of regeneration. By historical acts and secret
counsels of mercy, God imputes the divine righteousness to
man and thus regenerates him. All this comes to issue in conversion — visible, recountable effects of grace. To separate
God's act and declaration from their impact on man's experience suited the enemies of an "awakening ministry" only
too well.

The Vocation of the Ministry

Out of its involvement with these two doctrinal problems —
law and grace, and regeneration and conversion — the call to
the ministry obtained large significance. Candidates for the
ministry were traditionally examined by presbyteries. The
second act which the Synod of 1738 had directed against the
revival had transferred this privilege to the Synod. It was
aimed at the custom in the Presbytery of New Brunswick of
examining young men to determine whether they were "gracious." At Nottingham, Tennent asserted flatly that no unconverted person could possibly be called to the ministry because
"our Lord will not make men ministers 'till they follow him."
Men may try to "make ministers" but "God sends not such
hypocritical varlets" into his own ministry.

Thomson answered by arguing that nothing in the Westminster position justified Tennent in declaring that the "in-

ward call " was the more critical, even though presbyteries expected candidates to be earnestly persuaded that they should become ministers. It was the " external call " of the church that was all-important. Thomson went so far as to assert that the action of the church is valid " even if the candidate is a hidden dissembling hypocrite." [7] " The truth of the matter in short is this," wrote Thomson; "whatever gives a person authority and lays an obligation upon him in the sight of God and man to preach the Gospel is the call of God to that work; but it's only the external call according to the Word that can do this." While he desired a sanctified ministry, this had nothing to do with calling proper, which was an ecclesiastical matter.

Tennent's position that God does not call anyone to the ministry who has no " inward experience " of grace is distinguishable from the idea that calling is itself wholly subjective. He affirmed full support for ecclesiastical processes in ordination. " We believe that there is a necessity of previous Tryals and ordination in order to the ministry; and that such who are regularly set apart . . . however their inward state may be, are true ministers in the sight of the church and that their ministrations are valid. But in the mean time we think that none should undertake the ministerial work but those that are truly gracious, . . . for we know not how a graceless man can be faithful in the ministry. Now whether those inward pious dispositions aforesaid are termed the inward call of God to the Gospel ministry or only qualifications necessary, or pre-requisite in the persons whom God calls, it seems to be the same in substance." [8]

---

[7] John Thomson, *An Examination and Confutation of Several Errors Relating to Conversion* (Philadelphia, 1741), 70.

[8] G. Tennent, *Remarks Upon a Protestation Presented to the Synod of Philadelphia*, June 1, 1741 (Philadelphia, 1741), E4820, 23. Further light on Tennent's insistence upon full theological education is contained in a letter to Stephen Williams, apparently written soon after a visit to New England. Tennent wrote: " You mentioned in your's of laymen being sent out to exhort and teach." In his response he clearly coupled ordination with personal calling and strongly advised against lay preaching. HSP, Gratz, Case 8, box 25.

The sting in the question of calling lay in Tennent's insistence that regardless of whether spiritual experience *is* the calling to the ministry or simply accompanies it, no man can be a minister of God without it. Samuel Finley regarded the experimental phase of calling as evidence that God had taken the initiative, observing that " none can justly expect assistance from God whom he does not employ." [9] At his worst, Tennent affirmed that presbyteries that neglected or refused examination into the question of the divine initiative in calling were unconverted, "ungracious," and wicked.

Tennent proposed two policies designed to counter the two Old Side acts of 1738 that promised to defeat the revival. First, he defended itinerant preaching — " intrusions " as the Old Side men regarded them. Why should laymen in whom the Spirit was working be required to feed on the " dry breasts " of an ungracious preaching? It was the merest tyranny to legislate against their leaving their parish or against the freedom of laymen to invite a revivalist to preach to them. While he later recognized that grave problems in churchmanship arose around this view, Tennent deemed it critical for the revival to sustain this point.

As a second remedial measure he declared that "the most likely method to stock the church with a faithful ministry, . . .

In the *Irenicum* of 1748, Tennent went the whole way toward reconciliation: he declared flatly that he would not impose his views of conversion and spiritual experience as a term of communion. The church, like wheat and tares growing together, is a mixture of good and bad and " we ought to let it remain so." (*Irenicum Ecclesiasticum* [Philadelphia, 1749], E6423, 23.)

It is understandable that the Old Side would be slow to accept the *Irenicum* at face value and as late as 1765 Tennent was still working at peacemaking. " We should rather die than deny the least truth," he told the united Synod, " but there is a wide difference between our love to it and our imposing of it as a term of communion upon others. The former is our duty and the latter our sin." (*The Blessedness of Peacemakers Represented* [Philadelphia, 1765], 5. PSL, Sprague Collection, I, Vol. 143, item 9.)

9 Samuel Finley, *The Approved Minister of God* (Philadelphia, 1749), 5. PSL, Spr., I, 118:21.

the publick academies being so much corrupted, . . . is to encourage private schools or seminaries of learning which are under the care of skilful and experienced Christians; in which only those should be admitted who upon strict examination . . . have the plain evidences of experimental religion." [10]

Perhaps the most significant difference between the two Sides, from the theological standpoint, lay in Thomson's denial that it is necessary, desirable, or proper to experience the terror of being lost before grace could enter. The revival Thomson calls a " new fangle stir," a " spiritual phrenzy," terms as distasteful to Tennent as Tennent's adjectives were to Thomson. Here is the doctrine of " convictions." To Tennent it was inconceivable that a man should rise to the heights of love to God demanded by the gospel and made possible through grace without having first been seized by a conviction of the wretchedness of his condition. Ministers must " wound before they heal." [11] Graduates of the Log College believed that the minister too must pass through such an agony of conscience as the English Puritan Smyth depicted if he would find rest to his soul. If the revival demanded pain as the price of peace, it also held out the prospect of a " comfortable assurance " of the soul's salvation.

In a sermon on *The Righteousness of the Scribes and Pharisees Considered,* Tennent appealed specifically to children, youth, adults in middle life, and older people, asking them whether they did not in fact suffer from the complacency of natural religion. But to John Thomson, the evoking of preparatory " downcasting convictions " is not justified by the Westminster Standards or the Bible. [12] If man believes himself wholly without hope apart from faith, there is no need for him to *feel* the exceeding sinfulness of sin. To Tennent, this was mere carnal security, a form of knowledge not yet

[10] G. Tennent, *The Danger of an Unconverted Ministry,* 11.
[11] G. Tennent, *Love to Christ a Necessary Qualification* (1743), E5497, 19.
[12] John Thomson, *The Government of the Church of Christ* (Philadelphia, 1741), E4828, 24.

significant. Advising a newly ordained youth, he said: " After the understanding is informed by a calm and methodical explication of divine truth, doubtless all the other powers of the soul should be pathetically addressed, . . . all the arts of persuasion should be used in order to compel sinners to come in to the gospel feast." [13] If these two are separated, the ministry cannot perform its proper roles of preaching and pastoral reproof.

After devoting more than half the above-quoted ordination sermon to the problem of preaching, Tennent counsels on the uses of " *private reproof,*" which should be " marked with much caution and tenderness . . . lest persons be enraged instead of being reformed. The bitter pill of reproof should be dipt in sugar." This was the main purpose of pastoral conference. While the revivalists defined pastoral work narrowly, their practice led to a serious penetration of the home and family. As with Joseph Morgan, life in the home was to complement and seal the effects of preaching. But now the minister himself went there to probe the heart, evoke confession, lead in prayer, give content to repentance, and comfort and assure the converted. The ministry is less exclusively focused on preaching. It is a complex of activity designed to effect the conversion of nominal Christians through preaching, pastoral visitation, church discipline, and teaching.

The administration of the sacrament of the Lord's Supper is also a minister's business. Tennent remarked: " By this golden conduit the blessed head of Influence is wont to communicate much strength and sweetness to his people." Discipline he characterized as the " key to the kingdom of Heaven, or of the visible church, . . . put into the hands of Christ's ministers." Extremes in its use were to be avoided: there was to be neither exclusion from fellowship for minor differences of view nor toleration of immorality and heresy. Elsewhere he spoke gravely of governmental duties beyond the adminis-

[13] G. Tennent, *A Sermon Preach'd in Greenwich, September 4, 1746. At the Ordination of Andrew Hunter* (Philadelphia, 1746), E5472, 18.

tration of discipline in local congregation and presbytery. These were necessary for "building up the converted," a task that "does not make so great a noise yet it is a valuable mercy." [14]

Tennent's teaching of the doctrine of vocation differed in one signal regard from John Calvin's: "that secret call, of which each minister is conscious before God, . . . does not have the church as witness." [15] Calvin assumed the necessity of "piety and the other gifts of the good pastor," noting that "those whom the Lord has destined for such high office, he first supplies with the arms required to fulfill it, that they may not come empty-handed and unprepared." But he granted the church no right to examine the inward call; this was solely for God's scrutiny. On the other hand, the "outward and solemn call," Thomson's concern, occupied Calvin at length. The entry of men into lawful exercise of church ministry who could not or would not furnish evidence of a valid inward call was a problem of a degenerating church life. But Calvin was engrossed in establishing order in a newly constituted church.

Calvin all but forbade the movement of ministers from parish to parish. "We do not deny that a pastor bound to one church can aid other churches — either if any disturbances occur which require his presence, or if advice be sought from him concerning some obscure matter. But to keep peace in the church, this order is necessary: that to each be assigned his task to keep all from being in confusion, at the same time dashing about aimlessly without an assignment, rashly gathering together in one place, and forsaking their churches at pleasure, because they are more concerned about their own advantage than about the upbuilding of the church . . . . As generally as possible . . . each person, content with his own limits, should not break over into another man's province. This is not of human devising but ordained by God himself." [16]

[14] Ibid., 35.
[15] John Calvin, Institutes of the Christian Religion, IV. iii. 11.
[16] Ibid., IV. iii. 7.

Calvin was confronted with the intrusion of sectarians, which was the light in which Thomson regarded the revivalists. But what of Tennent's perspective — " intrusions " in behalf of the gospel in a decadent church? Calvin granted that the " extraordinary offices " of apostles, prophets, and evangelists might be exercised on rare occasions when " the Lord . . . now and again revives them as the need of the times demands." [17] Tennent could have been justified by this had it not been for the crucial question of judging which candidates and ministers were truly converted. At this point Tennent introduced an innovation long prepared in Puritanism: it is possible to determine, he affirmed, who is truly converted from the outward and visible signs of the inward transformation. Calvin never went so far: " We are not bidden to distinguish between reprobate and elect — that is for God alone, not for us, to do — but to establish with certainty in our hearts that all those who, by the kindness of God the Father, through the working of the Holy Spirit, have entered into fellowship with Christ, are set apart as God's property and personal possession; and that when we are of their number we share that great grace." [18] Whether Calvin would have applied so tolerant a principle to the ordained ministry itself in a time of spiritual decline, Tennent himself may have wondered.

The Purpose of Theological Education

It may be doubted that Thomson grasped Tennent's reason for urging thorough education for the ministry. In the logic of historical " enthusiasm," of which Thomson suspected the revivalists, the gift of the Holy Spirit sufficed to qualify the would-be minister. But Tennent was no enthusiast. God has given all that man needs to know for salvation and right conduct in the Bible. Only by studying the Bible can a man acquire the knowledge that is prerequisite to salvation. " Men's minds must be enlightened before they be reconciled to God.

[17] *Ibid.*, IV. iii. 4.   [18] *Ibid.*, IV. i. 3.

Reasonable creatures must be dealt with in a reasonable way." [19] The revivalists, like the Dickinsonians, talked much of conscience; yet conscience was not authoritative. "Not their conscience," wrote Samuel Blair, "but God's Word is to be a rule to the judicature. Upon this ground it is that churches require subscriptions or declarations." [20] Only on a foundation of thorough knowledge of the Bible does the Spirit act. The teachings of the Spirit are not something apart from the Bible but are "the Word of God brought with light and energy to our minds and hearts so as to affect us deeply with the sinfulness and danger of sin and a state thereof and make us despair of help in ourselves and depend on Christ alone for acceptance with God." [21] There are two ways of "understanding" the Bible: with the mind and "experimentally," by which there occurs within each man the redeeming event described in the Bible. This is the very nerve of the revival: the Bible should become for men not only a body of propositions to be received by the intellect but an illumination of human existence capable of altering the springs of action.

Theological education is essential to an awakened ministry but it is lifeless without the gifts of the Spirit to fructify it. Tennent was aware of continuing danger from heresy and prelacy. Spiritual manifestations notwithstanding, no young man should be granted a license to preach until educated. "An unlearned ministry . . . tend to disparage the gospel of Christ and open a door to error and delusion."

To the Old Side, on the other hand, theological education was a bulwark against the attacks of heresy. The experience with Anglicanism in Scotland and the growing success of Samuel Clarke's rationalizing Trinitarianism among Presbyterians in England were uppermost in the Old Side mind. Training for conversionist preaching involved a general re-

[19] G. Tennent, *A Sermon Preach'd in Greenwich*, September 4, 1746, E5872, 9.

[20] *A Vindication of the Brethren Who Were Unjustly and Illegally Cast Out of the Synod of Philadelphia* . . . (Philadelphia, 1744), E5343, 23 f.

[21] G. Tennent, *A Sermon Preach'd in Greenwich* . . . 1746, Spr., I, 28.

orientation of theological education. It was to take one's eye
off the enemy outside the wall. To educate young men to
believe that their principal enemy was inside — " carnal security, complacency " — could only enfeeble theological education. The Old Side preferred men trained in Scotland, where
this menacing alteration of theological education had not occurred, and Old Siders tended to doubt the New Side's sturdi-
ness against heresy. They never seem to have felt the force of
the main point made by the revival: coldness within the church
and among the clergy is a persistent invitation to Arminianism,
Unitarianism, and other heresies.

The conflict over theological education was a root of bitterness as schism approached. John Rowland, a young product of
the revival, offered himself for training at William Tennent's
Log College at a time when the Synod of Philadelphia was increasing pressure against it. Francis Alison, perhaps the ablest
Old Side man, had commented that " the Synod conceived, not
without Ground, that there was some slackness in particular
presbyteries in the examination of candidates, at their admission
into the ministry and that some of late were admitted who
were remarkably deficient in some parts of useful learning,
particularly Messrs. Alexander Craighead, Charles Tennent,
and John Rowland." [22]

The Synod of 1738, dominated by Old Side sentiment, passed
the requirement that before any presbytery might ordain, the
Synod itself must issue a document approving the applicant's
educational qualifications. Alison took the high ground of a
defender of a strong standard of education for the ministry.[23]

Revivalists vehemently denied that the Synod was motivated

[22] T. C. Pears, Jr., and Guy S. Klett, *Documentary History of William
Tennent and the Log College* (Mimeographed). (Presbyterian Historical Society, 1940.) *An Examination and Refutation* (1742), 161.
[23] *Ibid.*, 168. Alison's career in education supported his claim, and no
doubt he sincerely believed " the credible reports we received of Mr.
W. Tennent's great slackness in educating scholars under his care."
However, informed testimony indicates that Tennent was " celebrated
for his accurate and profound acquaintance with the Latin and Greek
classics . . ." and exhibited " laudable zeal in the promotion of knowledge."

by concern for educational qualification in passing the detested
Act of 1738; Gilbert Tennent " cried out that this was to prevent his Father's school from training gracious men for the
ministry." In this he was supported by Gillespie, an Old
Sider. In defense of the Act, Alison claimed that it merely
provided that Synod examiners might be substituted for university theological examiners in the absence of a college of
theology in the middle colonies.[24]   Gillespie commented:
" Here is fair speech but there is poison here." The New Side
termed the Act a Synodal intrusion on Presbytery's rights, and
in 1739, in deliberate scorn of it, William Tennent invited
Rowland to preach at Neshaminy.

THE CONFLICT IN NEW ENGLAND

It is instructive to note the relation between Old Side opposition to the revival in the middle colonies and the hostility to
Whitefield, Tennent, Edwards, and Davenport in Boston.
Charles Chauncy, pastor of the First Church, and Edward
Wigglesworth, Hollis Professor of Divinity at Harvard, had
little to say at the crest of the revival in 1741, but by 1743
both had produced lengthy treatises arraigning the Awakening
for a range of offenses already identified by John Thomson.

Criticism of the educational quality of the Log College was uniformly associated with charges of a palpably partisan character. The
literacy and competence of the graduates of the school suggest that
however sincerely Alison may have desired a highly qualified Presbyterian clergy, his judgment on the work of Tennent was mistaken.
It was not the Old Side that established the College of New Jersey,
the only institution comparable to Harvard or Yale to be implanted
in the middle colonies before 1750. Theological education was at a
very low ebb in Glasgow, where Alison himself was trained, as it was
throughout Scotland. The College of Philadelphia, with which Alison
was associated after 1752, was not trusted by Presbyterians of either
party. (Cf. Letter of R. Peters to Wm. Smith, New York, June 27,
1763 [HSP, Brinton Collection]; Letter of William Smith, London,
August 11, 1763, and others of about the same date [HSP, Penn-Peters
Correspondence, II].)
[24] Letter of Alison to Clap, May 30, 1746, *Documentary History,* 162.

Theirs was an answer not only to the preaching of the Awakeners — Tennent, Whitefield, Davenport, and Edwards — but a defense of the modified Calvinism that had carried Boston and much of English Puritanism away from the doctrine of the era before Dort.

Perry Miller has outlined the evolution of Puritan thought in the first third of the eighteenth century. The conflict within it achieved its harshest American form when Jonathan Edwards attacked popular Boston orthodoxy as actually a betrayal of the divine sovereignty, an illicit promotion of man to the critical role in redemption.[25] It was not the openly unitarian, of whom there were none, but the established leadership that was at fault. Edwards impassioned Chauncy and his allies. He alleged that renegation of God was already well advanced in the New England mind and did it with such trenchancy and subtlety that he was not answered, nor perhaps even comprehended. Smear words — notably, Arminian — figured prominently in his assault, and his associates in almost any enterprise were bound to feel the counterslashing of the wounded.[26]

Into this situation came Whitefield with his gifts of irresponsible utterance and social inflammation. Later Tennent and Davenport were to concede the truth of many antirevivalist accusations in both New England and the middle colonies,[27] but in the teeth of the storm the debate in the former provinces was not confined to provable offenses but touched the larger question of whether the reigning ecclesiastical and social mon-

[25] Perry Miller, *Jonathan Edwards*, 26–34; 101–126.
[26] Cf. Edw. Wigglesworth, *A Letter to the Rev. Mr. George Whitefield* (Boston, 1745), 58.
[27] Cf. Davenport's *Recantation*, July 18, 1744. The original in his own hand is in HSP, Gratz, Case 8, box 22. It was sent for publication to Kneeland and Green of the *Gazette*. Edwards wrote Eleazer Wheelock July 13, 1744: " I believe he is much fuller of the Spirit of God than he was in years past when he seemed to have such a constant series of high elevations and raptures. I think he is now fully satisfied in his duty in making a publick, humble and suitable recantation and confession of his great errors that have been of extensive and extremely hurtful consequence to the interest of religion." HSP, Dreer, III.

archs would accept a raw, new sweep of religious vitality in any form. The works of Chauncy and Wigglesworth are notable for their total neglect of any but the most marginal concessions to the critics of New England religion. There existed in their minds almost nothing of the conscientious uneasiness about the state of the church that distinguished Thomson and Gillespie and touched the Presbyterian division with tragedy.[28] Chauncy and Wigglesworth contended for the *status quo*. The ministry was orthodox, spiritual, properly educated in a proper seminary, and revival was simply not needed. Thomson, by contrast, recognized that Arminianism was an enemy of truth and that experimental religion had ebbed dangerously; and this divergence signaled very different destinies for Presbyterianism and Congregationalism. Presbyterian antirevivalism underwent transmutations that issued in Old School Calvinism. One large wing of New England antirevivalism ended in Unitarianism and Universalism.

The charges laid against the revival, however, corresponded: "rash-judging"; itinerant intrusion upon established parishes; disorder arising from disrespect for law, custom, and the teachings of the fathers. Chauncy and Wigglesworth bitterly resented the maddening charge that the ministry was unconverted and that any exception taken to the revival marked a man as an "opposer of the work of God."[29] Harvard had not sunk into a "meer seminary of paganism" from which prayer, orthodox instruction, and Christian experience had vanished. Wigglesworth exegeted in detail Eph. 4:11, as did Presbyterian

---

[28] Chauncy's bitterness is visible in a letter to Solomon Williams, December 9, 1747. "I trust by your question [whether any answer to Edwards' book was contemplated] that . . . you are meditating an answer yourself to Mr. Edwards; if you are, I wish you success in it and that you may be hereby instrumental in doing much service to those churches. I think Mr. Edwards has been greatly imprudent; especially considering after all the difficulty he has rashly run himself into he has no more to say in defence of what he has undertaken." HSP, Dreer, II.

[29] Charles Chauncy, *Seasonable Thoughts on the State of Religion in New England* (Boston, 1743), 392.

antirevivalists, to prove that the office of evangelist was temporary and primitive and that itinerants were usurpers of an
extinct function.[30]

Resistance to revival in New England was more thorough
and more categorical because it drew power from seasoned
hostility to Edwards. Both Chauncy and Wigglesworth argued
that the revival was reviving nothing but the incubus of Fam-
ilism, fifth monarchism, Münzerism, and the worst of the anti-
Reformed movements of the sixteenth and seventeenth centuries [31] and cited the most respected Puritan fathers — Owen,
Baxter, Increase Mather — against the agitators.   Chauncy
carried forward his riposte to Edwards' New Haven [32] sermon
in an extended and crushing documentation of revivalist excesses, devoting the first 331 pages of *Seasonable Thoughts* to
accounts of ecstasies, emotions, and enthusiasms calculated to
discredit not only Whitefield, Tennent, and Davenport but by
association, Edwards' far-reaching theological critique as well.

It is a paradox of the Great Awakening and a fact that dis-
tinguishes it from its successors in the history of American
religion that it was the revivalists who were the philosophers
and their enemies who were tempted by anti-intellectualism.
Chauncy wrote movingly of the power of the sufferings of Christ
to convert anyone who would contemplate them. "Mourning
for sin," he wrote, "is a sorrow taking rise from faith in
Christ and a view of sin as occasioning those sufferings. . . .
There is nothing, no not the torments of hell itself, that
will so effectually move the heart as a believing sight of Christ
in his bitter suffering and dying agonies for our sins. . . . An
eye to Christ is the only gospel ground of a gospel repent-

---

[30] Edw. Wigglesworth, *Some Distinguishing Characters of the Extraordinary and Ordinary Ministers of the Church of Christ* . . . (Boston, 1754), *passim*.

[31] Chauncy, *op. cit.*, Preface, iv–xiv; Wigglesworth, *Some Distinguishing Characters*, 2–23.

[32] Jonathan Edwards, *Distinguishing Marks of a Work of the Spirit of
God;* Charles Chauncy, *The Late Religious Commotions in New England Considered* (Boston, 1743). PSL, Spr., I, 567:5.

ance." [33] Chauncy's vision of the dying Lord had the advantage that it evaded the Edwardean philosophical analysis in favor of something positive, not to say romantic. Two generations later the prince of Presbyterian Old Calvinism, Ashbel Green, wrote similarly against the successors of Edwards. It is "not enough to indoctrinate . . . in knowledge of God as the Creator, preserver and judge of the world and by this knowledge to rouse the attention and alarm the fears," he told the General Assembly of 1825; it is necessary to speak of the "Lamb of God . . . coming from heaven to suffer, bleed and die." Only this can convert; "God blesses nothing else." "All your merely metaphysical, logical, rhetorical, moral and philosophical preaching in which the name of Christ is seldom heard and the doctrine of the cross never clearly set forth is lacking in [power to convert]." [34] Chauncy, of course, was actually drifting away from doctrinal rigor, while Green insisted on "the proper divinity and atonement of our Lord Jesus Christ"; but romanticism and humanism were common to both and they were equally hostile to the task of critical theology.

It was James Davenport, the mad evangelist, who drove the New England revival into disrepute. If Thomson did not deny the need of revival in the middle colonies, neither did Tennent, for all his sanguine temper, behave like Davenport. Edwards was early with an analysis of the true and false in revivalist conduct; he blunted but could not turn the thrust of Chauncy: if this be revival, it is a work of Satan. Edwards labored to distinguish illusion from conviction. "True Grace distinguished from the Experience of Devils," published in 1752, and *Religious Affections* in 1746 stated at length what he had already said publicly and published in 1743 in *Distinguishing Marks of a Work of the Spirit of God* in New Haven. But Davenport had already been judged *non compos mentis* by a Massachusetts Grand Jury in 1742 and the revival was

---

[33] Chauncy, *The Late Religious Commotions*, 12, 13.
[34] Ashbel Green, *Christ Crucified, the Characteristick of Apostolical Preaching* (Philadelphia, 1825). PSL, Spr., I, 63:10, 16–25.

ruined. After that, whatever so eminently sane a man as Chauncy, whatever so creditable an academic as Wigglesworth had to say, even though it touched upon the aching doctrinal dispute with Edwards, obtained immediate acceptance.

EDUCATION FOR AN AWAKENED MINISTRY

The violent polemic of the period immediately following 1740 did not quickly disappear from the memories of offended Presbyterians. The New Side deeply resented the charges of the *Protest* drafted by Robert Cross, and the Old Side was lastingly injured by the flogging of Nottingham. Tennent soon realized that the schism must eventually be surmounted and recognized real difficulties in itinerant evangelism. The fact was that for all his vindication of it, he had never seriously relied on nonresident preaching. The real need was for a whole corps of awakened and converted clergymen, resident pastors who knew the spiritual and social needs of their people. A visiting revivalist might preach to the needs of the heart and in that sense deal personally with his hearers. But he could never cope with private problems. Only an awakening among parish ministers could consolidate the revival; no amount of visitation could lift the dead weight of a moribund clergy. For this reason, the leaders of the revival urged congregations to be most cautious in their choice of pastors and advocated strict examination of candidates.

There was pressing need of a permanent school for the training of ministers in America, the Log College having terminated its work sometime between 1742 and 1746, when William Tennent, Sr., died. In October, 1746, a charter was issued to the " College of New Jersey," destined to grow into Princeton University. The genius of the new college lay in its peculiar union of the New England experience of Reformed faith and churchmanship with a chastened revivalism.

IV

A REFORMED THEOLOGY OF REVIVAL

DID AMERICAN REFORMED REVIVALISM imply a theological revision or simply the vitalizing of familiar orthodox positions? Around this choice the history of theological thought developed from Jonathan Dickinson, a sympathizer with revival who attempted no general revision; through Edwards, whose "new Calvinism" was partly motivated by the questions arising out of the experience of revival; to John Witherspoon, who extinguished Edwardean Calvinism at Princeton.

JONATHAN DICKINSON: GRACE AND THE EVANGELICAL APPEAL

The revival brought a shift from controversy with Anglicans and sectarians, who were nevertheless not wholly forgotten, to concern with the state of the heart and mind in relation to conversion. But the prominence of such topical heads as "Original Sin," "Conversion," and "Sanctifying Grace" was only a symptom. Implicitly, the revival demanded that the attention of the people be directed less to the explanation of the divine order than to their own predicament. The minister's function was to describe God's way of working with individual men and the church in order to conversion and sanctification. The theological problems that interested the revivalists simply were different from the problems of apologetic orthodoxy.

In his didactic treatises, Dickinson constantly dealt with the doctrinal heads in terms of revival experience. This was inevitable, since the renewal of the ministry demanded by Tennent and others raised fundamental questions about the acts of God and man. Conversion, so central to revivalism and its special view of preaching, immediately projects the theological problem. Conversion is effected when man arrives at a "just view of things as they are," wrote Dickinson.[1] This is accomplished by the Holy Spirit using the preacher as instrument. Sermons give the sinner a "lively sight of his sin and danger powerfully applied to his mind and conscience." By this he may be awakened to "an earnest inquiry after the way of salvation."[2] Dickinson understood that to see "things as they are" would *necessarily* change the will of man. The great danger is "a cold and unactive assent."[3] "Notional knowledge" alone cannot effect conversion; if associated with faith at all, it is "dead faith." Now the problem: Is it not "impertinent to press the duties of religion upon them when their utmost endeavors will give them no title to salvation"? Dickinson furnished more than one answer. "If God can bestow grace . . . , we should be the more in earnest to obtain it from him."[4] But that reply does not satisfy the question about man's natural ability. If he is impotent to respond, he is incapable of carrying earnestness from resolve to action.

In his treatment of original sin, Dickinson affirmed the orthodox Calvinist position that "nature" is fallen; but at the same time, he never went so far as to say that man's faculties are so gravely damaged as to render him incapable of responsible apprehension of God's communication. Dickinson was standing on the threshold of a theological problem that he did not clearly discern. If man's nature is fallen, does this mean that he possesses no capacity to respond? If he can, why doesn't he?

Dickinson took it for granted that the corruption of nature inherited from Adam and confirmed a thousandfold in "nu-

---

[1] Jonathan Dickinson, *The True Scripture Doctrine Concerning Some Important Points of Christian Faith* (Elizabethtown, 1793), E4710, 149.

[2] *Ibid.*, 145.

[3] *Ibid.*, 146.

[4] *Ibid.*, 159.

merous actual sins" still left reason capable of arriving at a "rational conviction of the sad truth" about man's "perishing circumstances."[5] The problem was that, having seen all this, so many "sleep on in a fatal security and perish forever." Here the work of God is altogether critical — along with the work of the awakening preacher and counselor. Dickinson urged his readers to "labour for a realizing affecting apprehension of [their] extream misery." The "improvements" of Dickinson's treatises assume the competence of the natural faculties. Man's problem lies in his lack of motive.

Beyond the psychological problem of the natural faculties lies the problem of election and predestination. Human freedom may, it is true, be discussed wholly within the sphere of the psychological and social, thus escaping the vexing problem of reconciling freedom and election on the metaphysical level. Even so, it remains necessary to explain the meshing of the metaphysic of divine determination with the human experience of free choice.

Dickinson's argument rested on this distinction. While "the futurity of the decreed event must be certain and infallible . . . yet we find by experience that we are at full liberty and freedom, that we act in all our moral behaviour according to our own wills. . . . Don't this consideration make it necessary that the liberty of the creature is consistent with the decree of God, whether we can see through it or not?"[6] Having thus distinguished election and freedom in quality as in logic, Dickinson justified them with an argument almost identical with that of Jonathan Edwards in his treatise on free will.[7]

Human freedom consists in man's ability to choose what appears to him "most fit to be chosen"; slavery, oppositely, is the necessity of "choosing" what is abhorrent. Men do not will-

---

[5] *Ibid.*, 129.
[6] J. Dickinson, *The True Scripture Doctrine Concerning Some Important Points of Christian Faith: Discourse on Election* (Boston, 1741), 32.
[7] Both depend on Locke's *Essay Concerning Human Understanding*. Cf. J. Edwards, *Freedom of the Will*, edited by Paul Ramsey (Yale University Press, 1957), 163.

ingly choose what appears bad to them. It is rather that evil masquerades as good and beguiles them.[8] The notion that freedom is "a power to choose indifferently either the one or the other of two contrary objects" simply misunderstands the psychology of choice.

This leads to the paradoxical assertion that "every free agent must necessarily will what his understanding, appetites and affections represent to him the most fit object of choice; he can't do otherwise." Whenever he does otherwise, it can only be because "a power extrinsical to him . . . must move his will as a clock or watch is moved; and is utterly inconsistent with freedom." The opposite of freedom is "coaction or constraint." "He that can act according to his own will and do what he does of choice, without any constraint, is therein free."[9] Freedom is not a "power to do everything which man might choose to do"; this prerogative is God's alone. It is rather "a power to act of choice in all that he does do."

Thus understood, it is not inconsistent to say that in election God fixes what a man "does do" and man chooses it freely since no violence is done to the inclination of his mind toward the object of its choice. "From which it necessarily follows that the infallibility of the decree of God can no ways obstruct the liberty of the creatures."

Dickinson was conscious of his departure from the orthodox distinction between the natural as the realm of freedom and the spiritual as the realm in which divine grace is necessary. He found it an "inaccurate and obscure way of speaking to attribute freedom . . . to the will." John Locke had taught him, he stated, that the will is a "faculty of the mind." Freedom may be predicated of a person but not of his faculties. A person deluded about the good persistently wills what destroys him; yet he remains free since he makes his choice unconstrained.

[8] J. Dickinson, *The True Scripture Doctrine Concerning Some Important Points of Christian Faith: Discourse on Election* (Boston, 1741), 37.

[9] *Ibid.*, 35.

When grace intervenes, it clarifies man's vision of the worthy and alters his motives. "I fully agree with the meaning of these [orthodox] devines . . . no man has a power to will the exercise of saving grace . . . until the Spirit of God . . . represents these to him as most fit to be chosen and makes such a powerful impression upon his mind as conquers his natural aversion and excites him to will them." [10]

By this means did the incipient theology of the revival argue that awakening preaching was not only justified by circumstance but actually an instrument of divine election. At one stroke, opponents of the revival were put at odds with election and deprived of the argument (which they shared with secular rationalism) that in a predestined world, appeal to human motivation was not only bootless but betrayed an Arminian view of man. As a by-product, the intellectualism of the revival laid open the distasteful fact that rationalism had so fully invaded the Old Calvinist mind as to render its ministry at once incapable of preaching for decision and unable to distinguish its intellectual substructure from that of the worst enemies of the gospel. Not only to vindicate the revival but to amend this well-nigh fatal weakness, Dickinson enunciated a position that was to be elaborated in the Edwardean theology.

Not all that was implied by Dickinson's scanty pages on human freedom was apparent to him, and no new theology broke free until Edwards ventured upon a fresh treatment of the orthodox assertion that by his bond with Adam, man is deprived of his capacity to respond to the gospel.

It befitted the times that the later writings of Dickinson should ponder the problem of free will, even though in the main he defended the revival and formulatd orthodoxy to that end. But Edwards and his succession were looking to the coming age whose overwhelming problem was to be the vindication of the Calvinist view of the human predicament, with its peculiar solution, faith in the Savior, in the face of the

[10] *Ibid.*, 37.

swiftly rising challenge of humanism. Was not God unjust to distribute his gifts of grace arbitrarily? Did he not rob some men of due opportunity? Did he not make a farce of human freedom? And was not the Calvinist attitude that human nature was poisoned at the base a root of many other problems?

Fear of the softened Calvinism of Samuel Clarke had been abroad among Scottish Presbyterians in America from the outset of the century, as the subscriptionist controversy amply testifies. "Latitudinarianism" and "catholicity" were extant in Boston by 1710.[11] As early as 1734, John White of Boston had boldly put the Arminian tag on views prevalent in New England, while in 1731 Jonathan Edwards had charged that Americans were harboring "schemes of divinity" that were "repugnant to the design and tenor of the gospel."[12] As the century advanced, the books of French and English social philosophers were disseminated in the colonies and Arminian modification of Calvinism increasingly became an open hostility to its basic precepts. The revival had met the threat of "coldness" among church members; but the church now needed an intellectual instrument capable of destroying a more sophisticated enemy that intruded even into the minds of the clergy itself. If Arminianism was to be repelled, there must be fresh thought about the predicament of man and a thoroughgoing vindication of the ways of God and his scheme of redemption.

JONATHAN EDWARDS: THE VINDICATION OF DIVINE INITIATIVE

Dickinson had implicitly assumed unimpaired natural faculties, while affirming the depravity of man's nature; but he had attempted no fresh statement of the situation of man in relation to the bondage of sin and the possibility of escaping it. Yet it was precisely upon the situation of man — whether God deals with him justly, whether man's "rights" are duly acknowledged by orthodoxy, and the question of inborn possi-

---

[11] Cf. Perry Miller, *op. cit.*, 9.   [12] *Ibid.*, 29.

bilities — that the new assault focused. It was absolutely essential to Calvinism to define the "nature" of man more precisely and vindicate his relation to the order of God.

In an era when prescientific psychological categories were swiftly developing, the task of defining the situation and nature of man was vastly more complicated than when Calvin borrowed the undifferentiated term "nature" for use in expounding original sin. Criticism in this epoch revolved upon imprecise notions of man's "faculties" and their bearing on man's freedom and God's justice. Jonathan Edwards plunged into an effort to define the vocabulary that the occasion required.

The crux of the criticism of the Calvinist view of the "nature" of man lay in an alleged deprivation of ability — or if he was believed to retain ability, of freedom — to choose the good.

In his treatise of 1754, Edwards defined "natural ability" and "moral ability" and their opposites. "We are said to be *naturally* unable to do a thing, when we can't do it if we will, because what is most commonly called nature don't allow of it, or because of some impeding defect or obstacle that is extrinsic to the will; either in the faculty of understanding, constitution of body, or external objects. *Moral* inability consists not in any of these things; but either in the want of inclination or the strength of a contrary inclination; or the want of sufficient motives in view, to induce and excite the act of the will, or the strength of apparent motives to the contrary. . . . Moral inability consists in the opposition or want of inclination." [13] The word "ability" is tricky. "In the strictest propriety of speech a man has a thing in his power, if he has it in his choice or at his election; and a man can't be truly said to be unable to do a thing, when he can do it if he will." The fact is, Edwards insisted, that if man will, he can; to say anything else is to say that "he can't will if he does will." So the word "ability" ought to be reserved for the natural, as

[13] J. Edwards, *Freedom of the Will*, 159.

when a man who wills to drink from a cup is unable for lack of arms. But if he has arms and chooses to drink, with what justice can it be argued that he *cannot* drink? It is rather that he *will* not. If we use the term "moral inability" at all, it must mean then that there are insurmountable habits, disinclinations, or counterattractions that prevent a man from willing an act. Thus a man may have the natural ability to drink — arms and sane mind — but "moral inability," as when a physically normal man, bidden to drink poison, cannot bring himself to do it. To come closer to our own case, a man may have a natural ability to choose God — a functioning intellect — but be morally unable through insurmountable prejudice. But he nonetheless possesses the necessary natural ability required for the choice. Thus Edwards brought into the field of controversy an explicit conception that Dickinson never defined.

From this followed Edwards' definition of freedom: "Let the person come by his volition or choice how he will, yet, if he is able, and there is nothing in the way to hinder his pursuing and executing his will, the man is fully and perfectly free, according to the primary and common notion of freedom." [14] Man is a "moral agent" because at creation God implanted in him "those faculties and principles of nature whereby he is capable of moral agency. Herein very much consists the natural image of God; as his spiritual and moral image, where in man was made at first, consisted in that moral excellency that he was endowed with." The latter of these images — the excellence by which man once actually exercised his natural capacity for moral agency in conforming with the divine will — is lost in the Fall. Only the "natural" image of God remains: man's possession of "understanding to perceive the difference between moral good and evil; a capacity of discerning that moral worthiness of blame or punishment; and a capacity of choice, and choice guided by understanding, and a power of acting according to his choice or pleasure and being capable

[14] *Ibid.*, 164.

of doing those things which are in the highest sense praiseworthy." [15]   While all this survived the Fall, the inclination by which the will is moved to exercise these capabilities was lost through Adam's sin.   The "excellency" in man from which once flowed the necessary inclination — the spiritual and moral image — is lost.

In his treatise *The Doctrine of Original Sin Defended,* Edwards granted that "men come into the world with a corrupt and ruined nature." [16]   This means that "men . . . actually are born into the world with a tendency to sin."   "None ever fail of immediately transgressing God's law . . . as soon as they are capable of it." [17]   This is a "moral tendency," since "it must be remembered that it is a moral depravity we are speaking of." [18]   It is no more than fact that "all mankind come into the world in such a state as without fail comes to this issue, namely, the universal commission of sin; or that every one who comes to act in the world as a moral agent, is, in a greater or less degree, guilty of sin." [19]   But what has this to do with the sin of Adam?   "When the doctrine of original sin is spoken of, it is vulgarly understood in that latitude as to include not only the depravity of nature but the imputation of Adam's first sin: or in other words, the liableness or exposedness of Adam's posterity, in the divine judgment, to partake of the punishment of that Sin." [20]   We have now arrived at "the grand point" of the debate: Just what is meant by "imputation"?

Taylor's *Scripture Doctrine of Original Sin,* against which Edwards wrote his treatise, charged that it was unjust "that men should come into the world with a corrupt and ruined nature without having merited the displeasure of their Creator by any personal fault."   Edwards said: "Dr. Taylor . . .

[15] *Ibid.*, 166.
[16] J. Edwards, *The Doctrine of Original Sin Defended,* Worcester Ed. (New York, 1844), I, 311.
[17] *Ibid.*, 326.
[18] *Ibid.*, 311.
[19] *Ibid.*, 314.
[20] *Ibid.*, 309.

speaks of the conveyance of a corrupt and sinful nature to Adam's posterity as the grand point to be proved by the maintainers of the Doctrine of Original Sin." [21] The Scriptures, in Edwards' view, are clear: " Moses' account does, with sufficient evidence, lead all mankind, to whom his account is communicated, to understand, that God, in his constitution with Adam, dealt with him as a public person, and as the head of the human species, and had respect to his posterity, as included in him." [22] Contrary to this, Taylor had asserted that " nothing comes upon us in consequence of Adam's sin, in any sense, kind or degree, inconsistent with the original blessing pronounced on Adam at his creation; and nothing but what is perfectly consistent with God's blessing, love and goodness, declared to Adam as soon as he came out of his Maker's hands." To reveal the enmity of this view toward the Biblical position, Edwards pointed out that this means simply that men possess of themselves " sufficient power and ability . . . to do all their duty and wholly avoid sin." Taylor himself said that " when men have not sufficient power to do their duty they have no duty to do. . . . God requires of them no more than they have sufficient powers to do." [23]

Affirming that the Scriptures teach a quite different doctrine, Edwards proceeded to a " right stating of the doctrine of the imputation of Adam's first sin." Before all, it is necessary to understand that " God in each step of his proceeding with Adam, in relation to the covenant or constitution established with him, looked on his posterity in this affair." Although Edwards inserted " covenant" and " constitution" as synonyms, these words were by no means synonymous in the minds of later Calvinists. The word " covenant" presupposed both the solidarity of mankind and a federal headship, and both these were vividly apparent in Adam's parenthood of the entire human race. The unique significance of the word " constitution" in the history of Calvinism in America arises from the fact that it defined the solidarity of mankind and the federal headship of

[21] *Ibid.*, 314.   [22] *Ibid.*, 405.   [23] *Ibid.*, 463.

Adam substantially apart from his genealogical priority.

Edwards elaborated his own understanding of the covenant by affirming that the first sin of a newborn man is not the original sin but the " extended pollution of Adam's transgression . . . by virtue of the constituted union of the branches with the root." [24]   " The first being of an evil disposition in the heart of a child of Adam whereby he is disposed to approve the sin of his first father . . . is not to be looked upon as a consequence of the imputation of that first sin . . . but rather prior to it in the order of nature." In the moral sphere, the child is not helplessly determined by an act of God, imputation; sin arises from the human circumstance that the child is born into a previously constituted moral unity with Adam and thus experiences at the very outset of life " an evil disposition in the heart." Thus Edwards avoided a determinism that entered deeply into the thinking of his student Samuel Hopkins a generation later, and produced a doctrine of predestination as rigid as any that Calvinism has known. Furthermore, Edwards' doctrine denied that imputation is the visitation of sin as punishment for Adam's sin. To affirm, as Edwards did, that all human sin occurs in unity with Adam on account of the moral solidarity of the race is very different from the more linear view that Adam's sin is conveyed to man by a divine declaration (imputation) that is itself the immediate cause of subsequent sinning.

Taylor objected that this arrangement was unreasonable and unjust, and Edwards replied that " Adam and his posterity are not one but entirely distinct agents." [25]   This is not a contradiction; the key word is " agents." Men are constituted one, argued Edwards, but in respect of agency, which is each individual's responsible activity within the grand scheme, each person and each act is distinct. God's constitutive acts relate to more than racial solidarity. Such personal identity as man has is also a product of divine constitution, and Taylor had no right to protest the rights of man in one constitutional relation-

[24] *Ibid.*, 481 f.   [25] *Ibid.*, 484.

ship against facts that arise from another. Imputation is a word that describes the bonds between persons within the constituted unity of the race; other words, also describing relations, define the unity of the parts of personality. All at bottom rests on God's "sovereign constitution."

Numerous variants of Edwards' thought arose during the two decades after his death among his ablest students, notably Joseph Bellamy, Samuel Hopkins, and Edwards' namesake son. The revival had created a warm regard for Edwards among the New Side men in the middle colonies, and in 1757 he was summoned to the presidency of the College of New Jersey, the critical academic enterprise of the epoch. Edwards died before fairly assuming his duties, but for a decade his thought and much that arose from it entered freely into the education of the Presbyterian clergy in New Jersey. It was this body of modified Edwardean thought that John Witherspoon found entrenched at the college when he left Paisley, Scotland, at the importuning of American Presbyterians who needed a strong hand in both college and denomination. The death of Samuel Finley, the last revivalist president, marked the end of an epoch in the history of the Presbyterian ministry of America. The coming of Witherspoon, corresponding with the onset of the Revolutionary upheaval and internal church changes, founded another.

V

THEOLOGICAL EDUCATION IN MANSE, ACADEMY, AND COLLEGE

THE PRESBYTERIAN CHURCH had depended, before 1746, on the Scottish universities, the New England schools, and the tiny academy in the woodland at Neshaminy for the education of its clergy. With the founding of the College of New Jersey, first in Elizabethtown, then Newark, and finally at Princeton, the forming of the Presbyterian clergy and the theological and practical mentality of the church passed to the middle colonies. Not until 1825 was a second center of theological education authorized by the Presbyterian Church, and for twenty years thereafter the new school at Alleghenytown, Pennsylvania, Western Theological Seminary, barely subsisted. For nearly a century, therefore, Princeton, New Jersey — first in the college and after 1811 in the seminary — nursed the clergy of American Presbyterianism.

In the colonial period most candidates for the ministry studied theology under the guidance of a senior pastor principally engaged in parish labor. Something comparable had existed at Glasgow before the time of Thomas Melville in the " regentship "; divinity was taught by tutors responsible for the subject matter of the entire liberal curriculum as well. At first involved in this system, Melville eventually withdrew into the fields of divinity: Hebrew, Greek, Syriac, Chaldee; Old Testament backgrounds, exegesis, and systematics. Even with this formidable range of material, Melville was better situated in the late sixteenth century than Dickinson, Burr, and their immediate successors from 1746 to the end of the century, for Dickinson and Burr were pastors while they taught both the classics and divinity, and President Samuel Davies and his successors until the founding of the seminary in 1811 were obliged to shoulder the administrative and promotional work of the college while instructing in theology. The presidential predicament was eased somewhat by the appointment of tutors in classical languages and literature, science, and rhetoric; but the early presidents had little assistance in teaching theological subjects proper. The founding of the college greatly advanced general education. But "field education" — the domiciling of theological students with qualified clergymen for guided reading and the practice of the ministry — was not greatly bettered in a college where presidents could do little justice to the chair of divinity.

Given the unusual gifts of William Tennent, the academy at Neshaminy had many advantages. There was a community of candidates, which furnished an interchange of thought not possible when a student resided alone with his instructor. Such structured curriculum as the eighteenth century afforded was at the pretheological level, and men who had graduated from Harvard or Yale might as easily take up residence in the manse of a well-reputed minister as remain at college to read divinity with an overbusy president or a youthful tutor. The nuclear American universities aimed at the engagement of full-time professors in divinity, but this was accomplished only briefly at Princeton with the appointment of John Blair (1768–1769) and later of Henry Kollock (1803–1806). In its heyday the Log College with its congenial company of a half dozen eager divinity scholars compared creditably with the best the College of New Jersey was ever able to offer.

The classical pretheological curriculum varied little between the woodland academies and the New England universities. Variation lay rather in the quality of the instruction. The manuscript texts composed by David Evans (d. 1751) for the use of his sons yield considerable knowledge of the learning transmitted at Yale, where he graduated in 1713, and the general structure of classical instruction in the academies. Evans wrote four books ranging from 21 to 165 pages in length. The shortest, *Technometria,* exhibits the hierarchy of the " arts " of logic, which is basic, through grammar, rhetoric, geometry, arithmetic, and physics to the supreme art, theology. His other three books fall within these classes: logic, rhetoric, and physics and natural philosophy. Evans did not compose texts on the other heads.[1] This curriculum Evans had learned at Yale, where he had read William Ames, whose *Technometria* set forth "the limits and ends of all disciplines and faculties." [2] Evans' own subtitle read: " definitionem et distributionem artis in genera."

Within this framework the Greek and Roman authors were read, some in connection with logic, others with rhetoric, still others in pursuit of a grasp of "natural philosophy." There was little variance in the selection of these from the end of the sixteenth century to the beginning of the nineteenth century. In Scotland, Melville had prescribed Aristotle and Ramus, the French logician whose mind underlay Ames's *Technometria* and the Puritan curriculum. Plato, Cicero, and the Greek and Roman poets were read in Scotland in 1584, and in northern Ireland in 1820 by order of the Synod of Ulster.[3] The curriculums of Emmanuel College, Harvard, and Yale and their imitators remained loyal to this corpus of classical literature and the Ramist scheme until the acids of the Revolutionary period began to cut away the Renaissance heritage.[4]

---

[1] David Evans, MSS., 1733–1737, in the Presbyterian Historical Society.
[2] Perry Miller, *The New England Mind: The Seventeenth Century* (The Macmillan Company, 1939), Ch. 6, *passim.*
[3] *Records of the Synod of Ulster* (1778–1820), III, 280.
[4] T J. Wertenbaker, *Princeton, 1746–1896* (Princeton University Press, 1946). There is an excellent discussion of the moral philosophy of William Paley in Wilson Smith's *Professors and Public Ethics: Studies of Northern Moral Philosophers Before the Civil War* (Cornell University Press, 1956), 3, 44 ff. Smith shows how Paley's half-theological utilitarianism was gradually rejected by the Presbyterians as the

Education in divinity was recognized as a distinct body of learning demanding proportionately more attention for ministerial candidates. A number of ministers, unlike William Tennent, Sr., did not attempt to instruct in the classics but received candidates in divinity as members of their households. In the mid-eighteenth century, there was free movement of students between the colonial colleges and eminent pastor-theologians of New England. Early bonds between Makemie and Increase Mather and later contacts, such as those between Tennent and both the elder and younger Mather, had been fortified by revival in both regions. Princeton College men read theology in New England, and candidates trained there became pastors in the middle colonies. Among the members of the Synod of New York, Robert Smith and Samuel Finley, before becoming president of the College of New Jersey, received many students. Other candidates for the Presbyterian ministry sought out Joseph Bellamy, Jonathan Edwards, and Samuel Hopkins.[5]

This early milieu of theological learning is visible in the diaries of Samuel Hopkins. While at Yale, Hopkins had been influenced by David Brainerd and determined to read under Edwards' guidance. " In the month of December," he wrote, " being furnished with a horse, I set out for Northampton, with a view to live with Mr. Edwards, where I was an utter stranger. When I arrived there, Mr. Edwards was not at home; but I was received with great kindness by Mrs. Edwards and the family and had encouragement that I might live there during the winter. . . . I was very gloomy, and was most of the time retired in my chamber. After some days, Mrs. Edwards came into my chamber and said, as I was now become a member of the family, for a season, she felt herself interested in my welfare; and, as she observed that I appeared gloomy and dejected, she hoped I would not think she intruded, by her desiring to know, and asking me what was the occasion of it, or

---

realism of Witherspoon and his successors increasingly dominated the field.

[5] Trinterud, *The Forming of an American Tradition*, 128.

to what purpose. I told her the freedom she used was agreeable to me. . . . I was in a Christless, graceless state. . . . Upon which we entered into a free conversation; and . . . she told me that she had peculiar exercises in prayer respecting me . . . that she trusted I should receive light and comfort, and doubted not that God intended yet to do great things by me." [6] Association with charismatic personalities was no less important than study of theology.

The American divines accumulated libraries that were impressive in range and size, considering the remoteness of the colonies from European publishing centers. Joseph Bellamy supplied readings to his tutees from the pens of Quakers, Anglicans, and anti-Trinitarians as well as standard Calvinist authors of England, Scotland, and New England. There were usually very few books in French or German and none of the scholarly tools that have since released Biblical interpretation from the thralldom of dogmatic exegesis.

There were, inevitably, irregularities in field education. In 1775, Cotton Mather Smith, of Sharon, Connecticut, was serving as chaplain at Fort Ticonderoga and he left his wife in charge of his household, with its normal complement of children, servants, and theological candidates. "At this time there were five such students in our house," wrote Mrs. Smith. "My husband provided for them by engaging his beloved friend, the Rev. Dr. Bellamy, of Bethlehem, to come and reside in our house, prosecute the education of the young theological students, supply the Sharon pulpit and attend to pastoral duties; a young friend of Dr. Bellamy engaging to perform like brotherly services for him in his parish. As Dr. Bellamy had two students of his own he brought them with him, which added to those already in our house made my family to consist of twenty-two persons besides the servants." Small wonder that Bellamy's "pathetic" preaching was needed to keep this household tranquil.[7]

---

[6] Roland Bainton, *Yale and the Ministry* (Harper & Brothers, 1957), 56.
[7] *Ibid.*, 58.

THE FOUNDING OF THE COLLEGE AT PRINCETON

There was much uneasiness among Presbyterians about Harvard. Even at Yale, whose founders had specifically designed it to restore all that was passing away in Cambridge, a defection of the president and tutors to Anglicanism in 1722 created an uproar. But it was not principally these problems that led to the founding of a new college in the middle colonies. It was, rather, that the system of field education could not produce enough men to satisfy the demands of a growing church. The majority of pastor-theologians training Presbyterian ministers was favorable to the revival, but the expansion of Presbyterianism southward into Virginia and the Carolinas, added to the settlement of the valleys of the Alleghenies, warned that some more systematic method must soon be devised for supplying a ministry. The death of William Tennent and the lapse of his pioneering venture at Neshaminy left Presbyterianism without even the vestige of a formal theological curriculum.

During the months preceding the founding of the Synod of New York in September, 1745, Jonathan Dickinson, together with three New York laymen — William Smith, Peter Van Brugh Livingston, and William Peartree Smith — " first concocted the plan and foundation of the college " of New Jersey, modern Princeton University.[8] President Clap of Yale was openly hostile to the Great Awakening and the school was too remote in any case to serve the churches of the middle and southern colonies. After refusal by Governor Morris, Dickinson and his colleagues secured a charter from the interim governor who succeeded him, John Hamilton, in October, 1746, and a permanent charter from Jonathan Belcher in November, 1748. In two steps of enlargement and reorganization, the board received to its membership, first, four Log College alumni and Richard Treat, a Yale graduate, and then, with the

8 Quoted by Wertenbaker, *op. cit.*

election of Belcher to the presidency of the board and the granting of the charter, four members of the Council of New Jersey. The latter step was opposed by Gilbert Tennent, who feared dilution of church influence, but it had the merit of putting the new enterprise beyond the reach of its numerous Anglican critics and orienting the new college toward public service as well as the preparation of clergymen for Presbyterianism. Of the twelve ministers on this newly constituted board, only three were not New England trained; and these, William Tennent, Jr., Gilbert Tennent, and Samuel Blair, were Log College men.[9] It is the kinship in viewpoint and party affiliation between these founders and the graduates of the Tennent academy that justifies the common assertion that the College of New Jersey was the successor institution to the Log College. It is obvious, also, that the College of New Jersey was much more.[10]

In the familiar pattern of field education, classes were first held in the home of Jonathan Dickinson in Elizabethtown, where he was assisted by Caleb Smith, a Yale graduate and the first tutor of the college. Dickinson's death in October, 1747, brought the transfer of the small student body to Newark, where it was guided by the second president, Aaron Burr, also a resident clergyman. The first class (1748) numbered six, five of whom became Presbyterian ministers. Seven completed their studies the following year; again five became Presbyterian ministers. Of the first thirteen men trained in the college, four are known to have been Scottish born.[11]

For admission, these youths were required to demonstrate a reading knowledge of Latin and the Greek of the four Gospels. Although the loss of the faculty minutes makes it impossible to furnish an exact account of their training, many of the books they studied are known. The correspondence of Joseph Ship-

[9] Trinterud, *The Forming of an American Tradition*, 125.
[10] Wertenbaker, *op. cit.*, 23.
[11] John Maclean, *History of the College of New Jersey, 1746–1854*, 2 vols. (Philadelphia, 1877), I, 128; S. D. Alexander, *Princeton College During the Eighteenth Century* (New York, 1872), 1–4.

pen, a freshman at the college in 1750, speaks of readings in Cicero's *Orations* and Vergil. Readings in both New Testament and Attic Greek were continued, with Hebrew grammar added. Among the Greek authors were Xenophon and Horace. "Natural philosophy" was rudimentary science, principally astronomy, geography, and mathematics. The writings of Isaac Watts were plentifully used: on "ontology," astronomy, and logic. To instruct young scholars in the movement of the heavenly bodies, Witherspoon obtained from David Rittenhouse the first orrery built in the colonies. During the Revolutionary War it was ruined by uniformed American hearties who wanted to see the planets go round. Later in the course, young Master Shippen records that Homer was read and Martin's *Natural Philosophy*. The school owned a friction device that generated static electricity, and Aaron Burr, president of the college from 1748 until 1757, experimented with this "electrical machine" in hope of relieving Governor Belcher of a rheumatic ailment, but without benefit to health or science. Although probably not required, navigation, French, and advanced readings in ethics were offered; Grove's volumes on moral philosophy are mentioned.

Responsive to the urging of Governor Belcher, whose piety was altogether notable among colonial leaders,[12] and the readiness of the residents of Princeton to give two hundred acres of wooded land, ten acres of cleared land, and one thousand pounds outright, the trustees settled the college in its permanent location in 1752. Ground was broken for Nassau Hall in July, 1754, which was completed at the end of 1755 along with a home for the president. The main structure accommodated one hundred forty-seven students in forty-nine rooms. Eleven other rooms served for recitation, library, eating, recreation, and storage. The chapel was designed for the assembled student body. The trustees proposed to call the building Belcher

---

[12] Cf. Letter to George Whitefield, June 23, 1752. *Proceedings of the New Jersey Historical Society*, VIII, 84–86. Cf. also Belcher to Edwards, *Panoplist* (edited by Jeremiah Evarts at Boston, 1814), 407.

Hall in recognition of the governor's services, but he suggested that the house of King William be honored, whereupon it was ordered "that the said edifice be in all time to come, called and known by the name of Nassau Hall." [13]

The erection of Nassau Hall committed the college to a program of growth and incurred an expense that taxed the faith of the most sanguine. Gilbert Tennent and Samuel Davies now accepted a commission of the trustees to raise money in Great Britain for the new enterprise. The case for the college was set forth by the Synod of New York in a communication to the Scottish General Assembly. "The difficulty (and in some cases the impossibility) of sending youth two, three, four, or five hundred miles or more, to the colleges of New England, is evident at first sight. Now it is from the College of New Jersey only that we can expect a remedy of these inconveniences; it is to that your petitioners look for the increase of their numbers; it is on that the Presbyterian churches through the six colonies above mentioned [New York, New Jersey, Pennsylvania, Maryland, Virginia and Carolina] principally depend for a supply of accomplished ministers; from that has been obtained considerable relief already, notwithstanding the many disadvantages that unavoidably attend it in its present infant state; and from that may be expected a sufficient supply when brought maturity. . . . The young daughter of the Church of Scotland, helpless and exposed in this foreign land, cries to her tender and powerful mother for relief. The cries of ministers oppressed with labours, and of congregations famishing for want of the sincere milk of the word, implore assistance. . . . Your petitioners . . . humbly pray that an act may be passed by their venerable and honourable Assembly for a national collection in favour of said college." [14]

The Old Side sent copies of Tennent's Nottingham sermon to England and convinced a few that "the College was a party design." Davies wrote in his *Journal:* "I am shocked to think

[13] Maclean, *op. cit.,* 140–146.   [14] *Ibid.,* 151.

of the inveterate enmity of the Synod of Philadelphia." [15] But the mission was immensely successful. Although the exact sum cannot be ascertained, the whole cost of the two college structures was met and some means furnished for the support of indigent students.

At the death in 1766 of Samuel Finley, fifth president of the college, enrollment stood at about one hundred. During these twenty years, the college had survived a grave struggle for solvency, despite persistent disorder in accounts and collections. Only two of its five presidents had lived more than eighteen months after appointment. Aaron Burr's administration was by far the longest — nine years — making him the principal personality of this earliest, most difficult era. Dickinson had not lived to see the confirmation of the charter; Edwards died before his family could move to Princeton; Davies lived only a year and a half from the date of his appointment, July, 1759. Finley was chosen promptly upon the death of Davies and survived for five years but throughout the latter part of his administration he was in poor health. The school was without a president for more than two years until John Witherspoon, Finley's successor, arrived in Princeton. For all its gains, the college was greatly in need of a strong hand.

The trustees had long hoped to appoint regular professors but funds were lacking. Instruction was conducted principally by a succession of young tutors among whom few remained more than three years. The college was fortunate in having able men, however, in the tutorships. Jeremiah Halsey served from 1757 until 1767, when the trustees recognized his immense service to the school, not less important for its duration than its quality, by voting him the entire " graduation money," sixty-one pounds.[16] Samuel Blair, son of the graduate of the Log College, was elected tutor in 1762 and served for three

---

[15] W. H. Foote, *Sketches of Virginia*. First series (Philadelphia, 1850), 248 f. Cf. Letter of Tennent to Stewart, January 5, 1755. HSP, Gratz, Case 8, box 25.

[16] Quoted from the minutes of the Board by Maclean, *op. cit.*, 266.

years. He became president-elect in 1767 when he was but twenty-six years of age but withdrew upon learning that Witherspoon, the first choice of the trustees, was willing to come if invited again.

Except for James Thompson, who served eight years, no other tutor served more than three years and most not more than two. Eleven different tutors served in the nine-year administration of Burr. A few, such as Joseph Periam, subsequently ventilated theological views that gave considerable dissatisfaction to the friends of the college. When Witherspoon arrived, he found only four members on his staff: John Blair, newly appointed professor of divinity and moral philosophy; Joseph Periam, who had just succeeded the veteran Halsey as senior tutor; James Thompson; and Jonathan Edwards, Jr., who had also been recently appointed. This, in fact, was the strongest faculty the college had ever enjoyed, despite the resignation of so outstanding a man as Halsey.

Blair's appointment was to have been the first step in an ambitious plan of faculty development. According to an action of the board of October 2, 1767, Jonathan Edwards was to be advanced to the professorship of languages and logic; Hugh Williamson, of Philadelphia, an Old Side sympathizer, to be engaged as professor of mathematics and natural philosophy; Samuel Blair, to be president (Witherspoon at that date having refused the position) and professor of rhetoric and metaphysics. As it turned out, Edwards remained a tutor until his resignation in 1769; John Blair resigned in the spring of 1769 for lack of funds to support him; Samuel Blair withdrew from the presidency-professorship in favor of Witherspoon, who then assumed John Blair's duties; and no date was ever set for Williamson's removal to Princeton.

The general orientation of the staff in regard to the theological and philosophical issues of the day is noteworthy. The last three presidents — Edwards, Davies, and Finley — had been leaders in the revival, and the college had become progressively more hospitable to the theology of the successors of

Edwards, principally Joseph Bellamy and Samuel Hopkins. The former had persuaded Jonathan Edwards, Jr., not to despise his father's views,[17] and the younger Edwards proved to be an independent and analytic mind. Before Blair was selected for the chair of divinity, he joined with Alexander McWhorter and James Caldwell in an effort to bring Samuel Hopkins, the rising theologian of the new divinity, into the faculty of the college at Princeton. To Bellamy, Caldwell wrote in March, 1767: "You will be informed, I expect by Mr. McWhorter and more particularly by the bearer, Mr. Edwards, what steps we are taking to obtain Mr. Hopkins as a professor at the college. . . . Mr. Edwards is to try him. I hope you will go with Mr. Edwards to assist. . . . We shall push the matter with spirit. We want the fountain clear that the streams may be so too." [18]

In the circumstances, this meant that the college was hostile to the Old Side. Accounts of the maneuvering of that party after Finley's death for dominance of the burgeoning school may be found in both Maclean and Trinterud; what is important for this study is that the selection of Witherspoon amounted to a serious effort to heal the wound of the church.

Richard Stockton pleaded with Witherspoon to accept in April, 1767. "What shall I and my brethren, who have the inspection and care of that rising Seminary do? Shall we turn to our old antagonists and thereby let him in wholesale, or shall we make them greater enemies than ever by totally neglecting them? I am pained when I think of the consequences of your determining against us." [19]

But so much more was entailed for the future of the Presbyterian ministry in the selection of the mighty Scot that the irenic intent of the board was but the preface to an academic administration that founded a new era in the history of Presbyterianism and its clergy.

[17] Cf. Bainton, *op. cit.*, 56.
[18] *Proceedings of the New Jersey Historical Society*, VI, 173 f.
[19] Letter of Richard Stockton to John Witherspoon, London, April 14, 1767. PHS, MS. W771.

VI

THE WITHERSPOON ADMINISTRATION

THE COLLEGE OF NEW JERSEY was, in 1758, the most successful educational venture in the middle colonies. Its only rival was the College of Philadelphia, founded in 1755. Under its Episcopal provost, William Smith, the latter was capably served by Francis Alison but was slipping into Anglicanism and already losing the confidence of Presbyterians.[1] In September, 1758, sixty-six men had completed their training for the ministry at Nassau Hall. Thirty-eight were Presbyterian; twenty-two Congregationalist; two entered the ministry of the Dutch churches; there was one Episcopalian. Several ordained graduates entered educational mission work.[2] A full half of the clergy of the reunited Presbyterianism of 1758 were graduates of a school founded by the friends of revival and led by men friendly to the theology of Edwards and the fellowship of New England.

When commencement services ended in 1768, the first which John Witherspoon attended, seventy-three more clergymen had graduated from the college, forty-five of them Presbyterian. Again the second group was Congregationalist. Four Baptists,

---

[1] William B. Sprague, *Annals of the American Pulpit*, 3 vols. (New York, 1858), III, 74. Cf. Trinterud, *The Forming of an American Tradition*, 159, 214 ff. Cf. Richard Webster, *A History of the Presbyterian Church in America*, 440–443.

[2] S. D. Alexander, *Princeton College During the Eighteenth Century*, 1–56.

three Episcopalians, and three Dutch clergymen were readied for the ministry, and at least seven graduates became eminent in education, some of these having studied theology.[3]

In the two decades from its founding until the arrival of Witherspoon, 313 men had graduated from the college, of whom 47 per cent (148) had entered the ministry. Presbyterians had reason for confidence. The total ministerial membership of the Synod of New York and Philadelphia was impressive. From its beginning in 1706 with six ministers in a single presbytery, the church had now grown to include at least 102 ministers on the rolls of ten presbyteries. But the rate of growth was not the only index of strength, for the outcome of the great Presbyterian controversy had, on the whole, been favorable. Before the division in 1741, the total ministerial membership of the Synod of Philadelphia had stood at forty-seven. At its first meeting after the expulsion of the " new lights," the Old Side claimed thirty-eight members; but after the Dickinson group gave up its effort of reconciliation and joined the expellees in the new Synod of New York in 1745, the Synod of Philadelphia was reduced from a claimed forty-four to an actual membership of twenty-eight. During the seventeen years that elapsed before reunion, the Old Side church received five men from abroad and New England and ordained seventeen. To the reunion of 1758, they brought twenty-three ministers.

The New Side, at the formation of the Synod of New York in 1745, enrolled twenty-two ministers. In the interim before reunion, sixty-six were ordained and fifteen received, all but one from New England. Ministerial supply from Scotland and Ireland having completely dried up, the early New Side support of American theological education had proved fateful. Of the young men ordained by the Synod of New York before 1758, a full third were New England men. About twenty were Irish born and American educated; except for two Englishmen and one Welshman, the rest were American born.[4] The total

---

[3] *Ibid.*, 57–116.   [4] Webster, *op. cit.*, 250 f.

membership of the Synod of New York in 1758 was seventy-two, a net gain of fifty. The first official listing of the reunited church was ninety-four.[5]

It had been an uneasy decade since the reunion, but with so full a company of ministers and the lively hope that with Witherspoon in Princeton some of the old rancors could be surmounted, Presbyterianism appeared in a promising situation.

WITHERSPOON AS EDUCATOR

Although few could have guessed just how apt the decision was, Witherspoon was well chosen for the new era. To the American Presbyterian, Witherspoon's stinging criticism of the spongy theology of Moderatism identified him as a man who demanded a living religion. But in Scotland the patronage issue was a national cause, and by aligning himself against the Moderates, who supported it, Witherspoon proved his concern for causes public and political as well as private and ecclesiastical. Such gifts and interests were to dominate his career in North America.

Churchman though he was, Witherspoon's ultimate influence as an educator lay on the side of civism. Ashbel Green commented that "his improvements . . . mainly consisted in rendering the college life better adapted to qualify his pupils for active life." [6] Witherspoon introduced French, the language of the philosophy of revolt; insisted on proficiency in written and spoken English; greatly expanded the library; and argued the importance of a "very general knowledge of authors, books, and opinions of all kinds." [7] "The Dr. in his lectures does not go on in the order that System writers generally do," wrote a friend to Philip Fithian, "but chooses out the most important subjects in divinity . . . and treats them in as concise a manner as possible to give us a clear notion of them

[5] Cf. Trinterud, *The Forming of an American Tradition*, 150 ff.
[6] Sprague, *op. cit.*, III, 299.
[7] Ashbel Green's MS. account of Witherspoon's Administration. PHS, MS. W771g, 1841. Cf. Witherspoon's *Works*, IV, 17.

and gives us the several opinions of the ablest writers." [8]
Witherspoon's first professional appointment was in mathematics and natural philosophy: William Churchill Houston in 1771.

Witherspoon's sermons were conventional and his oratorical style drab, but he had distinguished himself as a satirist. His famous *Ecclesiastical Characteristics,* a biting attack on the policies of Scottish Moderatism, was compared in its time with the work of Dean Swift. In this tour de force, Witherspoon burlesqued the views and attitudes of his opponents with such effect that he was hounded in the church courts of Scotland until his departure for America. "It is not only unnecessary for a moderate man to have much learning," he wrote, "but he ought to be filled with a contempt of all kinds of learning but one, which is, to understand Leibnitz's scheme well; the chief parts of which are so beautifully painted and so harmoniously sung by Lord Shaftesbury, and which have been so well licked into form and method by the late immortal Mr. Hutcheson." After reciting the "Athenian Creed" of the Moderates, Witherspoon concludes with this article: "I believe in the divinity of Lord Shaftesbury, the saintship of Marcus Antoninus, the perspicuity and sublimity of Aristotle, and the perpetual duration of Mr. Hutcheson's works, not withstanding their present tendency to oblivion. Amen." [9]

Witherspoon gave steady support throughout his career to the ideal of literary excellence and its classical correlate, public life. He wrought no revolution in the curriculum at Princeton but bent the established classical course markedly toward preparation for law and public life and less exclusively toward the pulpit.

The curriculum at the close of Finley's administration was similar to that in the European schools of the eighteenth century and not much changed from that described by Joseph Shippen twenty years earlier. The standard division of under-

[8] Letter of Hunter to Fithian, *Journal and Letters, 1767–1774* (Princeton, 1900), 29.
[9] Varnum Lansing Collins, *President Witherspoon,* 2 vols. (Princeton, 1925), I, 36 f.

graduate students into four classes was by then fully established. Freshmen studied Latin and Greek: Horace, Cicero, the *Dialogues* of Lucian, Xenophon, and the Greek Testament. In the sophomore year, classical reading continued with introduction to geography, rhetoric, logic, and mathematics. Scientific studies received increasing emphasis as the student advanced through the junior year, where he added moral philosophy, metaphysics, and — for the theological student — Hebrew. The last year was spent in the practice of the arts learned in the first three: writing, debate, and declamation were accompanied by analysis of the literary style of the classical authors. Orations were delivered in Latin. In form these academic exercises were medieval: subjects for disputation were announced in advance. On Sundays, topics in the field of religion were publicly debated. The library was open to upperclassmen, and final examination of candidates for the bachelor of arts degree was conducted by the trustees in the third week of August each year, assisted by the staff of the college. The student's showing on this occasion determined his place in the formalities that ended the college year in September.

With the resignation of John Blair, Witherspoon himself assumed the instruction of divinity and continued to take considerable responsibility in other fields of learning as well, such as philosophy, French, English literature, and the adjudicating of disputations. He instructed in Hebrew and exegesis as well as theology and history. Only student notes of his lectures in divinity are preserved, but he appears to have proposed nothing that went materially beyond the treatment of theology then current in the Scottish universities. Witherspoon's creativity was not great. His innovations lay in the liberal curriculum: modern languages, instruction in the sciences, and the art of public address. Green speaks of "daily orations" during his student days after 1782.[10]

At the outset, Witherspoon's knowledge of the College of

[10] PHS, A. Green's MS. 771g, 8.

New Jersey cannot have been very great. He was sent a copy of *A General Account of the Rise and State of the College,* a booklet prepared by Samuel Blair in 1752 to support the mission of Davies and Gilbert Tennent to the British Isles. Richard Stockton and the young Benjamin Rush, then a medical student in England, had discussed the college with him.[11] What impressions Witherspoon may have retained from his encounter with Tennent and Davies fourteen years earlier can only be conjectured. So far as is known, he possessed only one of the major writings of Jonathan Edwards, the *Treatise Concerning Religious Affections,* to which he had subscribed. Beyond that, he had read Edwards' *Life of Brainerd* and some lesser essays. He probably thought of Edwards as a revivalist and preacher rather than as a philosopher and theologian.

EDWARDS' IDEALISM AND WITHERSPOON'S REALISM

Witherspoon's celebrated encounter with Edwardeanism on the campus of the college in 1769 was rich in misunderstanding, and in microcosm exhibited the nuclear truth about Presbyterianism's latest age: within a short span after Finley's death, Princeton was already losing contact with its hard-won colonial character.

Stirrings of the Spirit had persisted on the campus since the Great Awakening. In 1757, for example, Obadiah Wells of New York wrote: "Fourteen scholars in the Senior class are truly esteemed sincere converts and . . . every scholar in the college is seriously engaged in seeking an interest in the Lord Jesus Christ."[12] Some of the students enrolled in 1770 found

11 Letter of Stockton to Witherspoon, April 14, 1767; and Rush to Witherspoon, October 23, 1767. PHS, MS. W771. Cf. Collins, *op. cit.,* I, 97 ff.
12 Letter to Bellamy, March 19, 1757, *Proceedings of the New Jersey Historical Society* (Newark, 1853), VI, 170. Evidence of discussion of religion appears in correspondence between Finley and Eleazer Wheelock of Dartmouth, who asked Finley to explain the " pushing and setting up one above and so against another in matters of religion

Witherspoon "what we call a dull preacher"[13] and to gratify their enthusiasm, Jedediah Chapman of Newark accepted their invitation to preach. "I spent nearly a week there with great pleasure and satisfaction," he wrote Bellamy. "My time was wholly taken up in College, chiefly in private conversation. I preached three sermons — met several times in praying societies. . . . The truth prevails greatly but not without opposition. There are a number of ingenious fellows that are determined to study divinity under your inspection next winter."[14]

A similar awakening occurred in 1772 and Chapman again was invited.[15] But the preacher who came was Dr. Elihu Spencer, of Trenton, and he did not suit the youthful Edwardeans on the campus. Ebenezer Bradford, a member of the class of 1773 and later an eminent Congregational minister, was chief among them. To fortify the work of Spencer, Bradford circulated copies of Bellamy's *True Religion Delineated* with the title pages excised. The book having commended itself to the students, Bradford would then reveal its authorship with a view to bringing his fellows under the influence of Bellamy's evangelicalism. He succeeded in raising a subscription for two hundred copies of the book. The Rev. Mr. Chapman discovered on a return visit to the campus that this strategy had enjoyed considerable success.[16]

With due allowance for Bradford's enthusiasm, his judgment on Witherspoon holds considerable interest. "Both the Dr. and he [Witherspoon and Elihu Spencer] are great enemies to

---

in the college." Finley in his reply mentioned the coming of Whitefield in November, 1763. HSP, Gratz, Case 8, box 22.

[13] Philip Fithian felt differently. He wrote his father in 1770: "I am indeed much pleased with Dr. Witherspoon and think his sermons almost inimitable," *Journal*, 9.

[14] Letter of Jedediah Chapman, August 25, 1770, *Proceedings*, VI, 174.

[15] Letter of Jedediah Chapman to Bellamy, April 1, 1772, *ibid.*, 175.

[16] Letter to Bellamy, April 28, 1772. Cf. Letter of Andrew Hunter, Jr., to Philip Fithian, *op. cit.*, 21 f. Lewis Feuilleteau Wilson, a youth "thought to have got religion" at this time, became a minister but abandoned the ministry for medicine at the outbreak of the Revolutionary War.

what they call Eastward, or New Divinity, which was so much exploded by all in college that when I came here . . . I was advised by a particular friend not to let my sentiments be known." Bradford's views were more than impression. "The Dr. has lately been conversed with upon these things since they have made such progress in the College," he wrote Bellamy, "and declared that he is neither for nor against them; however, he both preaches and converses in contradistinction to them."[17] In a biography of Burr current in Green's time, it had been stated that Witherspoon was hostile to the revival. It is true that he condemned "rash-judging" as an effect of pride and malice.[18] Green admits that "he did endeavor to correct some irregularities and imprudences which usually take place when youth are under the excitement of strong religious feeling." But Green vehemently denied that this implied antagonism to revival. Witherspoon's very motives in coming to the colonies were consistent with the friendliest attitude toward revival, Green argued, and he explicitly denied that Witherspoon "thought or spoke lightly of this revival or that he was in fact opposed to it."[19]

The truth of the matter may be adduced from Witherspoon's "philosophy of revival." In his lectures on "Eloquence," he is quoted by a student as remarking that "there is a piercing, penetrating heat in that which glows from the heart which distinguished it both from the coldness of indifference and the false fire of enthusiasm."[20] There can be no doubt of Witherspoon's genuine concern for piety, which to him meant experience consistent with beliefs that conduced to their practice. Piety "gives a man the knowledge that is of the most service to a Minister. Experimental knowledge is superior to all others and most necessary to the perfection of every other kind of knowledge. . . . Experimental knowledge is the best sort in

---

[17] Letter of E. Bradford, April 18, 1772, *Proceedings*, VI, 176.
[18] PHS, MS. W771.
[19] PHS, MS. 771g, 12.
[20] PHS, MS. M157, 54.

every branch; but it is highly necessary in divinity because religion is what cannot be truly understood except as it is felt."

On the assumptions of Scottish realism Witherspoon inevitably distrusted any philosophy that contested the trustworthy correspondence of experience with reality. To him, the soul of revival was its validity as experience. To Edwards, its dynamic arose from man's rational vision of the perfections of God. No philosopher, Witherspoon did not venture upon a critique of Edwards. In the intellectual history of the Awakening we are here encountering philosophical positions that are clearly in conflict: the " idealist " theory of revival and its source, man's rational vision of the perfections of God; Witherspoon's " realism " of conversion and other " spiritual experiences." The choice was never so clearly defined as this in the eighteenth century, and the picture was muddled by the injection of a third " philosophy of revival " by Finney and his New England supporters in the nineteenth: the view that man is in himself, precisely as he is, altogether capable of marshaling the forces necessary to say, " I will." Thanks to Hopkins, Taylor, and Finney, the Old School realists who followed Witherspoon understood Edwardeanism not so much as a movement of revival arising in man's vision of God as a revision of orthodox anthropology in the direction of Arminianism. In this confusion, Presbyterian doctrinal history lost sight of the issue that existed between Edwards and Witherspoon.

How a Minister Knows God

The problem of the Scottish mind with the idealism of Edwards was pungently expressed by Robert Riccaltoun of Hobkirk, Scotland, in his comment on Bellamy's *True Religion Delineated*. " I am sorry to say that he appears to me deeply . . . tainted with the evil disease of regarding the nature and fitness of things and the eternal truths thence arising in the imagination, as the only thing worth a philosopher's notice. . . . Their fantastical, unmeaning terms — the nature of things, moral fitness, the true taste or moral sense, moral beauty, with much more such affected cant — run through the whole of his book. He carries them so far as to prescribe law to the Almighty, and dictate with assurance what he may do. . . . Instead of founding religion . . . on the love of God in Christ, and the plain facts by which it is evidenced and imprinted, he runs out into metaphysical excursions to raise and establish a sort of idea of God and his essential, and what he calls his moral perfections, (in the very words or phrases of that sort of man) abstracted from, and previous to, any discoveries he has made of himself in Christ." [21]

Berkeleianism argued that all a man can know of an object of thought is his own idea of it. Edwards presented an idea of God perfect in his moral excellency. An orthodox Scot found any "idea" of God far different from perceived *reality*, and Witherspoon was unwilling to commit himself religiously to an ideal of divine excellence that enjoyed at best an uncertain relationship to concrete experience of divine reality.

On the level of philosophy, Thomas Reid later undertook to demonstrate the unreliability of the Berkeleian position. But Riccaltoun was more direct. To him, the knowledge of God could never be grounded in metaphysics at all but only in historic acts of self-revelation.

Later Presbyterians would have done well to pursue the Christology of Riccaltoun, but they were determined experimentalists and assumed that the realism of the Scottish school must be the companion philosophy to revival if charges of enthusiasm in conversion were to be repelled. "Spiritual experience," that is, must be understood as a direct effect of ultimate reality. Far from recognizing the Edwardean vision of God as supremely capable of moving man to repentance, these Presbyterians believed that idealism threatened the validity of the revival by creating a doubt as to whether the convert had been moved by anything more than his own notions.

[21] Letter of Robert Riccaltoun to Erskine, quoted in Richard Webster, *op. cit.*, 630.

Witherspoon personally was friendly to revival understood as a veritable impression of divine reality on the heart and mind; he was unfriendly to philosophies that doubted the correspondence between external objects and man's inward apprehension of them.[22] Ebenezer Bradford was not wrong to construe Witherspoon's classroom critique of idealism as implicit opposition to Bellamy and his sort of revival. Following Witherspoon's example, Samuel Stanhope Smith, who ran the college during the war and became its president in 1794, assigned readings in Thomas Reid, professor of philosophy at Edinburgh and the leading contemporary critic of Berkeley.

THE REORGANIZATION OF THE FACULTY

Although the kinship of the Edwardean stream with Berkeleianism appears not to have been spelled out in the intellectual life of the college at this date, Witherspoon's preference for Scottish realism brought him none the less decisively into conflict with the new divinity. Upon his arrival in 1768, Witherspoon found on his staff Joseph Periam, an outspoken Berkeleian. Ashbel Green later wrote: " The Berkeleyan sys-

---

[22] To affirm that the Old School party was hostile to revival is too simple. Revival by the methods and theological and philosophical presuppositions of Nathaniel Taylor and Charles G. Finney was indeed feared by the Old School men, but at the same time the consistent emphasis upon the " state of the church " in Assembly reports cannot be dismissed. Ashbel Green put the case for revival on his own terms in *The Christian Advocate*, 1828, 329. The seaboard mentality of the Presbyterian conservatives, their insistence on doctrinal soundness and the standard of theological education they believed essential to protect it, their reluctance to accept different church habit on the frontier, and their emphasis on private piety as against social penetration as a proper consequence of revival combined to produce attitudes that amounted to hostility to revival as it actually flourished between 1810 and 1830 in Kentucky, New York, and other western regions. Nevertheless, revivals of a sort that suited the Old School were consistently reported throughout this period. Their problem lay in the interior character of revival — its theological presuppositions, methods, and effects — rather than being a matter of outright antirevivalism. Cf. *The Christian Advocate*, 1831, 64.

tem of metaphysics was in repute in the college when he entered. The tutors were zealous believers in it and waited on the President with some expectation of either confounding him or making him a proselyte. They had mistaken their man. He first reasoned against the system and then ridiculed it till he drove it out of the college." [23] Green's account is probably colored, since Bradford himself never alleged more than an implicit opposition to idealism; but that Witherspoon knew what he thought and did what he wanted can scarcely be questioned.

The position adopted by Witherspoon was vindicated in the minds of many when after leaving Princeton to study with Bellamy, Periam made statements that were damning in the eyes of the orthodox. Applying for licensure to the Presbytery of New York, he declared flatly that God was the author of sin, a view that with some justice was coming to be regarded as a symbol of the new divinity. The year 1769 was historic for both the new university and the church whose leadership it trained. Periam left; John Blair resigned; and so did Jonathan Edwards, Jr., the plan for his advancement to a regular professorship having failed. Thus, within a year of his assumption of presidential responsibilities, Witherspoon was no longer aided by three Edwardeans but had personally assumed the teaching of theology. Princeton divinity was henceforth erected on philosophical foundations laid in Scotland and designed to withstand the novelties of modern philosophy and theology.

The passing of the revival age in Presbyterianism nevertheless cannot be attributed to calculated hostility to revival or Edwardean thought. Witherspoon was not an Old Side man; in his relation to old American quarrels he was differently positioned, both theologically and ecclesiastically. The change that came so swiftly on the Presbyterian Church was the ef-

[23] Ashbel Green, *The Life of the Rev. John Witherspoon, D.D., LL.D., with a brief review of his writings and summary estimate of his character and talents.* New Jersey Historical Society Library, MS. The MS. is inconsistently paginated.

fect of the intrusion of powerful new currents of men and ideas from the Old World, personified and symbolized by Witherspoon, in an epoch of pressing social change. The new mold found the material soft, and it was the work of only half a generation to alter the character of the American Presbyterian Church.

THE PERSONAL INFLUENCE OF WITHERSPOON

Although under Witherspoon the College of New Jersey was increasingly oriented toward national affairs, it continued to dominate the development of Presbyterianism. New England trained a handful of Presbyterian clergymen during the last quarter of the century, to be sure, and not all Princeton men were hostile to the theology of Bellamy and Hopkins. But it was Witherspoon's mind that ruled the divinity classes at Princeton; and it was his graduates who filled the General Assembly. Despite a sharply decreased service of the college to the Presbyterian Church, Witherspoon could still remark to Ashbel Green in 1791: "You can scarcely imagine the pleasure it has given me in taking a survey of this Assembly to believe that a decided majority of all the ministerial members have not only been sons of our college but my own pupils." Of the thirty-six ministerial members present that year, twenty-eight were Princeton graduates and sixteen former students of Witherspoon himself. At the first registering of the reorganized church in 1789, the General Assembly reported a total of 188 Presbyterian ministers of whom ninety-seven were graduates of the school at Princeton and fifty-two of these former students of President Witherspoon.

Witherspoon's influence on Presbyterianism was multiplied many times by the extraordinary involvement of his graduates in educational activity. More than 11 per cent of those graduating in his administration became college presidents, many of them founders.[24] Jonathan Edwards, Jr., became the president

24 Collins, *op. cit.*, II, 223.

of Union College in Schenectady but was followed by John Blair Smith, a Witherspoon graduate. Witherspoon was succeeded by Samuel Stanhope Smith, who graduated in 1769 and whose leadership after 1794 was markedly different from that of Witherspoon. But Smith was succeeded by Ashbel Green in 1812, a "reform" president who held Witherspoon in as great veneration as any man he ever trained. John McMillan (1772) and Thaddeus Dodd (1773) founded higher education in western Pennsylvania. As presidents and professors, Witherspoon men labored in Virginia, North Carolina, South Carolina, Tennessee, Georgia, Kentucky, New Jersey, and New York.

Of the 114 men who entered ministerial service under Witherspoon, seventy-five were graduates of the years before the Revolutionary War. The high production of clergy remained substantially unchanged, therefore, from the founding of the school until the war; it was the radical reorientation of mind and interest in this troubled period that threw the church into revolution. From 1777 to 1794, when Witherspoon yielded to Smith, only thirty-nine Princeton men became ministers, a feeble 13 per cent of the modest total graduated.

The first substantial class to graduate after the war received degrees in 1784: twenty-seven men destined to a variety of occupations. The class of 1776 had been the last to graduate before the Battle of Princeton, also twenty-seven. Not until 1782 did more than six men graduate at any commencement.[25]

The total number of clergymen produced after the recovery of the college enrollment, the final decade of the Witherspoon administration, was thirty-one. The war appears as the hinge of the era. The power of a revived church to produce candidates for the ministry did not ebb until the outbreak of the Revolution; but the Presbyterian Church did not recover that critical gift even after the enrollment of the college had once again achieved reasonable size and stability. The zeal that

[25] Statistical information is derived from John Maclean, *History of the College of New Jersey, 1746–1854.*

had once lived in the churches now made the civil life of the community its temple.

It is indicative of the changing temper of American history that the sons of the great clerics of that earlier age now sought their public role at the bar. Alexander Cumming McWhorter, the son of the alumnus and trustee of the college, became an attorney, as did John Spencer, son of Elihu Spencer, trustee and preacher to the students in 1772. Pierpont Edwards, son of the president of the college, became a federal district judge, and his son, John Starke Edwards, filled a variety of civil offices during his career as an attorney and officer in the War of 1812. Timothy Edwards, eldest son of the president, was a respected businessman and became a judge in the state of Connecticut.[26] Witherspoon's son John became a medical doctor, and another son, David, practiced law in North Carolina. The college at Princeton was shifting its weight from the church to the state, from the clergy to the bar. Out of this circumstance, added to the insistent demand of the new western areas for a ministry, arose the impetus for the founding of the theological seminaries.

[26] S. D. Alexander, *op. cit.*, 45, 144, 292.

VII

THE IMPACT OF SECULAR CULTURE

THE FOUNDING of the fully independent theological seminaries was more than a device for educating more young men to a higher standard of learning; it was one form of the reaction of orthodox American Calvinism to the new orientation of the national culture. It coincided with and expressed a new understanding of the church's ministry and the function of its ministerial officers.

The colonial pastor was the pre-eminent figure of his community. The ecclesiastical order of the parish bore on the life of the whole town and determined acceptable forms of public behavior. As the Pennsylvania frontier in the colonial period shows, church government virtually corresponded with civil government before the organization of public order.[1] The minister was not only the public's moral administrator but its educator, not only in the congregation but through the academies commonly associated with churches. Preaching touched every issue of concern to the people, religious and civil, personal and public. The ministry was comprehensive and social and it placed the person of the minister at the heart of the lives of his people. In a way which can now be recaptured only by a strenuous effort of imagination, the minister was God's man. Church order symbolized the order of God's Kingdom; church censures bespoke divine judgment. This pattern of

[1] Guy S. Klett, *Presbyterians in Colonial Pennsylvania* (University of Pennsylvania Press, 1937), 116–126.

ministry and image of the minister presumed much but it also offered much, and when the world that was built around it passed away Calvinists scarcely knew how to rebuild the church and ministry or fix the role of the minister afresh.

THE NEW PUBLIC PREOCCUPATION

As the Revolution approached, the minds of the American settlers were forced to ponder problems that could not be solved by the application of the rules for living that had previously ordered the affairs of their villages. Colonial society was suddenly engrossed with ideas and decisions that were not churchly but clearly civil. The war forced Americans to decide and sustain policies on war and peace, and then new laws had to be framed. The country was precipitated into an absorbing debate on the natural rights of man and their bearing on public institutions. For the first time, the public at large recognized an area of debate and action that stood unmistakably clear of the church.

Churchmen were drawn into the vortex willy-nilly, Witherspoon conspicuously but others no less completely. His decision in 1782 to strike free of public affairs was due partly to the demands of the college, but he and his fellow clergymen faced at the same time a larger issue. Should a Christian become involved in public duty? What theological principles should guide him if he did? Should national issues be discussed in the pulpit as they had been during the Revolutionary War? At the Great Awakening the church was occupied with its own spiritual state. Could such a churchly concern be harmonized with involvement in the great national question?

The social upheaval had left a heritage of disorder and callousness. The prolonged religious depression after the Revolution was relieved only briefly by revivals in western Pennsylvania and Virginia in 1786–1790, and it continued regionally after 1800. Presbyterians prayed fervently for a new revival. It dawned on them only very slowly that they were living in a fundamentally changed society. " Since the French Revolution our congregations are become thinner and thinner," wrote Charles Nisbet to Jedediah Morse on the fourth day of the nineteenth century. " Those who continue to attend public worship are looser in their lives and opinions. The Sabbath is spent by many in traveling, idle visiting and amusement. Youth have no religious education and can scarcely do worse than by imitating the example of their parents. Family worship and family discipline are almost at an end and the youth are allowed by their parents to do anything that they please. Having never heard anything extolled or recommended except liberty, they think themselves entitled to all the privileges of Sovereign peoples. What a dismal presage this affords for the next generation need not be mentioned." [2] Against this trend the eighteenth-century Presbyterian brought the well-tempered sword of revival. Green made it clear upon assuming the presidency of the College of New Jersey in 1812 that any really pious student would inform on rioters.[3]

The situation was no less grave than this: for the first time in American history, a view of man deeply hostile to Calvinism was vigorously soliciting the loyalty of the American people. It was so manifold in its bearing on public order and so pervasive in the minds of both churchmen and nonchurchmen that the old tradition faced a major challenge to its dominion. At the very heart of established Congregationalism, Boston had been dabbling with Arminianism since 1730 and was now on the point of declaring for Unitarianism. The Calvinist revisionists, notably Samuel Hopkins, had been nurtured face to face with this problem and their publications, widely read in the middle states, were bent toward the issue of the new age in a fashion strange to Presbyterians.

[2] Letter of Charles Nisbet to Jedediah Morse, January 4, 1800. Dreer, V, HSP.
[3] Letter of A. Green to Benjamin Rush, January 2, 1813. LCP, Rush MS., Vol. 23, 51.

THE NEW ENGLAND REACTION

By 1795, New England orthodox leaders knew their situation was critical. Evangelicals were split by the increasingly sectarian spirit of the Hopkinsian party into revisionists and Old Calvinists. All Calvinists together, including Hopkinsians of a variety of colorations and Old Calvinists as well, were about to lose control of Harvard College. In 1795, Jedediah Morse, pastor of the Charlestown Church, preached on *The Present Situation of Other Nations* and sounded anew the classic conviction that although Satan had brought catastrophe to Europe, some hope of preserving faith and godly society remained in the new world and in 1798 he offered evidence that the root of the problem lay in the deceptive character of the French Revolutionary philosophy.[4] Between 1795 and 1800 orthodoxy in New England, led by Morse in Massachusetts and Lyman Beecher and Timothy Dwight of Yale in Connecticut, opened a vigorous propaganda against French infidelity and Unitarianism, the churchly beachhead of the atheistical spirit of France.[5] In the next ten years, the *Panoplist* was founded, Hopkinsians and Old Calvinists politically reconciled, Andover Seminary and the American Board of Commissioners for Foreign Missions founded, and a covey of societies for home missions, Bible publication, and promotion of morals established in the villages of New England. By these means, New England orthodox men intended to maintain in the new situation their ideal of the Christian society.

Soon after his accession to the presidency of Yale, Timothy Dwight lectured on *The Nature and Danger of Infidel Philosophy*.[6] His indictment was thoroughgoing and well documented. Philosophy as "the use and the attainments of our

---

[4] Sermon of J. Morse at Charlestown, November 29, 1798. PSL, Spr., I, 94:4.

[5] Sermon on *The Present Dangers and Consequent Duties of the Citizens of the United States*, preached April 25, 1799. PSL, Spr., I, 94:3.

[6] Timothy Dwight, *The Nature and Danger of Infidel Philosophy* (published at New Haven, 1798).

reason in the candid and careful examination of every question within the limits of our understanding" Dwight both admitted and approved. The new philosophy, however, pretends to discover the "duty and supreme interest of man" without recourse to revelation. Christianity affirms that "to the discovery of man's supreme interest and duty it is absolutely necessary to discover, first, what is the preceptive will of God or what God requires man to do. . . . This, philosophy can never accomplish; and hence I assert it to be vain and deceitful in its nature."[7] Men are not competent to discern the will of God by analysis of past acts and formulation of general moral conceptions. "Analogical" argument may corroborate but cannot elaborate the Scriptures. Nor can God be "perfectly known from Creation and Providence"; man possesses neither the data, the capacity, nor the freedom from bias necessary to such an accomplishment. As "a rebel subject," man's first need is to discover the "means of restoration to the favour of God." Dwight deemed even Samuel Clarke, whom Witherspoon recommended, to have failed in his effort to prove the existence of God necessary, despite his undoubted fidelity and good intention. Comparison of philosophers reveals the utmost diversity among them, not to speak of impiety.[8]

Dwight warned his students against the deceitfulness of philosophy, whose object is "to unsettle every thing moral and obligatory and to settle nothing." This complaint the Calvinist clergy echoed again and again against the monster arising in France: a spirit of chaos, the great stone that shatters order in the nations, a harbinger of millennium, the oppressor of the church.[9] The New England Calvinist clergy were solidly Federalist in politics.[10]

Dwight noted that infidels indict Scriptures for obscurity

---

[7] *Ibid.*, 10–12.

[8] *Ibid.*, 35.

[9] James Gray, *Present Condition and Prospects of the Christian Church* . . . (Baltimore, 1821). PSL, Spr., I, 380:1.

[10] Cf. John Bodo, *The Protestant Clergy and Public Issues, 1812–1848.* Bodo traces the development of federalism among the orthodox Calvinists of New England.

and antiquity. This must be countered by sound literary and historical learning. Dwight recognized the prestige of the new philosophy and warned students against the arrogance and confidence that were making antireligious persuasion so effective. "It is boldly asserted that the world has neither lain in a state of ignorance and infancy; that it has been chained by authority, and influenced by superstition but that it has, at the present time, broken at once its bonds, roused itself into many exertions and seized intuitively upon the whole system of truth, moral, political, and natural." The achievements of philosophy are impressive indeed, conceded Dwight: "But that the knowledge or the happiness of mankind has been increased by the change" is yet to be proved.

As inducements to fidelity, Dwight pointed to the stability of Christianity against the amorphousness of philosophy and its failure to restrain social evil — indeed, its positive encouragement of vice. "All virtue is summed up in piety to God, justice, Truth, and kindness to our fellow men and the government of our own passions and appetites. . . . That piety is not encouraged by this philosophy will scarcely need to be proved. . . . This indifference to vice and virtue, sin and holiness, and to all their amazing effects . . . insensibly or surely steals upon the heart; none more thoroughly depraves the character; none more certainly conducts to misery and ruin."

The treatise concluded with an exhibition of the compassionate spirit and heavenly joy of the Christian life and the sturdy reminder that "misery produced here by sin may be unceasingly generated by the same wretched cause through ages which cannot end. . . . God doubtless is perfect in holiness as well as in power and knowledge" and thus "Christianity teaches . . . what reason dictates and the highest wisdom of man. But in all this, infidel philosophy has no part, nor let, nor memorial." [11] A note at the close of the book referred to the latest literary alarum, Robinson's exposé of the sinister schemes of the "Bavarian Illuminati," an international cabal

[11] T. Dwight, *op. cit.*, 50–94.

believed to be on the point of overturning the thrones of Europe and suppressing Christianity. Morse sounded the same warning in Boston, and Nisbet testified on the basis of personal friendship with Robinson that his book could be trusted.[12] Even though the panic evaporated when it was discovered that the society no longer existed, it left the conservative mind in New England all the more firmly fixed.

The Presbyterian Response

By 1800, Yale College was brimming with hopefully pious young men, many of them strongly directed toward the ministry, but in the middle states Presbyterians were a full pace behind. To be sure, the reaction against the French Revolution occurred instantly in America as in England. Nisbet spoke caustically of the "massacre of 10,000 prisoners at Nantes by the Sovereign people."[13] But that was France; the American republic was quite another thing. Only in 1818 was Philip Lindsley, the most effective professor at the College of New Jersey, able to identify the new menace. "Behold the progress of heresy and infidelity under the guise of rational Christianity," he warned. "The great destroyer has commissioned his emissaries to assume the garb and function of ministers of the gospel, that they may more effectually sap the foundation of the whole Christian edifice."[14] The answer proposed: the upbuilding of Princeton Seminary, a bulwark against an unconverted ministry. This term was not revived in the new century, but with a changed definition it was present. The menace was not lukewarmness to the splendor of God and the mercy of Jesus Christ but fascination with new thought. So

[12] Letter of Nisbet to Morse, January 4, 1800. HSP, Dreer, V.
[13] Letter of Nisbet to William Young, October 27, 1795. HSP, Dreer, V. Cf. JPHS, " Letters of Charles Nisbet to the Rev. William Marshall," XXXIX, 1, 43–61; 2, 98–106.
[14] A Plea for the Seminary at Princeton . . . preached before the Presbytery of New Brunswick, October 16, 1818 (Trenton, 1821). PSL, Southern Presbyterian Review, Spr., I, 446:1.

the church in this threatening new era must be secured by thorough education in trustworthy truths, relentless defense and counterattack, and the rigorous application of doctrinal and disciplinary standards to the ministerial corps.

The experience of Samuel Miller, second professor at Princeton Seminary, strikingly illustrates the difficulty of some Presbyterians in seeing that the culture had changed and the bitterness they felt when at length they realized that the American Revolution was not only a patriot's war but also a spiritual revolt against the Calvinist view of life. Miller had always assumed that Christian principle was both relevant and congenial to the public welfare. " Nothing has so great a tendency to promote and establish real liberty," he wrote, " as the practical influence of [Christianity]." [15] He once planned to address a pamphlet to the country's politicians, arguing the importance of Christianity to their vocation. The injection of religion into public affairs seemed, furthermore, wholly consistent with the new republican principles.

Change came in connection with Miller's support of Thomas Jefferson. Miller shared the going view that the new philosophy was a menace but, unlike many, considered it an alien force rather than a reality in American political life. In 1798 he inveighed against the enemy he saw. " The men who would rob you of this religion [are] your enemies and the enemies of all social happiness. . . . They may tell you ' that in casting off religion you will only free yourself from chains which cramp your faculties and degrade your nature. . . .' But O fellow mortals; examine well before you commit yourselves to their delusive guidance. Are you patriots and will you embrace principles which tend to dissolve all the ties of social order . . . ? "

Miller did not, however, associate these anarchic views with Jefferson. During the campaign of 1800 he supported Jefferson and deplored the charge that he was unfit for public office.

[15] Samuel Miller, *The Life of Samuel Miller, D.D., LL.D.,* 2 vols. (Philadelphia, 1869), I, 129.

"Because Mr. Jefferson is suspected of Deism, are we to raise a hue and cry against him as if he ought to be instantly deprived of his rights of citizenship? If he be an infidel, I lament it . . . but notwithstanding this, I think myself perfectly consistent in saying that I had much rather have Mr. Jefferson President of the United States than an aristocratic Christian." [16]   Miller's zeal cooled in 1808, when he wrote the President asking if he would welcome a formal request from a group of clergymen that he proclaim a day of religious observance. Jefferson refused. "I consider the government of the U.S. as interdicted by the Constitution from intermeddling with religious institutions. . . . I do not believe it is for the interest of religion to invite the civil magistrate to direct its exercises, its discipline, or its doctrines." [17]

Miller's loyalty to Jefferson had worn out by 1810 and in 1830 he wrote bitterly: "After the publication of his posthumous writings in 1829 my respect for him was exchanged for contempt and abhorrence. I now believe Mr. Jefferson to have been one of the meanest and basest of men. His own writings evince a hypocrisy, a selfishness, an artful, intriguing, underhand spirit, a contemptible envy of better men than himself, a blasphemous impiety and a moral profligacy which no fair, honest mind, to say nothing of piety, can contemplate without abhorrence. . . . I renounce and wish unsaid and unwritten everything that I ever said or wrote in his favor." [18]

Miller and the Calvinist clergy had never really believed that agitators like Ethan Allen and Tom Paine spoke for the Revolution, but as the age of American secularism dawned ever more unmistakably, the ministers shrank from the new republicanism and allied with federalism in a united counterattack. This provoked a spate of anticlerical literature from republican writers. Soon after 1790 there appeared from the hand of a Connecticut Yankee *A View of the Calvinistic Clubs in the*

[16] Letter to Gemmil, December 7, 1800. *Life*, II, 130 ff.
[17] January 23, 1818. *Life*, I, 236 f.
[18] Letter of S. Miller, June 2, 1830. *Life*, I, 132.

United States.[19] The anonymous author argued that the New England clergy had led the defection from the ideals of the Revolution after having taken the lead in the republican cause. The growing apparatus of voluntary churchmanship was one vast plot against the republic: the " concerts of prayer," missionary societies, and educational programs. " Connecticut is almost totally an ecclesiastical state ruled by the President of the College as a Monarch." Evidently a spokesman for anti-revivalism, the author simultaneously accused the clergy of adulation for Tom Paine's works and improper involvement in "polemic divinity."

Philip Lindsley drew such arrows from the church body. Would the seminary inevitably become " an engine of political power and ascendency," as charged by some? Would it "impart too much weight and influence and consideration to the clergy " in both church and state? On the contrary, sound religious education was essential to civil government. Lindsley echoed the thesis of Beecher that " human governments could do nothing were there no laborious teacher to . . . check the natural progress of vice and to train up the young in virtue's ways. Banish the minister of peace and this instruction is at an end." Lindsley sharply reminded the anticlerical republicans that " the Presbyterian clergy were pre-eminently devoted to the popular principles of 1776. Although they are sometimes pointed at now as the dangerous foes of that very system of equal liberty they themselves or their predecessors labored to establish – and on this ground the people are cautioned to guard against their acts and intrigues and especially against their growing numbers and influence." [20] Against all this is the truth that the seminary at Princeton " shall serve as the grand bulwark of evangelical truth and piety to the latest generation."

No American churchman was more ardent in support of the co-operation of church and state than Beecher, but he never-

---

[19] PSL, Spr., I, 485:1.
[20] Lindsley, *A Plea for the Seminary at Princeton*, Spr., I, 446:20.

theless cautioned the clergy against involvement in partisan politics. Miller and the Presbyterian leadership went even farther. "I was wrong in suffering myself to be so warmly and actively engaged in Politics as I was during that period," wrote Miller of his activities of 1800. "For though ministers have the rights and duties of citizens and probably in most cases ought to exercise the right of voting at elections; yet when party politics run high and when their appearing at the polls cannot take place without exciting strong feelings on the part of many against them; and when their ministry among all such persons will be therefore much less likely to be useful, I cannot think that their giving their votes can have an importance equivalent to the injury it is likely to do." [21] Archibald Alexander is reported never to have voted in his life. Ashbel Green, after sharing the enthusiasm of the Revolution, ceased to go to the polls. The onset of public debate in the 1830's aroused his interest afresh and he resumed voting about 1836 but in a mood far removed from his enthusiastic commitment to the Revolutionary struggle.

THE RESORT TO PIETY

By 1810 the Calvinist churches had experienced repulse in a land they had once called their own. The Presbyterian resort to revival and piety implied a relationship to public life quite different from that existing before the cultural upheaval. To a degree never anticipated before Witherspoon, piety lost its sense of relevance to the total society and pursued personal ideals of spirituality. The new era was already seeing the founding of numerous action societies designed to repel the demons of infidelity, immorality, and heresy but in the end, such societies became instruments of the church for its own defense. Beecher had originally conceived the action societies as God's new means of recalling American society as a whole to obedience to its divine Sovereign; but as the century wore

[21] S. Miller, *op. cit.*

on, the local, independent, highly motivated action groups became tiny wheels in the machinery of rival denominational boards and the vision of a Christly society became secondary to concern for institutional welfare.

The piety that waxed stronger as the century matured worked in partnership with the ecclesiasticizing of church life. The mission movement, for example, was promoted largely by the monthly " concert of prayer " for the heathen. " The Spirit of missions," wrote Henry A. Boardman in 1832, " is the spirit of piety," and increasingly the mission movement became the vehicle for the development of personalistic piety.[22] Piety consisted principally in a discipline of private prayer. In his diary, Ashbel Green wrote of one such day: " I observed this as a day of prayer with fasting so far as to abstain from food after breakfast till tea time in the evening. I began the exercises of the day with prostrating myself in my study and with confessing my sinfulness and imploring forgiveness." [23] The general object of this devotion was a renewal of " quickening grace," often felt concretely as a relief of tension. " In the former part of this day," wrote Green on another occasion, " I was very uncomfortable. My mind was full of discontent and a kind of sullen gloom. . . . I did not neglect my season of prayer in the evening. At length I obtained sweet relief in meditation and prayer. O, to be truly humble and truly submissive to God and to have a constant exercise of faith in his word and promises." [24] Green reflected the concern of the Awakening for a continuous sense of the sweetness of the divine presence. But in the new century, this was more a private exercise than a corporate church awakening and it existed in unprecedented isolation from the public philosophy.

[22] Letter of Henry A. Boardman to Mark Tucker, January 17, 1832. HSP, Gratz, Case 8, box 36.
[23] *The Life of Ashbel Green V.D.M.* (New York, 1849), edited by Joseph H. Jones, 453.
[24] *Ibid.*, 451.

VIII

SEMINARIES FOR CALVINISTS

THE SWING of the nation toward secularism became an acute problem for Calvinism when unitarianism invaded its parent institution in Cambridge, Massachusetts. The appointment of Henry Ware, the candidate of the liberal party in the Harvard Corporation and Board of Overseers, to the Hollis Professorship of Divinity in 1805 set off a train of events that carried American theological education out of the study of the pastor and college president into the fully institutionalized seminary.

THE ANDOVER IDEAL OF CALVINIST UNITY

The first step was taken in the Boston region by an alarmed orthodox party. Controversy between orthodoxy and the more pliant views of the Boston clergy had been continuous since the time of Jonathan Edwards, and the reaction against Calvinism received a fresh impulse from the sudden prestige of French rationalism after the Revolution. Ethan Allen, for example, argued that "though human reason cannot understand anything, yet in such things, which it does understand, its knowledge which is acquired by reasoning is as true and certain as the divine knowledge may be supposed to be." [1] Such views were later to be found at the heart of the Calvinist re-

[1] Ethan Allen, *Reason the Only Oracle of Man* (1784). Cf. W. H. Werkmeister, *A History of Philosophical Ideas in America* (The Ronald Press Company, 1949), 34.

visions of the nineteenth century, but in the perspective of orthodoxy in 1800 they threatened the supremacy of God and the
church in New English society.

Two men in particular led the counterattack: Timothy
Dwight, president of Yale, and Jedediah Morse, of Charlestown, Massachusetts. Dwight's career was spent in controversy with deism and its ecclesiastical kindred and in conduct
of the revivals that defeated them at Yale. But Morse united
New England orthodoxy against Harvard, most signally by his
indefatigable labor in behalf of Andover Theological Seminary, founded in 1808.[2]

Edwardean theology had maintained its momentum through
Bellamy to Samuel Hopkins, its proponents addressing themselves to the problem of anti-Calvinism while assimilating
something of its spirit. The *opus magnum* of Hopkins appeared in 1793, defining in intricate detail the special posture
of his party's theology; nevertheless, Morse argued that no ir-
reconcilable differences stood in the way of co-operation
among American Calvinists, regardless of party. Led by
Morse, Samuel Spring, and Leonard Wood, the last the leading
personality of the new seminary, Andover was intended as a
counterweight to secularism in general and Harvard in particular. In 1808, Morse and Wood were trusted in the middle
states and as late as 1820 it was to Moses Stuart, professor of
Biblical Studies at Andover, that the young Charles Hodge
went for counsel on his career.[3]

---

[2] James King Morse, *Jedediah Morse, A Champion of New England
Orthodoxy* (Columbia University Press, 1929), *passim.*

[3] Leonard Wood, *The History of Andover Theological Seminary* (Boston, 1885). " The Legal Aspects of the Andover Creed," *CH,* XV
(March, 1946), 34. Later controversy between Princeton and Andover is documented by the following sources: Moses Stuart, *Letters
on Eternal Generation;* Samuel Miller, *Letters on Eternal Sonship.*
Hodge attacked Stuart's position on Biblical interpretation in *BRPR,*
1830–1833, *passim.* Alexander wrote against Wood (*BRPR,* 1835)
and Emmons (*ibid.,* 1842, 529). This debate excited comment
among Unitarians: Cf. *A Unitarian Miscellany* (Baltimore, 1924),
325 ff. John Oliver Nelson has argued that Miller's writings were
primarily responsible for giving the intellectual product of Princeton

Andover was not only New England orthodoxy's principal supplier of clergymen forearmed against heresy and deism; around it there soon gathered a covey of *ad hoc* agencies. The revivals of the period after 1795 had produced volunteers for the ministry who were unable to pay for their theological education and in order to aid them a number of small local societies came into being. A great number of these were later gathered into the American Education Society. They directed many men to Andover and from among its students the American Home Mission Society and its antecedent agencies recruited missionaries to the West. Numbers of its graduates became foreign missionaries after the founding of the American Board of Commissioners in 1810. Substantial works of scholarship as well as periodical and ephemeral literature issued abundantly from its faculty.

Morse and his skillful colleagues had been compelled to work explicitly for co-operation between Hopkinsians and " Old Calvinists " because differences were solidly defined in New England by 1808, much more clearly than in New York and the middle and southern states. Until the dispute over the commissioning of Samuel H. Cox [4] by the Young Men's Missionary Society of New York in 1816, Presbyterians of Hopkinsian bent had enjoyed the usual privileges accorded ordained Presbyterian ministers by the presbyteries and independent church agencies. By 1808 the dispute had been repressed in New England but in 1811 it sprang up again in New York. In that year Ezra Stiles Ely published his *Contrast Between Calvinism and Hopkinsianism,* a columnar comparison of the teaching of Hopkins and others with Calvin and the Scottish, Dutch, and English confessions, in order to demonstrate that a mischievous difference existed between the New

---

a polemic color: " The Rise of the Princeton Theology; a Genetic History of Presbyterianism until 1850 " (Ph.D. thesis, Yale University, 1935), 286 and *passim.*
[4] S. J. Baird, *The History of the New School* (Philadelphia, 1868), 237 ff.

England revision and Calvinist orthodoxy. In 1816 the debate spread to Philadelphia, where the synod promulgated a pastoral letter, written by Ely, who had moved to a charge in that city, warning the faithful against the dangers to religion and morals implicit in Hopkinsian teaching.[5] In 1818 rival education societies were formed in New York, arraying such eminent Presbyterians as Elias Boudinot, president of the Continental Congress during the Revolution; Gardiner Spring; and Eliphalet Nott, president of Union College of Schenectady, against the Princeton group: Alexander, Miller, and Green, at that date president of the college and of the seminary board as well. Worried by the outburst of dispute in Presbyterianism, John H. Rice warned the General Assembly in 1820 against partisanship, "love of distinction and influence," theological innovation, and any "attempt to produce uniformity of opinion" in Christ's church.[6] But the debate was already launched and was destined to rush forward with increasing velocity in the lower judicatories of the church until it broke calamitously upon the Assembly of 1831 at the trial of Albert Barnes, a Philadelphia pastor sympathetic to the theology of New England.

Meanwhile, the Presbyterian Church was moving toward decisions of the utmost gravity for its future. Although Morse had taken pains to keep close to conservative leaders like Green, Rodgers, Miller, and the Princeton professors and held both the faculty and student body of Andover open to Presbyterians,[7] the fact remained that the school was too remote to serve the needs of the middle colonies, not to speak of the south and southwest. Furthermore, the genius of Andover lay in its united opposition to the gravest threat to the old religion of New England: the Unitarianism that had captured Harvard.

[5] *Minutes of the Synod of Philadelphia,* 1816.
[6] *A Discourse . . . before the General Assembly . . . 1820* (Philadelphia, 1820), 6–9.
[7] Morse tried to persuade Miller to join the Andover faculty: Letter of Rodgers to Morse, January 31, 1807. Rodgers concurred with Morse's judgment on the dark significance of the revelations of Robinson's book: Letter to Morse, August 25, 1798. HSP, Gratz, Case 8, box 26.

The inclusion of Hopkinsians — indeed, their virtual domination of Andover Seminary — meant that a reconstructive spirit
in theological writing and teaching was regnant there. The
Presbyterians of the middle colonies, by contrast, had been
moving toward the churchmanship and mentality of Scotland
during the era after Witherspoon. His role at the college and
his influence, with John Rodgers, on the founding of the General Assembly symbolized the emergence of a strengthened
Scottish consciousness. To many who understood the history
of their tradition in the eighteenth century but poorly, Scotland was quite simply the motherland of American Presbyterianism, as a mass of minutes, letters, and polemic references
testify. History and geography were allied against Morse's
hope for a comprehensive Calvinist front.

THE RESPONSE IN NEW JERSEY

The trustees of the College of New Jersey were well aware
that the need for clergymen was more acute than ever and the
threat to piety darker. Yet increasingly its graduates were
choosing public and scientific careers. Did this mean that the
school was moving from its primary kinship with the church to
the service of the new culture?

The issue was abruptly posed when the trustees applied to
the legislature of New Jersey in 1796 for assistance in rehabilitating the war-damaged campus. The board committee
reported that " an objection drawn from the idea of this institution being under the sole and exclusive control of one denomination of Christians was used with great force against the application; and was in the end surmounted to obtain the grant
only by the personal assurances of the Committee that the
reason which had originally placed this institution under the
entire direction of one denomination of Christians had ceased
with the Revolution; and that the present Board of Trustees
had determined hereafter to act upon all proper occasions and
particularly in the choice of Trustees, on a plan of most ex-

tended liberality." [8] Two non-Presbyterian trustees were subsequently elected, but there the Board balked. It sought no further aid from the public treasury.

Jonathan Belcher had been the first to insist on a broadly representative board of trustees. Gilbert Tennent did not doubt Belcher's piety but he questioned the consistency of the step with the motives of the founders. The cold fact at the end of the century was that the college could neither support itself nor man its faculty nor secure enough students on the old assumptions. All this the trustees learned during sixteen years of frustration and near-failure for the college.

The church's first disappointment in the college lay in the declining number of ministerial graduates. But other suspicions arose. Upon the death of Witherspoon, Samuel Stanhope Smith had been elected. He immediately proposed that room be made for more scientific instruction by abandoning study of the classics after the first year. A substantial portion of the money raised after the Revolution was spent on scientific apparatus. John Maclean, a highly qualified chemist and teacher, excited much student interest in science. Aggressive disrespect seized the students of many American colleges after the war.[9] To the Princeton trustees, these effronteries were a consequence of the decay of piety.[10] Punishment bordering on reprisal was imposed for misdemeanors which, to be sure, were altogether intolerable but should have been dealt with all the more judiciously on that account. Student malice was blamed for a fire that gutted Nassau Hall in 1802, but New England responded and by 1805 the student body was larger and the buildings better than before.[11]

[8] John Maclean, *History of the College of New Jersey, 1746–1854*, II, 13 f.

[9] In 1806, Archibald Alexander complained, for example, that " the conduct of the students (at Hampden-Sydney) became very irregular and I grew weary of governing them." James W. Alexander, *Life of Archibald Alexander, D.D.* (New York, 1854), 275.

[10] Cf. *Biblical Repertory*, 1833, 61 f.

[11] New England gave generously in response to a solicitation by Alexander McWhorter, a trustee, between April and June, 1802. Letters

Meanwhile, the first professor of theology since Blair's brief tenure in 1769 was appointed: Henry Kollock, pastor of the Presbyterian Church in Princeton and teacher of Hebrew, theology, and Biblical criticism. But ministerial candidates were few, and in 1806 Kollock resigned. Samuel Miller, then a pastor in New York, wrote Edward Dorr Griffin at the time of the General Assembly of 1805: "I wish you to have a full and free conversation with Dr. Green . . . on two important subjects: . . . The great scarcity of ministers, and the indispensable necessity of adopting speedy and vigorous measures for increasing their number. I consider our prospect on this score melancholy and alarming." [12] Student troubles continued and in 1807 culminated in a destructive riot. The trustees understood the times but poorly and the student attitude not at all. President Smith was blamed for failing to suppress irreligion. Smith himself believed that impiety was at the bottom of the trouble and made strenuous efforts to restrain it, but the trustees were not mollified.

Distrust of Smith's views had been frequently expressed, although he taught little that differed from Witherspoon,[13] and the rioting marked the effective end of his leadership. The trustees threatened the entire faculty with dismissal and suspended 125 students, of whom seventy never returned. The

---

of McWhorter to Jedediah Morse, July 16, 1802, and November 8, 1802. Also, McWhorter to Ashbel Green, July 23, 1802. HSP, Dreer, Letters of American Clergy.

[12] John Rodgers had sought the theology professorship for Ashbel Green, but Green, having once desired it, refused out of offense. Letters of Rodgers to Green, October 27, 1803, November 28, 1803, and February 15, 1804. HSP, Gratz, Case 8, box 39.

[13] S. S. Smith, *Lectures on Moral and Political Philosophy*, 2 vols. (Trenton, N.J., 1812): "Whatever medium in the opinion of these philosophers (Locke, Berkeley, and Hume), nature may employ to connect the object with the organ of sense, whether image or idea, or any other sensible phantasm, it is, beyond a doubt, the object itself, not its idea, which is discovered by the sense; any image or phantasm, in the case being unknown or unperceived, and at the time wholly unthought of. An idea is merely a conception of the fancy, or the reminiscence of the object."

enrollment dropped from 200 to 112 in the year 1806–1807 and student income with it. Bitterly the Presbyterians reflected that their college, the child of revival, was scarcely fit for candidates for the ministry. Miller wrote in 1807: "What is the great head of the church about to do with that seminary? Is it about to be purged and elevated, or totally destroyed?"[14] To the General Assembly, Smith pointed out that twenty-six men had graduated into ministerial service between 1802 and 1806, but this scarcely satisfied the ravenous appetite of the West. The threat of 1807 was fulfilled in 1812: Maclean was asked to leave and Smith deprived of his responsibilities. He thereupon resigned and the disastrous "reform" administration of Ashbel Green was inaugurated.[15]

THE NEW DIMENSION OF PRESBYTERIAN RESPONSIBILITY

In the decade of lowest fortune in the college, the Presbyterians began to realize the immensity of the task they faced in the West. The gateway at Pittsburgh stood open, and the movement of people across the Alleghenies was to grow steadily for a century to come. Some conception of the pace of the expansion may be derived from a glance at the decennial census reports.

In the year 1790, the American people numbered 3,929,827 in fourteen states and their extended territories.[16] Of the total, 697,897 (17.7 per cent) were slaves. By the year 1800, the

---

[14] T. J. Wertenbaker, *Princeton, 1746–1896*, 145. Rodgers wrote Green, then a trustee of the college: "You must get rid of your professor of Mathematics and I wish your Professors of languages would resign." (October 16, 1807.) HSP, Gratz, Case 8, box 39.

[15] Green furnished a full account of his experience as a college president in his autobiography, 338–438. Green was jarred by a serious riot in 1817. A letter pleading for the readmission of Edward Smith, expelled at that time, is included in the Gratz Collection. HSP, Case 8, box 39 (February, 1817). Cf. Breckinridge's account of that riot: Letter to G. Ridgely, February 14, 1817. HSP, Dreer Collection, II.

[16] Maine is included with Massachusetts in the census, and Kentucky with Virginia.

population had risen to 5,305,925 distributed throughout twenty states and territories and the District of Columbia and extending to the Mississippi River. There were 893,041 slaves (16.8 per cent). Ten years later the total stood at 7,239,903, of which 1,191,364 (16.4 per cent) were slaves, now heavily concentrated south of the Pennsylvania state line. In 1820, the total inhabitants of the nation numbered 9,638,131; slaves 1,538,038 (16 per cent). In 1830, the population had risen to 12,861,957; the number of slaves to 2,010,629 (15.6 per cent).[17]

There are no accurate statistics on total population before 1790 when the Congress first authorized a census, and before 1820 no precise analysis of the sources of immigration was made. It is estimated that immigration into the colonies or states from the outbreak of the Revolution to 1820 totaled about 250,000, of which at least 95 per cent were northern and western Europeans.[18] Immigration into the United States on a truly dramatic scale began in the 1840's; but by that date the Presbyterian Church had made its decision as to how it would react to the new masses.

Following the large influx of Irish there was a lull.[19] But again in 1770, reverses struck the linen industries on which the northern counties depended, and the exodus recommenced. Arthur Young reported that an average of two thousand persons sailed each year from Belfast for America during this period of emigration. Four thousand left in 1773, but improved conditions reduced emigration by 1775. Emigration affected chiefly Presbyterians, who were most active in linen manufacture: "the Catholics never went; they seemed not only tied to the country but almost to the parish in which their masters lived."[20]

Beginning in 1820 the United States census listed all immigrants from Ireland in a single category, irrespective of reli-

[17] United States census reports for 1830.
[18] G. M. Stephenson, A History of American Immigration (New York, 1926), 9.
[19] Cf. G. S. Klett, Presbyterians in Colonial Pennsylvania, 52–86.
[20] H. J. Ford, The Scotch-Irish in America, 204.

gious affiliation or previous county of residence, so Presbyterian elements of Scottish origin cannot be clearly distinguished from the Roman Catholic in this immigration. Nevertheless, the figures for the decade from 1820 to 1830 are revealing. A total of 7,691 Europeans entered the United States in 1820, of whom 3,614 came from Ireland and 2,410 from the remainder of the British islands. Irishmen arrived in comparable proportion throughout the decade, comprising the largest single classification of European immigrants in every year save one. The high point came in 1828 when 12,488 Irish arrived, a full half of the European total. During the decade, 50,724 Irish immigrants settled in the United States.[21] Emigration having begun in the northern counties, it is certain that a substantial proportion of the new arrivals became the responsibility of the Presbyterians.

It is more difficult to appraise the over-all influence of Scottish and Irish immigration on the developing ideology of Presbyterianism. The records of the severely subscriptionist Synod of Ulster mention only nine clergymen sent to America in the forty-two years between the Revolution and 1820, six of them officially discredited for taking part in the rebellion of 1798. The influence of the Irish in the Presbyterian Church was certainly greater after 1820 than before; yet in the year 1828, the high point of emigration to America, not a single Irish licentiate or ordained minister sought release from the synod in order to minister to the new world.[22]

The western areas in America received newcomers from both overseas and the eastern areas of the United States as well, and Pennsylvania and Virginia grew notably between 1800 and 1820. The second census reported 274,566 persons west of the Alleghenies in Pennsylvania and twenty years later a total of 1,049,488 in the state, western Pennsylvanians numbering 321,481. Eastern Virginia had been a stronghold of the Church of England, plantation agriculture, and slavery

[21] United States census, 1830.
[22] *Records of the Synod of Ulster* . . . , 1828.

from the beginning; but a fertile valley lying between the Blue
Ridge Mountains and the main Appalachian chain furnished
a highway for Presbyterian emigration south and west. The
movement was under way before 1750 and by 1820 the population of western Virginia stood at 147,534, including 13,000
slaves. The difference between the tidewater culture that developed from the sea and thrived on slavery and the Scottish
and Irish small holders who came overland persisted throughout the nineteenth century.

Reports to the General Assembly were notoriously incom-
plete, and the church sent repeated requests to its judicatories
for full statistical information. Bearing in mind this impreci-
sion, there is evidence of growth corresponding to the expansion of the country. Standing at 102 in 1768, there were 324
ministers in 1798. The files of the Assembly were lost about
1800, but in 1802 a reasonably accurate statistical system was
adopted and 334 clergymen were listed. In 1810 this had risen
to 485 ministers and licentiates in 772 churches; and in 1820,
national totals stood at 849 ministers and candidates and 1,299
congregations.[23]

Between the Revolution, when the nation's total population
did not exceed 2,300,000, and 1830, when it had multiplied five
times over, lay the explosion of the peoples that was the overarching fact of the social history of the United States. In this
period, the church increasingly accepted responsibility for mission to the slaves, whose numbers had increased fourfold. And
it was just at this juncture that there was born in the conscience of Western Christianity the conviction that the
churches must give themselves to mission on a worldwide
scale. In a single prolonged generation, therefore, the demands of history and conscience on the church for clerical service rose to a level never contemplated at the close of the colonial era.

[23] *MGA*, 1798, 1802, 1810, and 1820.

THE RESPONSE OF THE PRESBYTERIAN CHURCH

The General Assembly was well aware of the crisis. " While the population of our country has been rapidly extending; while new settlements have been forming; and new churches in quick succession rising to view; the increase in the number of ministers has been slow, and altogether incommensurate with the increasing demand for their services. . . . Large districts, within the bounds of old settlements, in which churches might easily be planted . . . are lying waste for want of their labors; and more than one thousand congregations, on the extensive frontier of the United States . . . are able and willing to support spiritual teachers, but cry for them in vain." [24]

At the instance of Miller, Ashbel Green brought an overture to the General Assembly (adopted in 1806) urging enlarged enlistment of young men for the ministry, increased assistance to candidates, and strict screening of volunteers.[25] President Smith confronted the rising sentiment for a new theological school by arguing that "the Trustees [of the College of New Jersey] have ever been attentive [to training up of men of piety and talent for the ministry of the gospel] and have made the most generous provision for the support of theological students." He described the school's preferential treatment of candidates, the strong curriculum, and the meticulous methods of instruction — perhaps an exaggeration of practice, although not of Smith's own idealism. But suspicion of the college was too deeply rooted. On March 12, 1805, Miller had written to Green: "Am I not right in supposing that at least two hundred more ministers might at this moment be advantageously employed within the bounds of the General Assembly; and that near half that number are imperiously demanded? It appears to me that we ought forthwith, either to establish a new theological school . . . or direct more of our attention to extend the plan and increase the energy of the Princeton establish-

[24] Report of a committee of the Presbytery of New York, October, 1805, of which Miller was a member. *Life*, I, 196.
[25] *Ibid.*, I, 201.

ment. On the latter part of the alternative many doubts occur to me." [26] This letter was the earliest impulse of the movement that issued in the founding of Princeton Seminary.

In his opening address at the Assembly of 1808, Archibald Alexander broached the question of a theological seminary. " Our seminaries of learning, although increasing in literature and numbers, furnish us with few preachers. . . . We shall not have a regular and sufficient supply of well-qualified ministers of the Gospel until every Presbytery, or at least every Synod, shall have under its direction a seminary established for the single purpose of educating youth for the ministry in which the course of education from its commencement shall be directed to this object; for it is much to be doubted whether the system of education pursued in our colleges and universities is the best adapted to prepare a young man for the work of the ministry. The great extension of the physical sciences and the taste and fashion of the age have given such a shape and direction to the academical course that I confess, it appears to me to be little adapted to introduce youth to the study of the sacred Scripture." [27] Presbyterians did not cease to oppose the modernizing of the collegiate curriculum for two generations.

One reason classical pretheological work was essential was that most orthodox theological texts were written in Latin. At his accession to the presidency of the college in 1812 Green found that " contrary to primitive usage, the junior and senior classes, after the Revolutionary War in our country, read nothing of the Greek and Latin classics. Their whole time was employed in mathematics, philosophy natural and moral, belles-lettres, criticism, composition, and eloquence." [28] The literary emphasis had been Witherspoon's; it was Smith who was the real culprit, with his bold shift to the sciences, and Green reacted by assigned recitations in the Latin and Greek authors.[29]

---

[26] *Ibid.*, I, 192.
[27] *Ibid.*, I, 315.
[28] *Life of Ashbel Green*, 347.
[29] Presbyterian publications were relentless in their hostility to modernizing trends in collegiate arts courses. Cf. Ashbel Green, *BRPR*, 1835, 529 ff. For Breckinridge, a learned ministry meant solid grounding

The founding of the first Presbyterian seminary at Princeton was undertaken not only to relieve an acute shortage in ministerial supply; it was also designed to sequester theological students, to protect them from the secularizing mood of the national life, and to control their curriculum.

Alexander's proposal for synodical schools came to the Assembly through an overture from the Presbytery of Philadelphia, but Assembly's committee recommended instead " one great school, in some convenient place near the center of the bounds of our church." When submitted for judgment to the presbyteries, it was found that they were equally divided between the Alexander plan and concentration on a single school. Green argued that " there were those who had voted in favor of the third plan [Alexander's] from an entire misconception of the nature and intention of the first plan [the single school] and on this ground, the committee recommended the latter to the Assembly." Having induced the Assembly to focus its energies in a single school, Green wrote a plan of the seminary which was approved by the Assembly in 1811.[30] The board of directors first met on June 30, 1812, and elected Green its president. He held that post until his death in 1848.

THE ROLE OF ASHBEL GREEN

Ashbel Green was, of course, fully aware of the softening of Calvinism already long in progress and he was in correspondence with the New England orthodox leadership. There is no evidence, however, that he considered the quarrel in New York provoked by Ely dangerous to the integrity of doctrine in Presbyterian circles. Green's record before 1816 reveals real

---

in the older theological systems, study of the classics, philosophy, and the Bible in the original languages. His animus against the scientific curriculum was not so much the effect of a theoretical or philosophical antagonism for science as resentment of its inroads on classical pretheological training. BRPR, 1835, 272, 541. The Presbyterians were opposed to unordained college presidents, ibid., 278.

[30] This Plan is discussed more fully on pages 121 f., 144 f.

friendliness toward New England. It was he who had made
the motion in the General Assembly to send representatives to
the General Association of Connecticut and he voted enthusi-
astically for the Plan of Union of 1801, urged by Jonathan Edwards, Jr., and foredoomed to become a cause of church strife.
Nevertheless, Green was a "Presbyterian man" by instinct. As
he matured he increasingly argued that the church should not
ask independent local groups to do its work. The Plan he
wrote exhibited his concern for the defense of sound doctrine
and his belief in responsible churchmanship but no anxiety on
the subject of Hopkinsian theology in particular.

Princeton Seminary, declared the Assembly in the words of
Green, would provide the church with men "who shall be able
to defend her faith against infidels and her doctrines against
heretics." To assure the former, the Plan provided that every
student "must have read and digested the principal arguments
and writings relative to what had been called the deistical controversy." As to heresy, the student must know the Bible and
its background and have studied "carefully and correctly,
Natural, Didactic, Polemic, and Casuistic Theology. . . .
Thus he will be preparing to become an able and sound divine
and casuist."

For safety from doctrinal aberration the Assembly chiefly
relied on the life of piety, but to assure purity at the fount, directors were required periodically to "inspect the fidelity of
the professors" in regard to doctrines "actually taught." The
board, of which Green was chairman for thirty-six years, completely controlled the faculty and the curriculum. "The Board
shall direct the professors of the Seminary, in regard to the
subjects and topic on which they are severally to give instruc-
tions to the pupils." The oath, subscribed by each professor
at inauguration, granted no liberty in theological investigation.
"I do solemnly and *ex animo* adopt, receive, and subscribe the
Confession of Faith and the Catechisms of the Presbyterian
Church . . . as the confession of my faith . . . a summary
and just exhibition of that system of doctrine and religious be-

lief which is contained in holy Scripture. . . . I do solemnly promise and engage, not to inculcate, teach, or insinuate anything which shall appear to me to contradict or contravene, either directly or impliedly, anything taught in the said Confession of Faith or Catechism; nor to oppose any of the fundamental principles of Presbyterian church government." Each professor was further required " to lay before the Board of Directors, as soon as practicable after his appointment, a detailed exhibition of the system and method which he proposed to pursue and the subjects which he proposes to discuss . . . and in this system he shall make such alterations or additions as the Board shall direct; so that, eventually, the whole course through which the pupils shall be carried, shall be no other than that which the board of directors shall have approved and sanctioned." [31] Later additions or variations had to be submitted to the board before introduction into the classroom.

By these measures, the Presbyterian Church believed it could be assured that the spring of the gospel flowed uncontaminated in the church and that the church membership could be safeguarded from the pollution of the ministry of Christ by the poisons of infidelity.

[31] *Charter and Plan of the Theological Seminary of the Presbyterian Church*, Princeton, N.J. Somerville, N.J., n.d. Cf. revised ed., Princeton, 1953. Also *MGA* . . . 1729–1820 (Philadelphia, 1847), 472, 449 f., 504. Also *Life of Ashbel Green*, 335 ff.

IX

THE FIRST THEOLOGICAL FACULTY

WITH SO MUCH staked on the seminary, great solemnity attended the election of its first professor. The commissioners to the Assembly of 1811 understood that a new era in the history of their church's ministry was being inaugurated.

ARCHIBALD ALEXANDER

Archibald Alexander was their choice. A Virginian by birth and culture, he was supported by the growing southern wing of the church and was highly respected for his personal and intellectual qualities in Philadelphia, where he had been a pastor for five years.

Alexander was not a graduate of the College of New Jersey but was a product of that distinguished frontier system, "field education." His tutor was William Graham (d. 1799), a graduate of the College of New Jersey (1773) and a scholar-clergyman in Virginia with strong affinities for New England.[1] Graham was a thorough student of the classics and deeply interested in the scientific investigations of the post-Revolutionary period. He shared the concern of Presbyterianism in that period for public affairs, volunteered for the Revolutionary Army, and wrote political articles.[2] Graham's special interest

---

[1] Cf. S. D. Alexander, *Princeton College During the Eighteenth Century,* 163 f.

[2] James W. Alexander, *Life of Archibald Alexander,* 17.

was "Philosophy of the Mind." Alexander wrote: "He carried on his investigations not so much by books as by patient and repeated analysis of the various processes of thought as these arose in his own mind and by reducing the phenomena thus observed to a regular system." This frontier philosopher had read the works of Reid and Beattie but "he thought he could construct a better system than any proposed by these writers." [3] Under Graham's guidance, Alexander read the Scots, Edwards' *Free Will, Original Sin,* and *Religious Affections,* and treatises by Owen and Boston.

Alexander was an avid reader as a youth and early in life digested the limited shelf of theology extant in Virginia: Flavel, Soxma, Jenyns, Burkitt, and Gill. Of the first of these, Alexander later wrote: "To John Flavel I certainly owe more than to any uninspired author." [4] While occupied with liberal studies, Alexander read Chauncy's anti-Calvinist writings " officiously put into his hands by a latitudinarian doctor," but he also read Whitefield's sermons. Between 1786 and 1790 Virginia was experiencing revival, and the young candidate heard a number of effective preachers, among them John B. Smith, father of Samuel Stanhope Smith and John Blair Smith, later president of Hampden-Sydney College. Alexander found the Seceders of Virginia implacably hostile to the revival; they said that " if ever any man was possessed of a devil in modern times, it was John Blair Smith." [5]

Archibald Alexander searched his soul, earnestly desiring conversion, but he was a sanguine person and in his youth not given to moodiness. He candidly confessed that his moments

[3] *Ibid.,* 18, 84.
[4] *Ibid.,* 47. It is noteworthy that although the books of Richard Baxter were found in New England libraries and were republished there as late as 1827, his name seldom appears in the lists of theological books read by American Presbyterians in the late eighteenth century. Cf. M. L. Gambrell, *Ministerial Training in Eighteenth Century New England* (Columbia University Press, 1937), 15. Of Flavel, Alexander is known to have read *Knocking at the Door, Practical Truths,* and *Method of Grace.*
[5] James W. Alexander, *Life of Archibald Alexander,* 49, 55.

of illumination were brief and too few. He was none the less serious and in 1789 he confessed his faith. Writing at the age of 77, he spoke gratefully of the preaching of William Graham and fixed the time of his conversion in the year 1788.[6]

Graham was "strictly orthodox, according to the standard of his own church," wrote Alexander, "but in his method of explaining some of the knotty points in theology, he departed considerably from the common track, judging that many things which have been involved in perplexity and obscurity by the manner in which they have been treated are capable of easy and satisfactory explanation by the use of sound principles of philosophy."[7] Graham was a protagonist of experimental philosophy. His affinity with the Edwardean current was revealed by Alexander's comment that "one of his radical principles was that the rational soul of man can undergo no moral change except through the influence of motives, or the presentation through the understanding of such subjects as excite the affections . . . He held that by the influence of the Holy Spirit truth is presented in its true nature by the rational mind and when thus perceived cannot but produce an effect correspondent with its nature. He therefore fully held what has been called in some places the 'light scheme'; believing that all moral changes must be produced by new views."[8] Graham believed that the fall of man in no way destroyed natural ability. It was only to be expected that his most notable scholar would be open to Hopkinsian theology when he visited New England in 1801.

During his tutelage with Graham, Alexander read Witherspoon's *Lectures of Moral Philosophy*, but by his own testimony they did not excite his mind. At this time Alexander first made the acquaintance of Francis Turretin, the orthodox Swiss Calvinist, whose *Institutes* he read in compendium. When Alexander settled in Philadelphia, he returned to works of this kind. "These Reformed divines," wrote James Alexander of his father, "he regarded as having pushed theological

[6] *Ibid.*, 72.   [7] *Ibid.*, 18 f.   [8] *Ibid.*, 107.

investigation to its greatest length and compacted its conclusions into the most symmetrical method." But Alexander was also widely read in current German thought and thoroughly acquainted with the New England controversies then reaching a new height. "As respects his own conclusions," continues Alexander's biographer, "he has left on record the statement that on his return from New England and during his residence in Philadelphia, his views, which had been somewhat modified by eastern suggestions, began to fix themselves more definitely in the direction of the common Westminster theology." [9]

SAMUEL MILLER

Samuel Miller, professor of church history at Princeton after 1813, was the son of John Miller, who was born in Boston in 1722, educated under the direction of a New England divine, and ordained in 1749 by an assembly of eminent Congregationalist clergymen that included Joseph Sewall and Thomas Prince.[10]

Samuel Miller's early education was private. He studied the classics under his father's guidance and entered the University

[9] A. A. Hodge, *Life of Charles Hodge, D.D., LL.D.* (New York, 1880), 48.

[10] Samuel Miller, *The Life of Samuel Miller*, I, 16. John Miller was, by the testimony of his grandson, no zealot for Presbyterian order and avoided identifying himself with either side in the schism of 1741–1758. Of his orthodoxy there was no question. At the forming of the General Assembly in 1788, there was last-ditch resistance to the Scottish principle of vesting large authority in the higher judicatories. The right of a congregation's elders to final jurisdiction was vigorously argued by Matthew Wilson, of Lewes, Delaware, a close friend of John Miller; and Princeton's second professor believed that his father sympathized with Wilson's view. After the conclusion of the debate, Wilson wrote bitterly to Miller: "The two Scots' Doctors and the poor wrangling wiseacres of our mountains carried all. . . . The Scots' unscriptural Hierarchy was determined beforehand to be adopted." (*Ibid.*, I, 25, notes.) Whether by reason of conviction or poor health or both, Samuel Miller's father failed to attend a meeting of the General Assembly.

of Pennsylvania at the age of eighteen. Miller at first was an irresolute student, unsure of his vocation. While in college he formed a friendship with Ashbel Green, seven years his senior and then embarking on his ministerial career as co-pastor of the Second Presbyterian Church in Philadelphia. Having visited the youthful student while ill, Green later counseled Miller at the time of his decision to enter the ministry. In a testimonial letter, Miller wrote of Green: " He took me by the hand with marked Christian affability and condescension. . . . I always considered my intercourse with Dr. Green as among the most decisively attractive and profitable that I could enjoy." [11]

Miller's grades improved as he turned toward the ministry, but actual decision awaited his graduation.[12] He had been deeply impressed during his college career by John Ewing, provost of the university and a redoubtable Old Side man. Miller's personal piety was greatly intensified by the experiences of this period. His mother died in November, 1789; his father was already suffering from illnesses that took his life two years later. Alone together, the two men resorted often to prayer, and Miller's diary contains many earnest religious effusions. The question of his worthiness for the ministry burdened him. " I confess and bewail, O Lord, the aggravation of my apostacy, the pollution of my original, and the exceeding vileness of my nature. My heart is corrupt, hard and rebellious; it is deceitful above all things and desperately wicked. My life has been contrary to thy will; I have transgressed thy holy and reasonable commandments times and ways without number; and deserved long ago, to be cut off from every hope and banished from thy presence and glory forever. . . . I desire with an affecting sense of this thine infinite condescension, to renew my own covenant engagements to thee and to consecrate myself and all my active powers to thy service." [13]

[11] *Life of Ashbel Green,* 524 f.
[12] Letter of John Miller to his daughter, August 27, 1789. *Life of Samuel Miller,* I, 45.
[13] *Ibid.,* I, 51 f.

In June, 1791, Samuel Miller underwent trials for licensure in the Presbytery of Lewes; in midsummer his father died and Samuel made a trip to Boston. After licensure in October, Miller resumed theological study under Charles Nisbet, an immigrant Scot at the head of Dickinson College in Carlisle, Pennsylvania.[14] Nisbet was a graduate of the University of Edinburgh in the class of 1754 and had pursued theological study there until 1760. He was a close friend of Professor Beattie, the notable realist of the University of Aberdeen. John Witherspoon regarded Nisbet so highly as to recommend him to the trustees of the College of New Jersey upon first refusing the presidency for himself. Witherspoon had perhaps once been an instructor of Nisbet.[15] The men together opposed patronage and theological moderatism in the Scottish Church.

Nisbet's college lectures paralleled those of Witherspoon at Princeton: logic, moral philosophy, philosophy of the mind, and belles-lettres. His theology lectures were arranged according to the heads of the Westminster Confession. It is no longer possible to identify the books assigned for Miller's readings with his father and President Nisbet, but the dominant influences of his theological education are revealed in the thought of Witherspoon and the writers upon whom this generation of Scots depended. "Dr. Nisbet was a thorough Old School Calvinist," wrote Miller. "He was a devoted friend of the Westminster Confession of Faith; considering it as a lucid and most happy exhibition of the system of doctrine taught in the Holy Scriptures."[16]

CHARLES HODGE

Charles Hodge was the third appointee to the seminary faculty. He became a tutor in language at the invitation of

---

[14] Miller's own estimate is contained in a letter to Samuel Prime, October 16, 1849. HSP, Gratz, Case 8, box 38.
[15] Sprague, *Annals of the American Pulpit*, III, 451.
[16] *Ibid.*, III, 457.

Archibald Alexander in 1822 and was installed as professor of systematic theology in 1840. He was active as a teacher until 1878, the year of his death, when he was succeeded as lecturer in didactic theology by his son Archibald Alexander Hodge and as lecturer in exegesis by his son Casper Wistar Hodge. Despite the universal affection for Alexander, by 1835 Hodge's personal influence upon the church was unrivaled in the seminary, largely owing to his prolific writing and its authoritative manner. He edited *The Biblical Repertory and Princeton Review* from its inception in 1825 (as the *Biblical Repertory*) until 1868, when he assumed a consultative function.[17] While all the major elements of the Princeton tradition were substantially defined by his predecessors — the philosophical assumption of its theology, the piety fostered there, and its attitude toward the civil responsibilities of churchmen — it was Hodge who brought these to their most systematic, influential, and persistent expression.

Hugh and Mary Hodge, Charles's parents, were married by Ashbel Green in 1790, and in December, 1797, Charles, the last of five children, was born. During childhood, he was catechized by Green, pastor of the Second Presbyterian Church of Philadelphia. After classical training, Hodge matriculated at the College of New Jersey in 1812, the year of Green's inauguration as president and the first year of the newly formed seminary. Green had assumed the teaching responsibilities traditionally borne by the president, and Hodge studied belles-lettres, moral philosophy, logic, and Bible under his direction. Hodge read Witherspoon's *Lectures on Moral Philosophy* and lectures prepared by John Blair, first professor of theology in the college. Alexander influenced Charles Hodge by his preaching. Hodge wrote in later life: "It was said of him that while most other ministers preached about religion, he preached religion. He recognized the fact that the religious and moral elements of our nature are universal and indestructible; and that these elements in Christian countries at

[17] *Life of Charles Hodge,* 249.

least are so developed that every man knows that there is a God on whom he is dependent and to whom he is responsible; that he is a sinner. . . . Dr. Alexander revealed such men to themselves." [18] Hodge had no startling experience of conversion but professed his faith in January, 1815, just before the descent upon the college student body of the " silent dew of revival" that was so coveted by the trustees.

It is noteworthy that Alexander, Miller, and Hodge all made journeys through New England, seeking out eminent pastors and theologians. Alexander traveled between its main centers during the spring and summer of 1801. He observed the ratification of the Plan of Union at the meeting of the General Association of Connecticut in 1801, later a thorn of schism among Presbyterians. He preached for Dr. Nathan Strong, of Hartford, a moderate Edwardean who had " drawn back from the ultraism of Hopkins, Emmons and others." Alexander here became aware of the distinction between " older Hopkinsianism " and such newer and less acceptable views as that " God is the author of sin, . . . willingness to be damned [is] a sign of grace and [that abstention from] the use of means in the case of the unregenerate " is required. [19] From Patton, reported Alexander, " I received a more satisfactory account than I had obtained of the entire system of Dr. Hopkins, who was still alive." Alexander preached for the aged Hopkins. He was received by Nathaniel Emmons, who inquired assiduously about the progress of the New England theology in east Tennessee, " whither Dr. [Hezekiah] Balch had carried the seed from Massachusetts." But Emmons avoided theological discussion with his Virginian visitor. Alexander was deeply impressed by the heterogeneous religious life of Boston, where a range of opinion from evangelical Calvinism to confessed unitarianism was heard. By contrast, Princeton's College appeared to him the acme of dignity and worth. [20]

[18] *Ibid.,* 27.
[19] *Life of Archibald Alexander,* 240.
[20] *Ibid.,* 265 ff. Upon returning to Virginia, Alexander wrote a cordial letter of thanks to his host in Charlestown, Massachusetts, Jedediah

During his trip to New England as a licentiate in 1792, Samuel Miller had visited Jedediah Morse in Charlestown.[21] He was there again in 1797 as delegate of the General Assembly to the General Association of Connecticut and preached in several pulpits. Later correspondence with Hopkins himself, Jedediah Morse, and other moderates suggests an unprejudiced attitude toward New England thought. Miller fell under the censure of Ezra Stiles Ely in 1811 for his acceptance of the Andover interpretation of Calvinism.[22]

Charles Hodge went to Boston in 1820 at the age of twenty-two. By this time the drift away from Edwards, visible in Hopkins and conspicuous in Emmons, had become wholly offensive to a majority of Presbyterians, in the thought of Nathaniel Taylor. "The pride of the southern part of Connecticut," Hodge called the founder of the New Haven variation and visited in his home en route to Boston. The visit was "one of the most improving incidents in our journey as this young man, (about thirty) who possesses uncommonly fine talents, differs very considerably in his theoretical opinions from the Princeton gentlemen."[23]

Alexander found the dynamic mentality of New England familiar, even congenial, owing to his training with Graham; but he recoiled from the views of Emmons. Hodge was the heir of Alexander's later decision. Confronted with Taylor's more radical modifications twenty years later, he reported "an animated though temperate discussion of our differences."[24] A critical turn had been taken.

It can be recognized in retrospect that the last occasion when there existed a serious possibility that Presbyterianism might share the dynamic theological mood of New England

Morse, and included a glowing account of the thriving Kentucky revival, December 2, 1801. HSP, Gratz, Case 8, box 36.

[21] Letter of Miller to Morse, October 4, 1792; Letter of John M. McKnight to Morse, July 23, 1792. HSP, Gratz, Case 8, box 38.

[22] *Life of Samuel Miller*, I, 62, 107–108, 303 ff.

[23] Letter to Hodge's mother, October 9, 1820. *Life*, 77–79.

[24] *Life of Charles Hodge*, 54.

was the period when in the privacy of his own reflections, Archibald Alexander was pondering the significance of Hopkins' innovations. They were indeed problematical, and it is not surprising that Alexander decided for the Older Calvinists. Yet his own spirit was not polemic but, rather, expository and practical with an inevitable lacing of apologetics.

All of the "first five" of the Princeton tradition — Witherspoon, Green, Alexander, Miller, and Hodge — were capable and well-read. Witherspoon and Green were particularly skilled as leaders, but Witherspoon's lectures are conspicuously eclectic and Green's writing was mainly hortatory and polemical. Alexander was widely read in theology, Miller in the literature of science and history. Miller's personal manner was polished, and his writing style elegant. Like Witherspoon, he encouraged high standards of oral and written expression. Green's was a rigid mind, the only one of the five whose conservatism was clearly radical.[25]

---

[25] Green's rigidity caused a breach with the Princeton professors during the dispute preceding the division of 1837–1838. Early in 1830, Green determined to precipitate controversy in Philadelphia by opposing the installation of Albert Barnes, a declared advocate of views that Green deemed heretical, as minister of the First Presbyterian Church of that city. To Green's request for support in this portentous move, Miller replied: "I have revolved again and again in my mind what you say with respect to your intentions . . . and I now feel prepared to tell you, with all frankness, that I think such a course will by no means be the wisest that can be adopted . . . if I were a member of the Presbytery and if a call for Mr. Barnes were laid before that body, I should utterly oppose a motion to allow it to be prosecuted." (Letter of March 20, 1830. *Life of Samuel Miller*, II, 151.) From this point, Green was not supported by Princeton Seminary. The *Presbyterian*, edited in Philadelphia, was so engrossed by the controversy, so influenced by Old School radicalism, and so cool to Princeton, that Alexander McGill, professor of homiletics at the seminary, wrote fearfully that "every other seminary has a journal devoted especially to its welfare and what shall we do, it being the fact that we are sectional now as much as any other?" (To John Layburn, April 23, 1835. HSP, Dreer, Letters of American Clergy.) The apogee of Princeton's moderatism was reached with Hodge's acid criticism of the "Act and Testimony" (*BRPR*, 1836, 506–508), which would have led Old Calvinists into secession. Confidential cor-

THE REALISM OF JOHN WITHERSPOON

In the next chapter we shall see how definitive of the practice of the clergyman the fundamental philosophy of the Princeton tradition was to be. The three first professors of the seminary were all adherents of the realism of the Scottish school presupposed by Witherspoon's *Lectures on Moral Philosophy.* "In [the five senses] are observable the impression itself or the sensation we feel and the supposition inseparable from it, that it is produced by an external object," wrote Witherspoon. "That our senses are to be trusted in the information they give us seems to me a first principle, because they are the foundation of all our after reasonings. . . . The reality of the material system, I think, may be easily established except upon such principles as are subversive of all certainty. . . . The truth is, the immaterial system is a wild and ridiculous attempt to unsettle the principles of common sense by metaphysical reasoning which can hardly produce anything but contempt in the generality of persons who hear it." [26] In easy yoke with realism was Witherspoon's natural theology. "If the Scripture is true, the discoveries of reason cannot be contrary to it," he declared in the introduction to his course at the college. "It is true that infidels do commonly proceed upon pretended principles of reason. But as it is impossible to hinder them from reasoning on this subject, the best way is to meet upon their own ground and show from reason itself the fallacy of their principles."

Without the slightest risk to his acceptability among Presbyterians, Witherspoon approved certain philosophical assumptions of Samuel Clarke and Francis Hutchinson and opposed Robert Riccaltoun, a Scottish Seceder of considerable theolog-

---

respondence between Samuel Miller and Ashbel Green was resumed only after January, 1838. (Cf. *The Christian Advocate,* edited by Ashbel Green, 1832, 20; 1833, 499; 1834, 63.) By then, Green and fellow radicals had forced a choice on the church, and Princeton had opted for the Old School.

[26] Witherspoon, *Works,* VII, 22 f.

ical discernment. The position of Witherspoon becomes clearer when we hear his criticism of Riccaltoun. Riccaltoun, wrote Witherspoon, " [has] written against the light of nature, showing that the first principles of knowledge are taken from information " rather than from the inward rational perceptions of natural man. But the latter, Witherspoon affirms, assure us that " a sense of moral good and evil is as really a principle of our nature as either the gross external or reflex senses. . . . This moral sense is precisely the same thing with what, in Scripture and common language, we call conscience. It is the law which our Maker has written upon our hearts and both intimates and enforces duty, previous to all reasoning." " The moral sense dictates to us . . . that there are disinterested affections that point directly at the good of others. . . . The moral sense implies also a sense of obligation, that such and such things are right and others wrong." [27] Witherspoon protested the reduction of these impulses to self-interest and concluded that all men know right, wrong, and duty by nature. Thrust aside by the rising stream of Presbyterian naturalism, Riccaltoun's contention that all that man knows of good, evil, and duty is given from beyond himself has a startlingly modern ring.[28]

Witherspoon's moral philosophy was transmitted to Archibald Alexander and Charles Hodge intact. " Man has naturally a sense of moral obligation, a perception of the difference between right and wrong," wrote Alexander. " These are what have been called his religious feelings. . . . These principles of our nature are so deeply radicated that they never can be moved." [29] The innate moral sense exists in harmony with natural reason. " Without reason we can form no conception

---

[27] Ibid., 25–28.
[28] Riccaltoun's thought was not without sequel in American Presbyterianism. See SPR, 1848, 206; BRPR, 1845, 381. Yet the mainstream of Presbyterian theology from Witherspoon to Hodge consciously excluded it. See Riccaltoun's " Treatise on the General Plan of Revelation," Works, 3 vols. (Edinburgh, 1772), II.
[29] Archibald Alexander, Evidences of the Authenticity, Inspiration, and Canonical Authority of the Holy Scriptures (Philadelphia, n.d.), 18.

of a truth of any kind; and when we receive any thing as true, whatever may be the evidence on which it is founded, we must view the reception of it to be reasonable. Truth and reason are so intimately connected that they can never with propriety be separated." [30]   Alexander's realism appears in his statement that "it is reasonable to believe what by our senses we perceive to exist; and it is reasonable to believe whatever God declares to be true." Hodge went beyond Alexander and asserted the innately rational character of the highest objects of faith; but Alexander retained Edwards' sense of the ineffable. "That a revelation should contain doctrines of a mysterious and incomprehensible nature . . . is not repugnant to reason; on the contrary, judging from analogy, sound reason would lead us to expect such things in a revelation from God. Everything which relates to this Infinite Being must be to us, in some respects, incomprehensible." Reason is vindicated by the reasonableness of divine ineffability rather than by the innate rationality of the mysterious.

Hodge went farther and stated that the laws of reason constitute the method of theology. "[The theologian's] method of ascertaining what the Bible teaches is the same as that which the natural philosopher adopts to ascertain what nature teaches. . . . He must assume the validity of those laws of belief which God has impressed upon our nature. . . ." [31] "We are required to pronounce anathema an apostle or angel from heaven who should call upon us to receive as a revelation from God anything absurd, or wicked, or inconsistent with the intellectual or moral nature with which He has endowed us. . . . It is impossible that He should by an external revelation declare that to be true which by the laws of our nature He has rendered it impossible we should believe." [32]   Hodge opposed idealism which, with Witherspoon, he felt could end only in skepticism. "Confidence in the well-authenticated testimony of our senses is one of those laws of belief which God has impressed upon our nature; from the authority of

[30] *Ibid.*, 10.   [31] *ST*, I, 10.   [32] *Ibid.*, I, 52.

those laws it is impossible that we should emancipate ourselves. Confidence in our sense is, therefore, one form of confidence in God." [33]

The natural theology of Witherspoon, Alexander, and Hodge enlisted them with the progressive spirits of the time, for trust in the senses meant acceptance of science and philosophy. Witherspoon believed that investigation of the natural world could reveal only the wonder of God's work, and Hodge's confidence extended even to Biblical criticism. " The relation between philosophy and revelation as determined by the Scriptures themselves, is what every rightminded man must approve. Everything is conceded to philosophy and science which they can rightfully demand. . . . It is admitted that theologians are not infallible in the interpretation of Scripture. It may therefore happen in the future as it has in the past that interpretations of the Bible long confidently received must be modified or abandoned to bring revelation into harmony with what God teaches in his works. This change of view as to the true meaning of the Bible may be a painful trial to the church but it does not in the least impair the authority of the Scriptures. They remain infallible; we are merely convicted of having mistaken their meaning." [34]

Although Alexander's philosophical assumptions were substantially the same as those of both his great predecessor and his influential pupil, throughout his life his orientation in theology was practical rather than metaphysical or systematic. Here lay his kinship with the Edwardean perspective in theological inquiry. His mind worked from the actualities in religious experience to the theological and philosophical views which he believed they validated. Hodge, by contrast, erected theology on first principles. He promoted piety, to be sure, but as an implication of principle and doctrine. Methodologically, Alexander found the beginning of man's thought on God in the " impression of divine truth on the mind by the Holy Spirit." To him divine truth, both natural and revealed, was the seal

[33] *Ibid.*, I, 60, 192.   [34] *Ibid.*, I, 59, 171.

of which piety was the impress; the meaning of the truth can be better read from the impress than any analysis of the seal itself. As long as he lived, Alexander preserved at Princeton something of the earliest tradition of revival, but his failure to write systematically left the field open to Hodge's more radical rationalism.

X

CHURCH MINISTRY
IN THE NEW NATIONAL CLIMATE

THE CALVINISTS OF AMERICA recognized by 1812 that a secular age had dawned. In both New England and New Jersey, the orthodox clergy were creating new seminaries to repulse Arminianism within the churches. What would the pious doctors of Andover and Princeton teach their students? What would be the relationship of the minister to his town and nation; of his message to the popular preoccupation with freedom and individual rights?

MINISTRY AS MORAL REFORM: LYMAN BEECHER

At this juncture there appeared several answers to the question that the new era put to the churches. The first was voiced by Lyman Beecher of Litchfield, Connecticut, later of Boston, and finally president of Lane Seminary in Cincinnati, Ohio.

The fierce Puritan concern for the realization of God's covenant with New England founders that underlay the establishment of Yale, the preaching of Dickinson, and the revivalism of Tennent burned brightly in the soul of Beecher. In the 1730's it had been a question of recalling the church from coldness; Beecher now returned to the other side of the Puritan ideal and propounded the divine purpose for the whole of America.

Before the disestablishment of Connecticut Congregationalism, Beecher looked to the state, with the support of the churches, to regenerate society. "The Kingdom of God is a kingdom of means," he declared in 1814, "and though the excellency of power belongs to him, exclusively human instrumentality is indispensable." The clergy were to expose social evil and persuade as best they might, but "in a free government, moral suasion and coercion must be united." The magistrate could not perform his task without a friendly public opinion, and this should be deliberately created by the church. "Local voluntary associations of the wise and good to aid the civil magistrate" were the answer "a sort of disciplined moral militia prepared to . . . repel every encroachment upon the liberty and morals of the state."[1]

Beecher's thinking was not superficially practical. He deplored the separatist and parochial spirit of the divisions a half century earlier and blamed "enthusiasm" for many social ills. Against it he argued that "the gospel recognizes no independent churches. All are the subjects of one Kingdom, . . . members of one body united in one common head. . . . There is a fellowship of Churches which Jesus Christ has constituted. . . . It is not a matter of discretion whether the churches of Connecticut shall help feeble churches. They are bound to do it."[2]

With the abolition of state congregationalism in Connecticut in 1819, what new means could be devised to regenerate society? First, said Beecher, the church must use the franchise: never vote for candidates who tolerate social evils such as dueling.[3] Christian citizens have a right to demand that their governors adhere to a generally Christian moral system. This did not mean that "churches are bound in point of duty . . . to confine their suffrages exclusively to persons of their own denomination" or even necessarily to professing Chris-

---

[1] Lyman Beecher, *Sermon at Woolcot, Connecticut,* September 12, 1814 (Andover, 1815).
[2] *Ibid.,* 21.
[3] L. Beecher, *The Remedy for Dueling . . . Occasional Sermons,* 1807. PSL, Spr., I, 13:18.

tians. But there must be " such belief in the being of God and of accountability and future punishment as lays a foundation for the practical influence of an oath; such exemption from immorality as will render the elevated example of rulers safe to the interest of public morals; such general approbation of the Christian religion and its institutions as will dispose them to afford to religion the proper protection and influence of government." [4] " It is both the duty and policy of legislators to countenance the Christian religion and its institutions." [5]

The crown of Beecher's thinking was his proposal to form a network of moral societies that would neglect no corner of the country. The public stands in constant need to be reminded of the gravity of apparently minor misdemeanors such as drunkenness, blasphemous speech, and profanation of the Sabbath. "A society . . . is calculated to do good from the influence it may have in the formation of public opinion." Furthermore, it is needed to educate the young in sound morals. [6]

Beecher was formulating a general conception of society with specific views of the duties of magistrates and churchmen. His source of authority was the Bible understood as a book of law. *The Bible a Code of Laws* revealed the charter of a comprehensive social order. "The Scriptures are to be regarded as containing a system of moral laws revealed to illustrate the glory of God . . . and the salvation of man," he said at the ordination of Elisha Swift, later an Old School leader in Pittsburgh. Man is so constituted as to be fully responsible to the law of the Bible. " The faculties of understanding, conscience, and choice constitute an accountable agent. Their existence is as decisive evidence of free agency as the five senses are of the existence of the body." The fundamental doctrines of the Bible are those " which are essential to the

[4] L. Beecher, *Sermon Subsequent to the Formation of the Connecticut Society for the Promotion of Good Morals* (Hartford, 1813), 16.

[5] L. Beecher, *The Faith Once Delivered to the Saints . . . October 15, 1823* (Boston, 1824), 8.

[6] *Panoplist,* edited by Jedediah Morse, III, 265.

influence of law as means of moral government and without which God does not ordinarily renew and sanctify the soul." The minister is an agent of God to remind men of the divine requirement. The good magistrate, irrespective of church affiliation and apart from any establishment of religion, allies himself with the church in this effort.[7]

The driving power behind moral societies, colportage, and missions is "real, experimental religion" to which any man, by his very constitution, may be challenged, argued Beecher. Summarizing the fundamentals of the Christian religion, he named first the doctrine "that men are free agents, in the possession of such faculties and placed in such circumstances as render it practicable for them to do whatever God requires, reasonable that he should require it, and fitting that he should inflict, literally, the entire penalty of disobedience." Beecher deprecated the halfway covenant and returned to the Matherian and Edwardean ideal of congregationalism: "a careful maintenance of the apostolic tenure of membership in the visible church, . . . a credible profession of repentance towards God and faith in our Lord Jesus Christ."

Beecher's support of the revival and the doctrine of the free agency of man and his conception of social control through voluntary church-based societies placed him in the forefront of the founders of the moral crusade of the nineteenth century. He willingly adapted his theology to practical goals that he believed to be right. To him revival was not so much the soul's vision of its utter wretchedness and a rapturous embrace of the God of salvation as a first step toward the moral rehabilitation of the nation. The troubled idealist, Orestes Brownson, whose experience of organized American religion began with the Presbyterians and ended in the Roman Catholic Church, reflected the culture created by this moral system. "I believe that every individual in the human family should be honest," he wrote in 1829. "I believe that every one should be kind and benevolent to all. I believe that every one should use his

[7] L. Beecher, *The Bible a Code of Laws* (Andover, 1818), 4, 24.

best endeavors to procure food, clothing and shelter for himself and labor to enable all others to procure the same for themselves." [8]   This idealism was a secular version of Beecher's crusade.

The ministers of the churches throughout the nation were to be the soldiery of Beecher's strategy of reform. He called for a proportion of one minister to every one thousand Americans to carry the movement of national regeneration into every village and town of the nation. Preaching would expound the Bible as a lawbook for believers and nonbelievers alike. Governments would hear, political radicalism would be exorcised. America could be saved by a reforming clergy. But the colleges were producing far too few clergymen: Yale graduated only nine students per year between 1775 and 1815, while Beecher's proposal called for eighty each year. By 1815, candidates were more plentiful than the funds to educate them. [9]

Beecher proposed to finance the ministry of moral reform by establishing local groups composed of church people — but not necessarily connected with official church structure — in order to raise money. In 1814 two such societies were formed in Connecticut and Massachusetts, the latter to become the formidable American Education Society after numbers of small local groups had declared themselves auxiliary to it. [10]

By 1815, New England was furnished with a seminary to train the candidates recruited by the smoldering revival, a method of financing their education, and access to the churches on the frontier through the Plan of Union, a co-operative arrangement with the Presbyterians that enabled Congregationalist ministers to serve Presbyterian and mixed congregations. The revival impulse was constantly stimulated by the foreign missions appeal and its New England sponsoring agency, the American Board of Commissioners for Foreign Missions. The New England program was furnished with its last essential

[8] *PR*, XXX, 127, note.

[9] *Panoplist*, IV (New Series), 45.

[10] Cf. "The Forming of an American Denomination," *CH*, XXXI (March, 1962), 2.

tool in 1826 with the establishment of the American Home Mission Society, a merger of several smaller agencies, for the purpose of subsidizing new congregations and winning the West for Calvinist reform.

This was the ministry of the "New School" — Presbyterian and Congregationalist. It had been shocked by the Revolution but it counterattacked. Its piety was a matter of public life; its gospel essentially social. At its heart it accepted the going American view of man: sin-ridden though he might be, he was a free and responsible agent, able to determine his destiny in heaven as on earth.

MINISTRY AS THE PRACTICE OF PIETY: WITHERSPOON AND ALEXANDER

It was not that a specific decision was made or a specific treatise written, nor did a General Assembly action specially mark it; nevertheless, in the second decade of the nineteenth century the Presbyterian Old Calvinists moved with glacial authority into a position of defense.

The strict provisions of the Princeton Seminary Plan illustrated Presbyterian reaction. Andover had taken precautions to protect itself from the Arminian threat but that seminary was planned to train soldiers for the orthodox army, not to ferret out the enemy within the camp. After 1816, when conservative Philadelphians warned against the subversion of the church, Presbyterian history was marked by a polemic not only against Harvard-style Arminianism but also against the writings of Samuel Hopkins and his followers, the professors at Andover Seminary, and the agents who itinerated the eastern seaboard in search of funds for the New England societies.

The mentality of defense made particular demands on the clergy. Major attention must be given to church discipline lest wolves infiltrate the flock or clergymen of good standing and high reputation begin to entertain dangerous thoughts. Students must be schooled to defend the faith and to preach it so as to enable the faithful to recognize false philosophies. Three lines of defense gradually took shape among Old School Presbyterians, all primarily concerned with the thought and conduct of the clergy: church discipline, apologetic theology, and "eminent piety."

The quantity of literature that poured from Presbyterian pens in the nineteenth century on the subject of piety for ministers is almost unbelievable. Piety had ever been praised but never with such manifest anxiety as now. The role of discipline in the Plan of the seminary adopted by the Assembly in 1811 has already been indicated; it also provided specific methods for fostering piety: stated times of private devotion and public prayer and worship. Sundays were to be wholly occupied with devotional exercises. "It ought to be considered as an object of primary importance by every student in the Seminary," read the document composed by Ashbel Green, "to be careful and vigilant not to lose that inward sense of the power of godliness which he may have attained, . . . to grow continually in a spirit of enlightened devotion and fervent piety; deeply impressed with the recollection that without this, all his other acquisitions will be comparatively of little worth." [11]   Every student was to spend one day a month in "special prayers and self-examination in secret" and he was to fast. For "levity or indifference in regard to practical religion, though it does not amount to any overt act of irreligion or immorality," a student was first admonished and then, if he persisted, dismissed by the faculty. Students were warned against the twin dangers of formality and enthusiasm. In the minds of the founders, such piety was a natural accompaniment of diligence in study and temperance of manner and a prime safeguard against wrong thought.

Princeton piety was rooted in the Great Awakening but an internal shift in philosophy of religion had occurred between the era of Bellamy and that of Hodge's *Systematic Theology*, which achieved substantial form by 1845.[12] The desideratum

[11] *MGA*, 1811, 338 f.   [12] *Life of Charles Hodge*, 323.

of true religion for the earliest revivalists had been "a deep sense of sin, an interest in Christ, a life of serious devotion, and a solicitous concern about [one's] eternal state." Their analysis of "meer profession" of religion was lengthy and their prescription specific: "The general answer then is, 'without holiness, no man shall see the Lord.' Holiness is necessary according to the very nature of things to naturalize you . . . to the heavenly regions." [13]

The theoretical foundation of these assertions of Samuel Davies had been enunciated by Edwards. It is "in the nature of things" that death should fall upon man entrapped by sin, even though God may hold it at bay to await man's repentance. It is "in the nature of things" that when divine power comes to bear on man, new motives are awakened and the heart is moved to repent. It is "in the nature of things" that this inward motion will appear openly in visible acts of piety.

To the earlier Edwardeans, acts of holiness were therefore ends and consequences in a causal chain beginning with a vision of God and inevitably concluding in piety. Because of the invariable connection, a discriminating person could read the sequence backward: authentic holiness would reliably indicate divine activity in the heart of the convert. The supporting philosophical idea is the Edwardean view of God: he exists in power as an idea accessible to the mind of man. The purpose of Edwards' preaching was to direct the eye of man to God. A clear view of his excellence would set piety in motion.

The piety of the Princeton tradition took religious experience with great seriousness also but Witherspoon's repudiation of Edwards' idealism gave it a very different meaning. For the Scot from Paisley and Princeton, all that theology postulated must be brought to proof — not only to light — by experience. Apart from experience, the hardheaded Scottish philosophy saw no sound reason for believing that a supposed invisible

[13] Samuel Davies' views were expounded in a number of sermons. Cf. "The Method of Salvation through Jesus Christ," *Sermons*, 3 vols. (Philadelphia, 1864), I, 109 ff.

reality so much as existed. As Alexander was accustomed to say: "There are two kinds of religious knowledge, . . . the knowledge of truth as it is revealed in the Holy Scriptures and the impression which that truth makes on the human mind when rightly apprehended. . . . When that impression is clearly and distinctly made, we can understand by contemplating it the true inscription on the seal more satisfactorily than by a direct view of the seal itself. Thus it is found that nothing tends more to confirm and elucidate the truths contained in the word than an inward experience of their efficacy on the heart. . . . Genuine religious experience is nothing but the impression of divine truth on the mind by the energy of the Holy Spirit." [14]

From this infallible interconnection arose the Princeton emphasis on the evidences of Christianity, not only in personal religious experience but in the curriculum. Edwardeans had affirmed the intimate bond between the reality of the divine and its impression on man, but they did not elevate impressions to the rank of evidence for the existence of God. But at Princeton impressions were precisely regarded as evidence of divine operations on the individual affected. Thus Princeton realism elevated experience to a role never contemplated by the Edwardean awakening. For Edwards, God would exist in his own excellence — and the mind could know it — if the world contained not one shred of holiness. For the Scottish realist, such a circumstance would call into question the existence of God.

The Princeton-trained minister was expected to reveal in his own life, visibly and convincingly, the evidences of God's work. His piety was, as it were, his most eloquent sermon; it taught the reality, not merely the idea, of God. A sound minister would never say: "Be like me"; he knew he was a sinner. But if men caught the point of his piety, they would want to be like him, for in his life he proved the reality of God.

[14] Archibald Alexander, *Thoughts on Religious Experience*, 3d ed., (Philadelphia, 1844), 5, 8.

The historic problem of works now asserted itself in the Princeton tradition of ministry: since works are moral actions, the fundamental communication of God to man appeared to Princetonians increasingly to be a matter of moral urgings to which the eminently pious could and would conform. Good works were " the impression which the truth of Holy Scriptures makes on the human mind," as Alexander was wont to argue. Since experienced truth is superior to announced truth, the minister's piety was supremely significant. Preaching directed the eye of man to evidence in human life.

The fulcrum of the Edwardean movement and its consequent piety was the character of God and his providence for the natural order; for the Princeton philosophy, it was religious experience. This difference produced variants in practice. As the Great Awakening discovered, a convert who had caught sight of the beauty and excellence of God was instantly precipitated into an overwhelming personal crisis. The first glimpse of divine holiness against the background of smugness and virtual blindness to the human condition would be completely shattering. Edwards himself had known this effect and radical emotional reactions were no surprise to him. The prominence of conversionism in the Great Awakening was wholly consistent, therefore, with its underlying philosophy. Piety was the lifelong extension of conversion, the first response to God.

The Great Awakening was gravely compromised by hollow emotional displays, and Edwards had struggled to distinguish the marks of the true vision of God from " animal commotion." The conservative attitude of Princeton toward conversionism cannot, however, be wholly explained by the chastening of the revival. After Alexander, the Princeton philosophy simply did not estimate conversion as highly as did Edwardeanism. What was important was that there should be no slackening of the flow of *evidence:* the religious experience upon which the realist relied for assurance that God exists and acts. The intensity of the conversion experience was clearly secondary to the continuity of piety — which could never have been said of Edwardean conversion. For the Edwardeans, it was natural and inevitable that a life of piety should follow the moment when the divine excellence first flashed brilliantly on the life of man. If it did not, this would suggest that the alleged conversion was a superficial emotional crisis. But for the Princetonian, continuing streams of evidence must flow, so his cardinal concern was to establish durable habits of piety. Meanwhile, revivalist excesses and schism in Kentucky continued to sap Presbyterian enthusiasm for high conversionism. In theory the specific experience of conversion might be all but dispensed with so long as believers could learn the rules of sanctification and adopt firm habits of personal piety.

The actual description of piety underwent remarkably little change. Tennent called for "a work of humiliation, or conviction, in order to a sound conversion." Dickinson declared that the sinner under conviction "mourns under a sense of his former sins; he groans under the burden of his remaining corruptions . . . and with earnest diligence follows after holiness. . . . Nothing can so banish the great concern from his breast as to make him habitually slothful and indifferent." Davies stated in 1755 that "holiness consists in the conformity of our hearts and practices to the sacred law of God. . . . It is the image and likeness of God formed in the soul by which we become 'partakers of the divine nature.'" Witherspoon taught his students that a minister's piety was "to have a firm belief of that gospel he is called to preach and a lively sense of religion upon his own heart." [15] This he grounded, however, on the Scottish estimate of experience — and at this point, not with respect to counsels of piety but as regards its philosophical base, the historic change from the first period of revival to the new pietism occurred. "Let me just take notice of the great advantage of true religion to one destined for the work of the ministry," said Witherspoon. "It gives a man the knowledge that is of the most service to a minister. Experi-

[15] Lectures on Eloquence, *Works,* VII, 274.

mental knowledge is superior to all other and necessary to the perfection of every other kind. It is indeed the very possession or daily exercise of that which it is the business of his life and the duty of his office to explain and recommend." [16] Witherspoon's earnestness about religious experience was not less than that of Tennent and Davies. "There is a piercing and penetrating heat in that which flows from the heart. . . . A man truly pious has often esteem, influence and success though his parts may be much inferior to others who are more capable but less conscientious." But Witherspoon was not so much preaching for conversion as encouraging piety.

The rules of sanctification that were taught ministerial candidates in Princeton underwent little change after Witherspoon. Men presenting themselves were expected to be "hopefully pious": that is, they should have already discovered true religion over and above conformity to the general morality. A youth with sound habits of piety was assured of the reality of God and well on the road to "ardent and eminent piety."

At a height of eminence, piety enables the believer "to apprehend in their truth and excellence" the things of the Spirit, taught Charles Hodge, "and thus to experience their power." In its supreme moment "the soul is changed into [Christ's] image, from glory to glory by the Spirit of the Lord." [17] The achievement of such an "essential change of character" depends on moral education. The "infusion of a new principle of life" is followed by "the removing more and more the principles of evil still infecting our nature and destroying their power . . . the growth of the principle of spiritual life until it controls the thoughts, feelings, and acts and brings the soul into conformity to the image of Christ." [18]

Hodge furnished the new pietism with a strengthened doctrine of the Holy Spirit. True piety is the work of the Holy Spirit,[19] but the Spirit functions in harmony with reason and the Bible. Nevertheless, argued Charles Hodge, an act of the

---

[16] *Ibid.*, 276.
[17] Hodge, *ST*, III, 229.

[18] *Ibid.*, 221.
[19] *Ibid.*, 472.

Spirit is indispensable and anterior to understanding the Bible.[20] The Spirit first establishes its content as authoritative for reason; it then makes spiritually alive these raw materials which would otherwise be useless to the soul. Piety, therefore, is first created by an act of the Holy Spirit without collateral aid from the Bible, and then, in the process of sanctification, in association with it. In the latter relation, the Bible is " essential to all holy exercises in the human soul." [21] Hodge was at pains to emphasize the freedom of the Holy Spirit to work independently of the Bible and criticized Luther for arguing that "the Spirit never operated on the minds of men except through the Word and sacraments." [22] Piety rests principally on "the power of the Spirit as a divine person acting with and by the truth, or without it, as in his sovereign pleasure he sees fit." [23]

Piety, in short, was an avenue to the knowledge of God and therefore a protective armor against untruth. The eminently pious Presbyterian clergyman was fully assured of the reality of God. His soul was refreshed by a steady flow of divine encouragement. He was equipped to share these blessings with seekers, to reassure the doubter, to preach from his own experience of God, and to refute the skeptic. In the Princeton tradition, piety had little to do with the world but everything to do with the church and the ministry.

Ministry as Apologetic Vocation

In an age when few doubted that the laws of God regulated the total life of man, the minister was the preceptor of his entire community. But the Revolution taught men that the foundations of public life were laid in the very nature of man. Calvinists might argue that God was the creator of man but that gave no pause to the rationalist whose trust in nature and reason emboldened him for criticism of religion and its traditional social forms. The Presbyterian clergy had, therefore, not only

20 *Ibid.*, 474.   21 *Ibid.*, 476.   22 *Ibid.*, 485.   23 *Ibid.*, 476.

to teach truth that corresponded with religious experience but also to vindicate the Christian claim of divine sovereignty in territory staked out by Tom Paine and Ethan Allen for the jurisdiction of man. Not only professors and writers but pastors must be prepared to persuade.

Precisely how the "ministry of apologetics" was fulfilled in the pastorate may be seen in the essays of Ichabod Spencer, minister of the Second Presbyterian Church of Brooklyn, New York. "On a very hot day in July," wrote Spencer, "a boy called at my house with a gentleman's card, saying that a lady had sent him to request me to visit a young man, who was sick." [24] The young Irish youth whom Spencer found was dying of consumption. He was trained in law, a child of the new age. "My mind is not so formed as to take things upon trust," he said. "I want knowledge. I am not prepared to yield to assumption and dogmatism." Spencer accepted these terms. He demonstrated that the truths of religion are a matter of knowledge, fully verified by experience, and that impartial reason demands that man should yield to faith. The story ended triumphantly. Scarcely hours before his death, the young rationalist capitulated and died secure in post-Calvinist hope.

The determinate system of rationalized Calvinism that the Old School believed essential to meet the critical problem of the age was stated fully by Charles Hodge. The theological consequences of Hodge's work were not clear to the loyalists of his branch of divided Presbyterianism but as we shall see, they were wholly consistent with the drift of the Calvinist tradition in this century, irrespective of party.

The purpose of theology, declared Hodge, "is simply to state what God has revealed in his Word and to vindicate those statements as far as possible from misconceptions and objections." [25] However, an enormous range of knowledge about

[24] Ichabod Spencer, A Pastor's Sketches or Conversations with Anxious Inquirers Respecting the Way of Salvation, 2 vols. (New York, 1853), 1–64.
[25] ST, I, 535.

God is available to man apart from the Bible, and large areas of Hodge's own thought consisted of inferences from his all-important conviction that knowledge of God "is innate [and] is a deduction of reason." [26] "The theory that God is infinite, absolute and first cause can in no sense be brought within the mind's thought or conception and must therefore be remanded to faith is untenable," he wrote in the *Biblical Repertory*.[27] Other essentials are open to reason. By an "intuition of the intellect" all men know the cause-effect relationship to be valid; man also by nature knows God as first cause. In addition, there are "moral truths which the mind intuitively recognizes as true, [e.g.,] the essential distinction between right and wrong." [28]

Knowledge given by revelation is different. "By innate knowledge is meant that which is due to our constitution as sentient, rational, and moral beings. It is opposed to knowledge founded on experience; to that obtained by *ab extra* instruction." Since the facts of the Bible are externally experienced, they fall in the latter category. Man could never have known them except by their happening by divine impulse in history.

What is the effect of the fall of mankind? Did it not clog the channels of natural knowledge? Hodge responded that man's "sense of justice . . . is indestructible in the nature of man . . . and in common with reason and conscience has survived the Fall." [29] Even fallen men know that they are sinners, are guilty, and that God is both just and holy. The Holy Spirit is not needed to produce these convictions, but may confirm them. Also undamaged by the Fall is man's certainty that he is a free agent. To deny this "does violence to our nature and contradicts the intuitive convictions of consciousness." [30] God does not need to avail himself of revelation to make clear his existence, his nature, and the moral situation of man.

---

[26] *Ibid.*, I, 191.
[27] *BRPR*, XXXII, 1861, 445.
[28] *ST*, I, 193.

[29] *Ibid.*, I, 421.
[30] *Ibid.*, I, 333.

Hodge agreed with Kant that intuition, not the deductive reasoning process, was the source of man's knowledge of moral truth.[31] Reason may be trusted, however, to extract truth by deduction from intuited knowledge of God and to exegete and systematize the Bible. To Hodge, "rationalism" was the doctrine that one may infer the existence and character of God and the fundamentals of morals from experimental evidence — or from such evidence deny his existence. There was no need to validate the "testimony of sense and consciousness in fact." [32] But reason and sensory perception were both inferior to the moral consciousness. "If a man is shut up to deny either the testimony of his senses or the truths of reason on the one hand or the testimony of his moral nature on the other, all experience shows that he will give up sense and reason and bow to the authority of conscience. He cannot help it. . . . These moral convictions involve in them, or at least, necessitate the belief in a God to whom we must give an account." [33]

Hodge described the predicament of the young Irishman of Ichabod Spencer's *Pastor's Sketches* as American Christians of many affiliations understood it. "Our religious feelings, our sense of dependence, our consciousness of responsibility, our aspirations after fellowship with some Being Higher than ourselves and higher than anything which the world or nature contains, necessitate the belief in the existence of God. . . . It is of great importance that men should know and feel that they are by their very nature bound to believe in God." [34] The young Irishman's difficulty arose from his refusal to face the truth of his own nature.

Hodge's scholastic view of the relation of faith and reason furnished another essential tool of the ministry of apologetics. Faith does not require acceptance of the incredible; God makes no demand that is inconsistent with the rational nature. "By knowledge is meant the intellectual apprehension of truth." [35] Christianity is knowledge, and Christian faith is ac-

---

[31] *Ibid.*, I, 43.   [33] *ST*, I, 279.   [35] *Ibid.*, I, 393.
[32] *BRPR*, 1855, 85.   [34] *Ibid.*, I, 200 f.; cf. III, 697.

ceptance of and living trust in our knowledge of God. There are truths that men can " know " without understanding them: for example, the doctrine of the Trinity. " It is not necessary to the rational exercise of faith that we should understand the truth believed," Hodge wrote.[36] " The unknown and the impossible cannot be believed, but every man does and must believe the incomprehensible," [37] which represents simply a larger extension of the knowable than man commands. Accordingly, " religion is the reception of certain doctrines as true and a state of heart and course of action in accordance with those doctrines." [38] Hodge accepted the going view of the Enlightenment that man's nature teaches him of God but he refused to concede that Christianity is a mystical pervasion of the world by the Divine.

The apologetic vocation concerned not only doctrine but morals. " The common doctrine of Christians . . . is that the will of God is the ultimate ground of moral obligation to all rational creatures." [39] Conscience is the voice not of man's will but of God.[40] As regarded the ground of God's own relationship to right and wrong, Hodge was vague. God is free to act in keeping with " his own sense of what is wise, right, or desirable." [41] But is he guided by law or his own " conscience "? Hodge replied that God's acts do not arise from " the necessity of his own nature." God always keeps his promises; but he does it freely, which is to say that he is at liberty to break them. Nevertheless, " it is indeed inconceivable that God should violate his word. But this only proves that moral certainty may be as inexorable as necessity." God's freedom is " limited," therefore, by the moral certainty that he will do

---

[36] *Ibid.*, I, 40.
[37] *Ibid.*, III, 81. " True philosophy cannot contradict the Word of God. . . . No philosophy should have a hearing which contradicts the fundamental truth of Christianity." *BRPR*, 1855, 416 f.
[38] *ST*, I, 176 f.
[39] *Ibid.*, I, 406.
[40] Cf. John Calvin, *Institutes*, II. viii. 1.
[41] *ST*, I, 403.

what he has promised. This is embodied in his decrees, which Hodge defined as "rational determinations founded on sufficient reasons." [42] It is these reasons that determine what is "wise, right, or desirable" for God.

Hodge did not refuse to discuss the explosive issue of human ability. The effect of the Fall is to render man unable to respond; but "inability does not arise from the loss of any faculty of his mind or of any original, essential attribute of his nature." [43] In his moral nature man retains undistorted the image of God. Hodge did not develop a doctrine of the image of God systematically or even consistently. In discussing sanctification, for example, he affirmed that "by their apostasy, men lost the image of God. . . . They are by nature destitute of spiritual life." [44] This definition of the Fall, Hodge never brought into relation with the view that the image of God is moral and rational and is not lost at the Fall.[45]

The problem of salvation hinges not so much on lack of knowledge, affirmed Hodge, as on inability. The critical problem " consists in the want of power rightly to discern spiritual things and the consequent want of all right affections toward them. And this want of power of spiritual discernment arises from the corruption of our whole nature by which the reason or understanding is blinded and the taste and feelings are perverted." [46]

The important term here is " spiritual things." These are simply the particular data of the evangelical history, which could never have been known without a divine intervention. " Spiritual things " compose " revealed knowledge," which is inaccessible to intuition or reason although indispensable to salvation. As Ashbel Green put it: " Revealed or Christian Theology . . . is that system of truth which God has made known to man in the Holy Scriptures." [47]

The " corruption of our whole nature," continued Hodge, blinds understanding. This is not to say that the Fall destroyed moral consciousness; the Christian apologist must know the resources within the man to whom he is appealing. In Hodge's system, " blindness " appears to mean that man has no access to the content of the Bible or, having access, he does not receive it as true. Hodge was not altogether clear on this point. Why would not the corruption of man's whole nature damage intuited knowledge of God? Hodge repeatedly affirmed, nevertheless, that it does not. If man's intuitive grasp of God and duty is unaffected by the Fall, a phrase such as " the corruption of our whole nature " can only mean that fallen man lacks a taste for the Bible. If, as Hodge asserts, natural man knows God as he is, his critical problem would seem to be want of conformity to perception. But Hodge affirmed that the chief problem is man's failure to discern the import of the evangelical history. Ministry brings the Bible to man; grace enables man to accept the Biblical facts. The result is an enlarged perception of God: to natural perception is added appreciation of the Bible with its consequence, total personal change.

The possibility of effective apologetics rested on Hodge's precept that grace performs no office in relation to innate perception of God. Conversion is essentially an extension of cognition: " rightly to discern." Since the " feelings follow the understanding . . . the illumination of the mind . . . is the necessary preliminary condition of all right feeling and conduct." Here lies the work of the minister as exegete, evangelist, and apologist. To say, with Hodge, that " true conversion is said to be effected by a revelation," [48] is to allude to a cognitive process.

THE KINSHIP OF PIETY WITH MAN'S KNOWLEDGE OF GOD

To what power, theologically considered, does the minister look in order to effect the essential transformation? In Hodge's thought, so far as piety is concerned, the Holy Spirit is the cru-

[48] ST, I, 262.

cial member of the Trinity. Men are lost, despite extensive and valid knowledge of God, primarily because they lack a proper relationship to knowledge. No man accepts the Bible or rightly relates himself to God apart from the testimony of the Spirit. Lack of piety is the sure mark of " dead faith," a wrong relationship to revealed knowledge. The hinge that joins piety with knowledge of God is therefore true faith.

Faith is defined by Hodge as man's relationship to whatever in the Bible would be unknown without revelation and undiscerned without the Spirit; but which, while incomprehensible, is not essentially unknowable. Faith exists as " a form of conviction in the human mind . . . rather because of the limitation than the impotency of human reason." " What lies beyond the sphere of knowledge lies beyond the sphere of faith." [49] Faith and reason are equally rational at base; but reason enables men to believe the comprehensible, while faith makes the uncomprehended acceptable. " Faith must be preceded by knowledge," he affirmed in 1862.[50] Faith is also piety: " the satisfaction which [men] experience in Christianity for their spiritual needs."

Hodge had no sympathy for definitions of faith that lost contact with cognition; the view of Delitzsch, for example, which " describes faith as the most central act of our being; the return to God, the going out of our inner life to Him." [51] " Limiting [the concept of faith] to a consciousness of reconciliation with God," affirmed Hodge, " is contrary to the usage of Scripture and of theology." The inexpressible personal bond of a believer to his Lord is strictly speaking no part of faith. " The object of faith is the whole revelation of God as contained in his Word," including what may be " deduced therefrom by necessary inference." Hodge was aware of the numerous New Testament assertions that speak of a relation between Christ

---

[49] *ST*, III, 85.
[50] *BRPR*, 1862, 31–36.
[51] *ST*, III, 45. " It is impossible to believe that of which we can have no conception." *BRPR*, 1861, 445.

and his disciples unmediated by any specific doctrine about him. "Our Lord repeatedly declares that what men are required to do . . . is to believe on Him." Hodge introduced a distinction: "*the special object of faith* which secures our salvation is the act of receiving and resting on Him as he is offered to us in the Gospel." [52] Hodge did not further pursue the question of the relationship between the personal object of faith and its rational object, Biblical data. But he insisted that "if the contents of the Bible did not correspond with the truth which God has revealed in his external works and the constitution of our nature, it could not be received as coming from Him, for God cannot contradict himself. Nothing, therefore, can be more derogatory to the Bible than the assertion that its doctrines are contrary to reason." [53] Revelation is actually subject, therefore, to the judgment of intuition and reason; and the latter are subject to the authoritative judgment of the Bible.

IMPLICATIONS OF NATURAL THEOLOGY FOR CHURCH MINISTRY

At this late stage in the history of natural theology its dangers were by no means evident to American Calvinist divines. Eminent regard for the powers of reason, so strong among Presbyterians and Congregationalists of all parties — Old and New Schools, Unitarians, Hopkinsians, and orthodox — was also foundational to less pious men who were prepared to carry the logic of the Enlightenment to its natural conclusion, denial of the essentiality of revelation. A series of topographical lines already marked the terrain of this question quite plainly in English philosophical history in the eighteenth century. Samuel Clarke's name was a byword among subscriptionist Scots and his tendencies toward Unitarianism amply publicized by the failure of latitudinarian English Presbyterianism.[54] Yet

[52] *Ibid.*, III, 95–97. The italics are ours.
[53] *Ibid.*, III, 83. Cf. BRPR, V, 101.
[54] The works of Clarke had been a subject of debate in Boston in the 1750's, as correspondence between Thomas Foxcroft and Joseph Bel-

Witherspoon used his books to demonstrate the character of God at Princeton. Such diverse personalities as William Law, John Leland, John Tillotson, and Joseph Butler argued that revelation and reason dealt in the same coin, except that certain data, although essentially rational, were in fact known only by revelation.

To theologians who wanted to remain Calvinist, the question was simply how far man's innate capacities should be permitted to invade the narrowing range of data that an earlier age had considered the domain of revelation alone. Apologists drew the line at different points, but only a marginal figure like the conservative Scot, Robert Riccaltoun, perceived that the defense of Christianity must be based upon a fundamentally new assumption. Neither Edwards nor his most discerning successors nor even his critics ever ceased trying to capture the intellectual vision of God; nor did they question the assumption of the age that reason was, in its own way, divine. Riccaltoun sensed the revolutionary character of his own position, for he rejected both Edwardean idealism and the subjective experimentalism of the revival in favor of the historical objectivity of the acts of Christ, " the plain facts by which [the love of God in Christ] is evidenced and imprinted." [55] It did not occur to the American Calvinist fathers that so simple a suggestion could furnish theology with a fresh beginning and free them from a dangerous courtship with rationalism, whether orthodox, Unitarian, or deist.

Modern scholars have underestimated the significance of the agreement of " scholastic " Calvinists with their most determined enemies. Professor Sidney Mead, for example, speaks of the emergence of " the theological issue of reason versus revelation " after the Revolutionary War.[56] There was, indeed, an

---

lamy indicates. Letter of Foxcroft to Bellamy, September 23, 1758. HSP, Dreer, III.

[55] Riccaltoun, *op. cit.*, 96.

[56] S. Mead, " Denominationalism: The Shape of Protestantism in America." *CH,* XXIII (December, 1954), 311.

obvious debate between orthodox figures like Jedediah Morse and Lyman Beecher and their opponents at Harvard; but the significant fact remains that conservative Calvinism never broke with the deep-rooted rationalism that had come down to it from Puritanism and therefore it remained fundamentally in harmony with its first cousins and worst critics, the anti-Trinitarian rationalists. What is altogether obvious in the literature of the post-Revolutionary period is the controversy among the branches of rationalist Calvinism. What is less apparent is that there could be no refounding of theology until a fresh methodological conception was injected into the debate. Meanwhile apologists like Hodge, profoundly impressed by the advances of science and convinced of its place in the divine providence, conceded large ground to reason, narrowing the sphere of revelation to the point where just those portions of the Bible that the mind could never have invented were the only unique content of revelation.

The theological and practical views of Charles Hodge did not go unchallenged during the century of his dominion in Presbyterianism, nor could he have brought the Princeton tradition to focus without the penetrating effects of Witherspoon's philosophical and moral positions and Green's foundational work of organization. But the precedent in Presbyterian theological education that was laid down in Princeton so saturated the church that views opposed to Hodge's never obtained sufficient strength elsewhere materially to offset his influence. Correspondence during this period exhibits the grip of these assumptions on the mind of the clergy. "Although the Bible does not teach mental, any more than it does natural philosophy," wrote L. P. Hickock to C. C. Vanarsdale, "yet the facts and assumptions of the Bible in reference to the human mind may doubtless be put into a philosophical system." [57] The *Repertory* itself published articles that disputed the fundamentals of Hodge's teaching (even though the editors de-

[57] Letter of L. P. Hickock to C. C. Vanarsdale, February 13, 1851. HSP, Dreer, Letters of American Clergy.

nied the contradiction was real) as did *The Southern Presbyterian Review*, its regional counterpart after 1848.[58] But no one seriously threatened the eminence of the institution at Princeton.

[58] *BRPR*, I, 204.

XI

MINISTERIAL TRAINING
IN SOUTH AND WEST

ANDOVER AND PRINCETON furnished the principal models for the establishment of new seminaries along the main routes to the South and West. Institutionalized seminaries usually emerged from "field education" or the work of a college professor, often also a president, who gave time to theological instruction. The earliest beginnings of Princeton reveal these mutations. The Log College, first a field project of William Tennent, Sr., became an academy; after his death its work was resumed on an enlarged basis by the College of New Jersey (1745), which was actually little but a field project before its settlement in Princeton, where the president taught theology. The action establishing the seminary followed in 1811.

This was also the situation of Hampden-Sydney College in Prince Edward County, Virginia. By 1818, a substantial number of graduates of the collegiate course were reading theology and by 1822 a total of forty-four men had been prepared for the ministry through resident study ranging from a few months to several years. The founding of the Union Theological Seminary of Virginia, successor to Hampden-Sydney's collegiate work in theology, came only in 1824.[1]

---

[1] *Centennial General Catalogue of the Trustees, Officers, Professors, and Alumni of Union Theological Seminary in Virginia, 1807–1907*, edited by W. W. Moore and Tilden Scherer (Richmond, n.d.). Cf. J. Gray McAllister, *The Life and Letters of Walter W. Moore* (Union Theological Seminary, Richmond, 1939).

Although not the earliest effort made by the Scottish-American traditions, the Seminary of John Mitchell Mason at New York City, inaugurated in 1805, was by far its most distinguished. Trained at Seceder Divinity Hall at Selkirk, Scotland, Mason became a pastor in New York at the turn of the century and was a friend of Samuel Miller. Although fully authorized by the Associate Reformed Synod, the seminary was generally called " Dr. Mason's Seminary " and was scarcely distinguishable from the better programs of field education, although Mason assembled a library of historic importance to American theological education and enjoyed the assistance of an associate in Biblical and historical studies for nine years.[2]

Western Theological Seminary at Allegheny, Pennsylvania (in 1912 incorporated into Pittsburgh), reproduced the Plan of Princeton and the Presbyterianism of Ashbel Green. Auburn Seminary, on the other hand, was founded by the Synod of Geneva, New York, in 1818, to supply clergymen to the expanding population of western New York and took as its model Andover Seminary. In authorizing Western in 1825, the Assembly provided that " the plan of the Seminary at Princeton ought also to be the plan of the contemplated Seminary in the West with no other alterations whatever than those which are indispensably necessary to accommodate it to the local situation and circumstances." [3] After prolonged dispute with the claims of Cincinnati and Charleston, Indiana, the seminary was officially placed at Allegheny.[4] In 1827, the Assembly elected Western's first permanent board of directors. It included Francis Herron, Elisha Swift, Elisha McCurdy, and Thomas Baird, all of whom were working in harmony with the

[2] John McNaugher, *The History of Theological Education in the United Presbyterian Church and Its Ancestries* (United Presbyterian Board of Education and Bible School Work, 1931), 29. Cf. Frank D. McCloy, "The Founding of Protestant Theological Seminaries in the United States of America, 1784–1840" (Ph.D. thesis, Harvard University, 1959), 137.

[3] *MGA*, 1821–1835 (Philadelphia, n.d.), 148. Cf. *Plan of the Western Theological Seminary . . . , Allegheny, Pa.* (Allegheny, 1884).

[4] *Ibid.*, 1827, 177. Cf. Protest of J. L. Wilson. *MGA*, 1827, 208.

Green-led group. Herron, for example, submitted a recommendation to the Assembly in that year eliminating a provision in the "plans of intercourse" with the Congregational Associations of three New England states that gave their delegates the right to vote in the General Assembly. The abrogation of the mutual voting privilege was one of the goals of the Philadelphia denominationalists.

Jacob J. Janeway, earlier the associate of Green in the Second Church at Philadelphia, was the Assembly's choice for first professor at Western. In 1828, a second professor, John McDowell, also a strong Old School man, was elected to teach church history. McDowell refused; Janeway hesitated, accepted, served a year and resigned in 1829, leaving the Western program completely disorganized.[5] There were eight students enrolled at that date and plans to build were afoot but the financial situation was disheartening. In 1829, Luther Halsey, the only New School man to serve at Western, was elected in Janeway's place, but Western was troubled by internal friction and for two decades was not sure of its survival.

Auburn Seminary represented the earliest application of the Andover model to Presbyterian theological education. In February, 1818, the Synod of Geneva declared that the remoteness of Princeton precluded both substantial service to western New York and successful solicitations on its behalf and asked the next Assembly "to express to this Synod their opinion on the subject" of a new institution for ministerial training within its bounds. The Assembly's response was cryptic: "The said Synod are the best judges in what may be their duty in this important business." Seven years later the Assembly founded Western, and the year after accepted responsibility for Union of Virginia. Both these institutions were Assembly controlled and soundly Old School. In view of the dispute astir in New York and Philadelphia and the strong ties of the New York region with New England, it is probable that the Philadelphia leadership not only wanted no rival to Princeton for the time

[5] Cf. *MGA*, 1828, 245; 1829, 261.

being but was unwilling to approve a center where theological opinion prevailing in the Synod of Geneva would be perpetuated.

If such fears existed, they were confirmed by the appointment of Matthew LaRue Perrine to Auburn. In 1816 he had published a controversial pamphlet defending the views of Nathaniel Emmons and the New England theology.[6] He was professor of church history and ecclesiastical polity from 1821 till 1836, when he was succeeded by Luther Halsey of Western. Other appointments reflected the same kinship with Andover and its alliance with Hopkinsianism. Dirck C. Lansing, professor of sacred rhetoric, was a strong advocate of New England thought; William Wisner, a critical figure in promoting Auburn, and James Richards, professor of theology, were soon to emerge as New School leaders. The professors' oath contrasted strongly with the Princeton text: " I do solemnly and sincerely affirm and declare that I believe the Scriptures of the Old and New Testaments to be the Word of God, and the only infallible rule of faith and practice; that I do receive and adopt the Confession of Faith and the Catechisms . . . as containing the System of Doctrines taught in the Holy Scriptures . . . and I do solemnly promise to maintain with zeal and fidelity the truths of the Gospel and to be faithful and diligent in the discharge of all such duties as may devolve on me as a professor in this Seminary." Within twenty years, Auburn became the capital of the New School Presbyterian Church. Although ready to submit to General Assembly control at the reunion of 1870, the bonds with presbyteries and synod remained primary and Assembly " control " over Auburn never had unequivocal legal status.[7]

6 Matthew LaRue Perrine, *Letters Concerning the Plan of Salvation as Deduced from the Scriptures* . . . (New York, 1816).

7 John Quincy Adams, *A History of Auburn Theological Seminary, 1818–1918* (Auburn, 1918), 82 f. James Richards, although sympathetic to New England, was no Finneyite. Like Beecher, he felt Finney's methods were unwarranted and a betrayal of New England thought. Cf. Letter to Dwight, July 5, 1832. HSP, Gratz, Case 8,

Still lacking an adequate system of internal transportation, the country could not be served by a single educational center in New Jersey. "The more I know the more I am convinced," wrote John H. Rice, of Virginia, "that northern men cannot live and do what we want in the southern country. And now we want at least one hundred native preachers in Virginia; besides all that they need to the south of us." Rice deplored the rising doctrinal debate in the church in the North. "I hear that there is a mighty ado made in Princeton and New York about Hopkinsianism. . . . I would to God that the brethren felt more love to Christ and less to a party. . . . I will never join any party in the Church." [8] Under such impulses, Presbyterians favored regional control of theological education. Rice was a prime mover in establishing a full theological course at Hampden-Sydney and in 1824 the Union Seminary was set apart from the collegiate program of Hampden-Sydney College in Prince Edward County. By 1826 it had twelve students.[9] In that year the General Assembly agreed to the request of the Presbytery of Hanover to assume control, which amounted to "a negative on all appointments to the offices of Professors and Trustees . . . and on general laws or rules adopted by the Presbytery for its government." [10] Initiative was left to those locally responsible — board and presbytery — but the Assembly reserved the right to intervene in case any professor should "inculcate doctrines repugnant to the word of God and to our Confession of Faith." Failure to dismiss a professor on complaint would terminate the tie with the Assembly. In 1827 Virginia and North Carolina agreed to support

---

box 39. Cf. Adams, 137–141. The "era of good feeling" in the 1860's did not obliterate New School preference for synodal control. Cf. *Presbyterian Banner* (Pittsburgh), June 12, 1862.

[8] Letter of John H. Rice to Micah Baldwin, April 17, 1824. HSP, Gratz, Case 8, box 39.

[9] Letter of John H. Rice to Jedediah Morse, April 2, 1826. HSP, Gratz, Case 8, box 39. Cf. Letters to Baldwin, December 9, 1823, October 4, 1823.

[10] *MGA*, 1826, 184. Cf. H. R. Miller, *A History of Union Theological Seminary in Virginia, 1807–1865* (Th.D. thesis, 1957).

the school, and it received the name of " The Union Seminary of the General Assembly under the care of the Synods of Virginia and North Carolina." [11]

Already it was becoming clear that the theory of "one great seminary" could not be realized and that a federal affiliation with the Assembly was better suited to a church so widely distributed. A major problem of the second quarter of the century was the undue multiplication of seminaries. To an overture from the Presbytery of West Lexington, Kentucky, deploring this trend, the Assembly replied: "They [the protestants] believe that much good that might have resulted from having a larger portion of our young men brought in a personal acquaintance with each other and educated upon the same plan must now be lost; and that we must content ourselves with less harmony of feeling and unity of sentiment." [12] But the Assembly still left the synods free to train their own clergy. The synods themselves wanted candidates kept close by so as to seize them for their own vacancies. This attitude was justified by the facts, even though it worked against thorough education by drawing students out of school prematurely.[13] Throughout the history of American Presbyterianism, there has been a close correspondence between the location of seminaries and ministerial supply in the several regions of the church.

The capture of Transylvania College by militant secularists had been a bitter blow to Kentucky Presbyterians.[14] Centre College at Danville was their riposte. From the beginning it was specifically oriented to the preparation of ministers. Sim-

---

[11] *MGA*, 1827, 212.

[12] *MGA*, 1830, 288.

[13] By 1844 there was a surplus of 100 ministers and licentiates in the four synods nearest Princeton, while in the other sixteen synods there were 530 churches without pastors. R. J. Breckinridge, *The Christian Pastor* (Baltimore, 1845), 20, note.

[14] Cf. Letter of James D. Blythe to John B. Romeyn, March 29, 1822, asking Romeyn to consider the presidency; and if not, to approach Philip Lindsley, of Princeton. HSP, Gratz, Case 8, box 36; *MGA*, 1825, 140.

ilarly, in 1819 a school had been founded at Maryville, Tennessee, by Isaac Anderson after Princeton had proved unable to send clergymen to the southwestern frontier. This venture, the Southern and Western Theological Seminary, was inaugurated under the auspices of the Synod of Tennessee, and had as many as three professors in certain periods following 1831. Its plan and curriculum were similar to Princeton's; evangelical students of all affiliations were welcome. The college department at Maryville successfully established itself, but theological instruction ceased about 1856. In all, between 100 and 150 ministers were prepared by the Southern and Western Seminary.[15]

The theological department at Centre fared little better. In 1824 theological instruction was authorized by a revision in the charter and in 1828 the first professor was appointed. In 1829 the Synod of Tennessee asked that the seminary at Danville "be taken into union with the General Assembly," consistent with the resolutions of the West Lexington Presbytery. The Assembly replied that while the plan of the seminary was satisfactory, the general organization of the project was not yet definite enough to warrant Assembly affiliation.[16]

At one stage of the struggle over the location of Western Seminary a resolution had been introduced that "a theological seminary under the care of the General Assembly of the Presbyterian Church ought to be located in some suitable place in the bounds of the synods to the westward of the Synod of Pittsburgh." [17] While not adopted, this spoke for the Presby-

[15] Samuel T. Wilson, *A Century of Maryville College, 1819–1919* (Maryville College, 1935), 102–109. Cf. Davidson, *The Presbyterian Church in Kentucky*, 299 ff.

[16] I. S. McElroy, *The Louisville Presbyterian Theological Seminary* (The Presbyterian Standard Publishing Company, 1929), 30 f. MGA, 1829, 256, 274. Cf. Robert Stuart Sanders, *History of Louisville Presbyterian Theological Seminary, 1853–1953* (Louisville Presbyterian Theological Seminary, 1953). Also, Constitution and Bylaws of Louisville Presbyterian Theological Seminary. Approved April 15, 1958, n.d., n.p.

[17] MGA, 1827, 208.

terians of the Ohio River Valley and in 1829 the "literary department" of Lane Theological Seminary was established at Cincinnati with funds provided by two Baptist businessmen.[18] Instruction in theology began in 1832 when Lyman Beecher brought prestige and leadership to its presidency and professorship of theology. Within two years, however, the school was disrupted by abolition revivalism.

At the time he was invited to assume the presidency of Lane, Lyman Beecher was regarded as the champion of orthodoxy in New England, and his close personal friendship with Nathaniel Taylor, the principal suspect of Old School Presbyterians after 1820, had been no obstacle. Joshua L. Wilson, the determined and vociferous Old School leader in Cincinnati, had pressed Beecher to accept the Lane position but before his arrival Wilson reversed himself and eventually brought Beecher to trial for slander and heresy. During the ensuing controversy, Beecher charged that Wilson's dramatic turnabout was triggered by communications from the "Princeton party" and their sympathizers in Pittsburgh who were alarmed at the prospect of a New England man rising to leadership in Cincinnati.[19] Whatever the reason for Wilson's decision, Old School hostility to Lane did not diminish. In 1850 the Old School Presbytery of the then divided church asked that Western and New Albany be consolidated at Cincinnati in opposition to Lane, but the Assembly remembered the debate over the location of Western and refused. The Old School men in Cincinnati then undertook to open a seminary independently, but it closed in 1853 when its leader, N. L. Rice, resigned his church.[20]

The location of Princeton hampered its usefulness to the dis-

---

18 John Vant Stephens, *The Story of the Founding of Lane*, rev. ed. (Cincinnati, 1940). Cf. Edward D. Morris, *Thirty Years in Lane and Other Lane Papers* (1897), n.p., 54 and *passim*.

19 Stephens, *op. cit.*, 14.

20 On this abortive effort, cf. correspondence of James Hoge with Nicholas Murray, June 30, 1846; November 1, 1849; June 8, 1850. HSP, Gratz, Case 8, box 37.

tant South as well as to the West.[21]   In 1829 the Presbytery of South Carolina with assistance from the Presbytery of Hopewell, which embraced northern Georgia, established the Columbia Theological Seminary in the capital city of South Carolina.[22] First titled "The Theological Seminary of South Carolina and Georgia," it was later supported and controlled also by the Synods of Florida and Alabama; but its obligation to the General Assembly remained the same as that of Union Seminary.   Classes began in 1831 with two professors; by 1860 the faculty numbered five and the student body fifty.   The Civil War disrupted the seminary and destroyed over half its assets, but it gradually recovered until by the end of the century it had recouped the lost ground.[23]

Some of the incipient institutions of Presbyterianism never matured sufficiently to display definite kinship with any parent seminary, but Columbia was influenced by both Andover and Princeton.   George Howe, one of its first professors, was a Massachusetts man and a graduate of Andover.   The Princeton plan was not overlooked in the seminary's organization, but the curriculum was modeled on Andover and the example of Leonard Wood influenced instruction in theology.   James Henley Thornwell, one of the most competent minds produced by American Presbyterianism, became Columbia's strongest voice

---

[21] One of the problems lay in the Constitutional requirement that candidates be licensed by their own presbyteries. This called for a long and difficult trip to the home region. Some South Carolinians were ready to grant authority to license to Princeton Seminary to overcome the problem. Letter of A. Flinn to Ashbel Green, November 21, 1810. HSP, Gratz, Case 8, box 39.

[22] Cf. George Howe, A History of Columbia Theological Seminary, the Memorial Volume of the Semi-centennial of the Theological Seminary at Columbia, S.C. (Columbia, 1884); William Childs Robinson, Columbia Theological Seminary and the Southern Presbyterian Church: A Study in Church History, Presbyterian Polity, Mission Enterprise and Religious Thought (Decatur, 1931), T. C. Johnson, History of the Southern Presbyterian Church, Vol. XI of the American Church History Series (New York, 1894), 311–479.

[23] See Report of Progress in Letter of William Plumer, November 1, 1870. HSP, Case 8.

during the slavery controversy. That debate estranged Columbia first from New England and eventually from Princeton and diverted Thornwell's considerable talents into the desert of proslavery controversy.

The last of the seminaries to be founded in the crucial decade before the schism of 1837 was organized specifically because of controversy: Union Seminary of New York was established in 1836. That city was already very conscious of its rising eminence in commerce and culture. Although Presbyterian moderates prevented an outbreak of strife in the General Assembly before 1835, in that year the Old School party obtained a majority for the first time and began to move specifically toward "reform" of the church. This provoked a severe reaction. The Assembly of 1836, for example, exhibited more New School partisanship than any of its predecessors. In New York City a group of Presbyterians resolved "to provide a Theological Seminary in the midst of the greatest and most growing community in America around which all men of moderate views and feelings, who desire to live free from party strife and to stand aloof from all extremes of doctrinal speculation, practical radicalism, and ecclesiastical domination, may cordially and affectionately rally." [24] The complaint of "ecclesiastical domination" implied repudiation of the restraints that held Princeton firmly within the Old School orbit. Three years after establishment, Union had admitted so large a student body as to rival both Andover and Princeton.[25]

Spurred by the success of the American Board of Commissioners for Foreign Missions, Presbyterians were becoming increasingly convinced that the grace of revival was not given

---

[24] George Lewis Prentiss, *The Union Theological Seminary in the City of New York: Historical and Biographical Sketches of Its First Fifty Years* (New York, 1889), 8. Cf. also Henry S. Coffin, *A Half Century of Union Theological Seminary, 1896–1945* (Charles Scribner's Sons, 1954).

[25] The reunion of 1870 produced a uniquely roseate view of the origins of Union. A General Assembly Committee stated that the Union founders were "largely members of churches known after the division as Old School." *MGA,* 1870, 60.

only to Americans but was intended for the blessing of all mankind. Furthermore, Old School leadership recognized that
without a denominational agency, Presbyterian donations
would increasingly pass into the control of the American
Board of Commissioners, already generously supported by
Presbyterians. The establishment of the Western Foreign Missionary Society at Pittsburgh in 1831 answered to Old School
anxieties. This enterprise was transferred to the care of the
General Assembly at the climax of the schism of 1837, becoming the Board of Foreign Missions of the Presbyterian Church.

For the preparation of missionaries, a special program of
theological education was conceived in 1829: the "Missionary
Institution" on the campus of Princeton Seminary. Professors
Alexander, Miller, and Hodge, with two associates, recommended a new "Professorship of Pastoral Theology and Missionary Instruction" for the seminary. The appointee was to
press the claims of missions on all students as well as to teach,
and the proponents of the plan believed it would stimulate "a
spirit of deep and elevated piety . . . [and] personal zeal for
the salvation of men." [26] The adoption of the recommendation founded the historic association of Princeton Seminary
with the missionary cause.

A potent cause of Presbyterian dispute was the problem of
financing the theological student himself. The Kentucky revivals and the arrival of many New Englanders in New York
and Ohio had sharpened the appetite of the West for ministers. To found a vigorous seminary did not of itself solve the
problem; there was needed a considerable increase in the number of candidates as well. Revival produced the men, but
those who offered themselves were scarcely ever able to pay
for their education. Concurrently with the establishment of
the seminaries, therefore, there grew up societies to aid "poor
but pious" youths who, if they could be trained, would answer
to the church's need.

The first general education agency was the American Edu-

[26] MGA, 1830, 285–293.

cation Society, organized at Boston in 1814. It affected Presbyterianism most directly through the operation of the Plan of Union of 1801, which provided for combined work in villages where Congregational emigrants were settling side by side with Presbyterians. A clergyman of either denomination might serve as pastor of a mixed group, whatever the preponderant affiliation of the congregation as a whole.[27] Andover was a major source of ministers for the areas touched by the Plan. To some Presbyterians in the middle states, this highly coherent structure of theological education and church extension was little more than an engine for subverting the faith of emigrant Presbyterians and filling the General Assembly with delegates of questionable theology and churchmanship.

THE PRESBYTERIAN MACHINE AND THE SCHISM

The creation of equally efficient machinery under exclusively Presbyterian auspices began, in effect, with the founding of Princeton Seminary in 1811. In 1818, Ashbel Green and Professors Alexander and Miller proposed a denominational plan for sponsoring candidates but a serious dispute arose with a New York group of Presbyterians opposed to Assembly control.[28] While the Assembly authorized a Board of Education in 1819, it enjoyed no substantial support for a full decade. By 1831, the year of the first trial of Albert Barnes, party consciousness was fully established and at that date Assembly's Board of Education was invigorated by the appointment of an Old School man as executive, John Breckinridge, later a professor at Princeton Seminary.[29]

[27] Cf. *Plan of Union*. MGA, 1789–1820, 224 f.
[28] Certain moderates committed to co-operation with New England agencies — Skinner, Romeyn, Wilson — refused to countenance " divisive measures," one of which they considered to be the denominational plan. At this date the Green group could not obtain appreciable support. Cf. the very illuminating letter of Jacob J. Janeway to Ashbel Green, December 28, 1818. HSP, Gratz, Case 8, box 37.
[29] The dispute of the denominationalists with the American Education Society is excellently reviewed in a series of three articles published

The Presbyterian Church had formed a Committee on Missions in 1802 to provide for the West. In 1805 this committee was effectually brought under the control of Ashbel Green's sympathizers by an Assembly rule providing that ten of the seventeen members of the committee must be from Philadelphia and its immediate vicinity. In 1816 it was constituted a board competent to appoint missionaries and disburse funds without reference to the General Assembly save for annual report. Presbyterians were already supporting a variety of independent societies and the Presbyterian Board of Missions encountered great difficulty. In 1826, for example, the American Home Mission Society reported contributions of $11,804; two years later the Presbyterian Board received only $2,996. Like the Board of Education, the Mission Board flourished only after the emergence of a clear-cut Old School constituency.

The extraordinary organization of the Plan of Union congregations prompted the Assembly in 1820 to urge them to conform as soon as possible to Presbyterian forms of government and discipline; but only after 1830 did the Old School radicals attack the Plan itself. Controversy over Hopkinsianism and a mood of denominational chauvinism had already attenuated the ancient ties with New England, and in 1837 the Assembly abrogated the Plan altogether. The Old School was persuaded that the four synods principally composed of churches formed under the provisions of the Plan were infected by the theologies of New Haven and Andover, and they were expelled. Although success had seemed impossible at the close of the Assembly of 1836, the Old School emerged from the contest of 1837–1838 and its ensuing legal struggle with control of a thriving seminary, two boards of missions, and a program for recruiting and financing theological students. Most of the cler-

---

in the BRPR, 1829, I (N.S.), 345 ff., 560 ff., and 602 ff. The first article contains a critique of the New England group; Moses Stuart replies in behalf of the American Education Society; and the rebuttal of the editors follows, composed by Charles Hodge. Cf. Life of Charles Hodge, 260.

gymen who issued from these foundations were not only protagonists of the Scottish philosophy of orthodoxy as against the
New England revision but also strong denominationalists, hostile to co-operation with New England and oriented somewhat
more to the South than the West.

Even in the teeth of the schism, however, moderatism had
always been strong and once the Old School radicals had imposed their will, there was a reaction against it. This immediately projected Princeton Seminary into leadership. In 1835
the professors, notably Charles Hodge, had boldly brought
their prestige to bear against the radicals — Ashbel Green;
George Junkin, the second accuser of Barnes; J. L. Wilson of
Cincinnati, Lyman Beecher's prosecutor; and Robert J. Breckinridge — by a vigorous criticism of the *Act and Testimony*, a
document designed by Breckinridge, its author, to marshal support for reforms or secession. Although the schism could not
be prevented, when the convulsion ended, Princeton moved
into a dominance that could not silence but nevertheless consistently overwhelmed its critics.

XII

THE NEW ECCLESIASTICISM

CONCEIVED for the defense of orthodoxy and the preparation of clergy for the new settlements, the denominational structure adopted by the Presbyterian Church had subtle effects on both church and ministry that came to light only gradually. These were first described by Robert J. Breckinridge, author of the *Act and Testimony* and a radical Old School leader.

Breckinridge was highly intelligent, the scion of a family eminent in the public service, trained in law, an incisive debater, and ambitious to realize in his ecclesiastical career what he had renounced in civil life. Furthermore, he was bred in the West and resented his church's myopic affinity for the seaboard. Between 1842 and 1845 these irritations issued in a controversy of Breckinridge's personal creation known to posterity as "the elder question." Far more than the issue of elders' rights in church government was involved.

In 1842, after some discussion in the lower judicatories, the General Assembly unanimously confirmed the custom of excluding ruling elders from the privilege of laying hands on young men being ordained to the ministry. The next year the Assembly ruled that a quorum of a presbytery should consist of three ordained ministers, omitting the Constitutional phrase "and as many elders as may be present." The suggestion was

176

that clergymen had a clear right to rule without any necessary association with elders.[1] Both these interpretations, Breckinridge believed, marked a drift away from colonial Presbyterianism toward "hierarchical government," by which he meant the domination of the church by its clerics.

Breckinridge presented two briefs to the Synod of Philadelphia in October, 1843, subsequently published as *Presbyterian Government, Not a Hierarchy but a Commonwealth: and Presbyterian Ordination, Not a Charm, but an Act of Government.* Recalling that the "reform" of the church in 1837 — abrogation of the Plan of Union and excision of the four New School synods — was essentially a disciplinary action justified by the absence of properly ordained elders from the New School churches,[2] Breckinridge held that the exclusion of elders was "counterrevolution" and could lead to nothing but "irresponsible clerical domination." Arguing that clergymen derive their ruling rights not from their ordination to the teaching office but from their membership in presbytery, fully shared by ruling elders, he proposed that his synod overture the Assembly to repeal the interpretation that excluded ruling elders from a quorum of the presbytery and to acknowledge that the Constitutional phrase " and as many elders as may be present" was a recognition that a representation of ruling elders was *indispensable* to the proper constitution of a presbytery.[3] On

---

[1] " Ruling Elders." *BRPR,* 1843, XV (N.S.), 432 ff.

[2] The precise point disputed by the Old School had to do with the right of " commissioners " from presbyteries exhibiting the mixed polity of the Plan of Union of 1801 to sit as voting members of the Assembly. The Constitution of the Presbyterian Church asserted that voting commissioners must be " elders," i.e., duly elected by the congregation, ordained, and functioning as rulers of the congregation. The delegates from the mixed polity areas were not ordained, nor were they " ruling elders," since in congregationalism most of the functions of the Presbyterian eldership are reserved to the congregation itself. The Old School argued that unordained " committeemen " had no right to sit and vote in presbyteries, nor to be elected by presbyteries to sit and vote in the General Assembly.

[3] Robert J. Breckinridge, *Presbyterian Government Not a Hierarchy. . . ,* 12.

this apparently minute question, he submitted, hung the vast question of whether the divine sanction is conveyed by the presbytery or by the clergy, the issue between puritanism and "prelacy." To Breckinridge it was incredible that gains so dearly bought in Reformed history could be unthinkingly abandoned.

Charles Hodge replied in a contemptuous review in the *Biblical Repertory* of April, 1844.[4] Stung by the scorn of Princeton, Breckinridge published in 1845 a polemic entitled *The Christian Pastor* and expanded his charge of clericalism into a general indictment of the boards and the seminary, "the great institutions which rule the church and the great men who conspire with them."

The exclusion of elders from the laying on of hands seemed to Breckinridge an ominous symbol. "If ordination is by the court and elders are part of the court, it has always been a mystery to me how they could be excluded from taking part." In the *Biblical Repertory*, Hodge was arguing that the ordained ministers, whether pastors or not, compose the "standing membership" of the presbytery, while elders are elected as delegates to only a single meeting of the presbytery. He remarked that it was impossible in the nature of the case for an elder to welcome a newly ordained clergyman to a "part in this ministry with us." Only ordained clergymen could convey "this ministry" to their successors.

Breckinridge spewed such high churchism out of his mouth. "One common mass of learned trash" he called it, "one vast *caput mortuum* of theological trifling." It is Christ in the person of the whole presbytery who ordains and not the single part of the ministry selected by the prelatical mentality of Princeton Seminary. Breckinridge harshly blamed "the whole business of theological seminaries like ours" for the clericalism of the Old School church and said that if a new beginning could be made, he would never countenance the training of the

4 *BRPR*, XVI, 276.

ministry in institutions calculated to sap the manliness of youth.[5]

The heart of Breckinridge's case lay in one crucial proposition: the church is antecedent to the clergy. The church's existence does not depend on the clergy nor is its being symbolized by its ordained personnel. To Breckinridge this principle was the cardinal defense of Christian people against the pretensions of ambitious clerics. He distinguished ordination to the "pastoral office" from the "ministry." The latter term to him describes a variety of services, some ordained and some not, but it certainly included ruling elders and deacons. Pastors were called and ordained to perform specific functions: to pray and to read the Bible publicly; to preach, teach, and reprove; to administer the sacraments, bless the people, and care for the poor; and with other elders, to rule the church. These functions were all "directed to the perfecting of its members or have direct reference to the work of gathering into the fold those who still wander without God." To such a vocation, only God can call a man. The church of its own power cannot summon youth to the pastoral office nor confirm them in it by ordination. Furthermore, church boards ought not to attempt to recruit ministers by spurious arguments, such as that all converts are called to be pastors unless specifically directed by the Spirit into some other work.

This last point actually launched an attack on a further practice which Breckinridge disapproved. Heedless of consequences, he declared, the church was abusing a sacred privilege by ordaining large numbers of "evangelists": young men without calls to specific pastorates, many of whom were ac-

---

[5] The total difference of view between Breckinridge and the Princeton men appeared in a letter from Charles Hodge to George Potts, March 20, 1860. Recommending Robert Dabney, a Southerner, for a professorship at the seminary, Hodge remarks: " Dr. Dabney I am told at one time sympathized with the ' critic ' published in Baltimore; but all that has passed away and those who know him say that he would not be at variance with our Board of Directors on any important ecclesiastical question." HSP, Gratz, Case 8, box 37.

cepting employment essentially secular in nature. Again and again during the eighteenth century, recalled Breckinridge, American Presbyterians had protested this practice because through it the Scottish Church had foisted incompetent men on the helpless colonial church. Ordination as "evangelist" had been originally intended to meet the need of a church in revival, claimed Breckinridge; evangelists were ordained to a general mission. But the status of evangelist had become a catchall for clergymen in a variety of nonpastoral positions, some of them actually quite lost to the church. An evangelist should fill an extraordinary office in the church while the Constitution defined both eldership and deaconate as "ordinary and perpetual" offices. Should such regular ordinands be excluded from their appointed function of ruling in favor of a "*ministerium vagum*" often lacking substantial connection with the church? [6]

Promotional and administrative jobs in agencies like the Bible society and church boards might be more appropriately filled by unordained personnel, claimed Breckinridge. In particular, he felt that the right of clerical administrators to share in the government of the church involved a conflict of interest. The governmental apparatus of the church, instead of dominating its agencies, was being manipulated by clergymen whose pressing interest was the welfare of the almost independent bodies that employed them. Among these, Breckinridge included the seminaries which, through the professors, were in his view insidiously clericalizing the Presbyterian Church.

These ills Breckinridge proposed to cure by a fresh understanding of the ministry in its original Biblical sense. In the Bible, he wrote, the term "is employed to signify all the offices which Christ has appointed in his church . . . they are all ordained not in a way of honour but for arduous labor, that the work required is in the proper sense a service of the

---

[6] R. J. Breckinridge, *Presbyterian Government Not a Hierarchy. . . ,* 10–14.

church not a dominion over it. . . . It is not only incredible but absurd to suppose that our church should first define that a ministry is divinely appointed and then define that it consists ordinarily and permanently of Pastors, Elders, and Deacons; and yet that it should mean that the word ministry can signify nothing but Preachers of the Gospel." [7]

An incorrect view of calling was at fault. If only God can call, it cannot be true that "God's action in raising up and sending forth preachers may be stimulated or its frequency increased. . . . Surely [this] increases the danger greatly that youths in the first stage of religious experience — of tender years — of circumstances in which a gratuitous education is itself very often a powerful temptation and the station of a minister of the Gospel a seduction nearly irresistible — are, to a great extent, the objects of these experiments. Suppose them to succeed perfectly — and the result is, almost inevitably a class ministry; and what is worse still, an eleemosynary class ministry."

Breckinridge objected to the whole scheme of free education for indigent candidates. This plan had arisen spontaneously in remote localities of New England where revival had produced volunteers for the ministry unable to pay the costs of Yale. Lyman Beecher had converted the practice into a movement that issued in the founding in 1814 of the American Society for Educating Pious Youth for the Gospel Ministry. The free education of indigent but hopefully pious youth effectively solved the chronic shortage of ministers induced by the Revolutionary situation and the demands of the West. It was wholeheartedly adopted by Ashbel Green and the Princeton professors, who made numerous addresses advocating the recruitment and financing of the ministerial corps from its new source, the less-favored economic groups.

Intending no prejudice to worthy individuals, Breckinridge believed that the policy had produced a ministry with the outlook and habits of the lower classes, actually not fitted to serve

[7] R. J. Breckinridge, *The Christian Pastor*, 8 ff.

any other class than that from which it came. It is utterly wrong, he stated, " to cultivate the idea, as is constantly done, that God calls a very great majority of his ministers from [the lower] class. . . . We may supplant a ministry called of God from all classes by a ministry raised up by ourselves from a single class." Such men are only too easily diverted from their duty by " influences stronger than the church courts." Recruitment practice had created the danger " that our church may gradually recede from its ancient position as its ministry is gradually transmuted in all its relations to society." The diversion of the ministerial mind from its proper objects was abetted by so-called evangelists " exclusively engaged in secular employments — yea, even ordained to them under pretence of being evangelists," to the utter subversion of Presbyterianism. In illustration of the power of these nonpastoral clergymen, Breckinridge bitterly recounted the quashing of his protest in the Synod of Philadelphia. He had been downed by Maclean and Dod of Princeton College; hostile editors and board agents; and Professors Hodge, Elliott (Western), and Wilson (Union, Virginia) — not one of them a pastor but nonetheless, taken together, " the influence which has become predominant in our church." [8]

Breckinridge enlarged his criticism to include the church's system of theological education. Any graduate of Princeton is assured of ordination, he charged, because of its professors' influence in the neighboring presbyteries. Furthermore, these presbyteries had assumed jurisdiction of a disproportionate number of students. In 1843, New York, New Brunswick, and Philadelphia presbyteries enrolled forty candidates in addition to a large body of ordained men who were not pastors. This last class actually outnumbered settled pastors. Candidates " have been gathered into these three presbyteries from many

[8] Cf. John Maclean, *Letters on the Elder Question.* Selected from the *Presbyterian* (Robinson, 1844). PSL, Spr. III, 64:4. Breckinridge's charge is supported by the founding statement of Lane that it was established " for young men who were not only pious but indigent." Morris, *op. cit.,* 59.

parts of the country and from the bounds of many presbyteries because of the proximity of these three to Princeton and who will therefore be examined, licensed, and probably ordained by persons who know almost nothing about them." Breckinridge observed acidly that the forty-four nonpastors and twenty-eight licentiates listed by these presbyteries in 1844 established not a single new congregation during the year. The church, in short, must resist this "vagrant ministry" with its whole strength.

In remedy, Breckinridge proposed that the church should altogether cease to ordain *sine titulo*. This would strip board agents, professors, and the whole nonpastoral ministry, of ecclesiastical power. A great variety of services, both ordained and unordained, should be recognized as true ministries, and respect for the ruling eldership restored by granting it full parity with pastors in presbytery, including the right to lay on hands at ordination. Ordination, with its governmental powers, should be confined to pastors and bona fide evangelists.

Breckinridge was not alone in wondering whether the new formal system of theological education was accomplishing all that was hoped for it. Gardiner Spring, pastor of the Brick Presbyterian Church of New York and an Old School man with sympathies for Hopkins' theology, remarked: "It is something to impart theological knowledge and another to form ministers of Christ. . . . Rigid orthodoxy and well-defined symbols of faith will not always bind men whose idol is a learned rather than a spiritual and useful ministry; . . . American pastors and churches must be blind indeed if they have not seen enough to convince them that the gradual incursions of error have crept upon them awares, from the institutions of theological learning." [9] While Spring approved the earliest professors at Princeton, he felt that the pastoral inexperience of their successors, among whom Hodge was foremost, was leading to a type of theological study dangerously detached from the realities of church responsibility. Spring also agreed that the

[9] Gardiner Spring, *The Power of the Pulpit* (New York, 1848), 389.

recruitment of ministers from the least advantaged class was a dubious practice. "The obligation of furnishing the pulpit from any other classes of society seems to be in great measure lost sight of," he wrote. "It were a calamity greatly to be deplored, should we act upon the principle that poverty and low birth are essential qualifications for the Christian ministry." [10]

However, Spring differed from Breckinridge's view that the "ministry" included the entire body of faithful servants of Christ. He sharply distinguished the "minister" from the "people," a term that approximates the contemporary "laity." "The people and the ministry are correlative terms," he said. "What then are the obligations of the people in view of the relation they bear to the Christian ministry?" Actually, the distinction did not rest upon a miracle, either sacramental or individual. "There is no miraculous call at this age of the world. . . . It is just the deliberate conviction of a devout mind, adopted in full view of all the light it can obtain, after having sought counsel of God and man and after no small schooling and self-discipline." The minister, in short, is a layman who has determined upon a churchly vocation and has been set solemnly apart to his office by the presbytery.

James Hoge, another Old School man, felt that there was need of " correcting the erroneous tendency in theological seminaries generally towards a mere scientific [theoretical] education of the ministry." He wrote Nicholas Murray concerning the projected Old School seminary in Cincinnati: "My aim is to establish a system of practical study in connection with scientific theology by which the professors shall not so much *teach* as direct and help candidates to educate themselves. Now if we can succeed in preparing young men through their own efforts chiefly to do the work of the ministry it will be . . . a great, extensive, lasting benefit to them and to the Church." [11]

[10] *Ibid.*, 350.
[11] James Hoge to Nicholas Murray, June 8, 1850. HSP, Gratz, Case 8, box 39.

Breckinridge stimulated thought among Presbyterians, but
so great was the momentum of churchmanship-by-organization
and the prestige of Princeton, its vindicator, that Breckinridge
lost every single test vote in the Assembly by wide margins.
In the heat of controversy, he had heaped a weight of blame
on the seminary that really belonged to the church itself. The
Revolutionary age had diverted into public service, science,
and the professions the wellborn youth whom the aristocrat
from Kentucky coveted for the pastorate. The Second Awakening was reaching the new rural lower classes, and the ministry had become an avenue of social betterment. Denominational recruitment policies frankly sought out ambitious
lower-class youth.

Having shared in the "reform" of the church, Breckinridge
had no claim on freedom from the characteristic institutional-
ism of the Old School church he had helped to shape. The
Old School instinctively grasped the fact that in the nineteenth
century any large enterprise must organize, and it advanced
steadily while the New School Assembly was slow to recognize
that its historic resistance to centralization was out of step with
the times. "Hierarchical government" — the guiding of the
church by highly efficient, semi-independent agencies and
their ordained executives — was a necessity of the new era.

Breckinridge was in no position to cite New England practice, but it is noteworthy that its churchmanship elevated laymen to the highest positions of responsibility. William Phillips,
Esq., is an outstanding example. One of the founders and a
director of Phillips Academy, he favored the realization of that
school's hope for a theological department through participa-
tion in Andover Seminary. He was the president of the Society
for Propagating Christian Knowledge Among the Indians and
Others in North America, a generally "Old Calvinist" group
by 1812; president of the American Board of Commissioners; [12]
and first president of the American Society for Educating Pious
Youth for the Gospel Ministry, a Massachusetts body, later

[12] *Panoplist,* V (N.S.), 377.

the famous American Education Society. All the three vice-presidents who served under Phillips were laymen.[13]   Judge Tapping Reeve was the first president of a counterpart of this group, the Connecticut Society for Charitable Education of Indigent Pious Youth for the Ministry of the Gospel.[14]   Jedediah Morse put the editorship of the *Panoplist* in the hands of Jeremiah Evarts, a young attorney, who left that position in 1821 to become General Secretary of the American Board of Commissioners. The first president of that eminent body was Judge John Treadwell.[15]   Caleb Strong, Governor of Massachusetts, was president of the Hampshire Missionary Society in 1811, whose board contained a number of other legally trained men.

During the period of denominational organization, the Presbyterians, however, were preoccupied with the problem of doctrinal deviation within Calvinism and believed theologically trained personnel were indispensable to soundness in the Assembly's agencies. As Breckinridge complained, the development of executive structures in Presbyterianism furnished a vehicle for the clericalizing of the church, since these new and powerful organizations came into the control of men ordained to the ministry as it was understood by Charles Hodge and his numerous sympathizers.[16]

Southern Presbyterianism was more disposed to agree with Breckinridge and never abandoned its resistance to the power of boards, even when Assembly controlled. Just before the division of 1861 there was a major debate in the Old School led by James Henley Thornwell and after the outbreak of war, the new church of the Confederacy renounced powerful boards. Although retaining a certain respect for decentralism, Presbyterianism in the South is now highly organized and operates much like other American denominations. The waning of the

[13] *Ibid.*, XII, 139 f.
[14] *Ibid.*, XI, 480.
[15] *Ibid.*, IV (N.S.), 178.
[16] Cf. Letter of Breckinridge to John M. Krebs, July 24, 1855. HSP, Gratz, Case 8, box 36.

era when churches were primarily movements united by common tradition and inclusive associations and the onset of the age when churches became organizations under strong executive direction mark a decisive stage in the development of denominationalism in American church history.

XIII

THE MATURING OF CHURCH–CONTROLLED THEOLOGICAL EDUCATION

THE "seminary system" of theological education, together with the ideas of church and ministry that had come to be associated with it, continued to flourish in Presbyterianism, and ironically a decade later Robert J. Breckinridge found himself in its vanguard. In 1853 he was chairman of the Old School Assembly's Committee on Theological Seminaries. Sentiment excited in 1825 for a school in the lower Ohio Valley was stronger than ever, and after considerable debate between St. Louis, Nashville, Danville, New Albany, and Cincinnati — in the last three, beginnings had already been made — the Assembly voted by a clear majority to found a "new" seminary at Danville, it being already agreed that the new foundation should be in slave territory and east of the Mississippi.[1] Danville was founded on the model of Princeton — plan, curriculum, and faculty. Robert J. Breckinridge was designated to work out the required changes in the previous charter granted to Centre. William Breckinridge, who had presented his brother's critique of the Princeton position energetically in the Assembly of 1843,[2] raised the funds for the school. Robert Breckinridge was immediately elected professor, and instruction began in October, 1853, with twenty-three students.

The Civil War worked great hardship on the Danville Sem-

[1] Cf. Letter of N. C. Rice to Nicholas Murray, May 2, 1853. HSP, Gratz, Case 8, box 39. Also, McElroy, *op. cit.*, 38.
[2] *BRPR*, 1843, 433.

inary, and the reunion of Old and New School in 1869 threw it into competition with Lane at Cincinnati. By 1883 all the Danville professors had resigned, one consenting to continue from year to year in order to sustain its token existence. An effort to bring the Southern Presbyterian Church into a united and reorganized seminary plan failed. Danville nevertheless maintained its identity until 1901, when it merged with the Louisville (Southern) Presbyterian Theological Seminary. Before this merger it had graduated over three hundred candidates for the ministry.

At Hanover, Indiana, sixty miles down the Ohio River from Cincinnati, a revival in the classical academy led to the establishment of a theological department under the patronage of the Synod of Indiana, which then embraced the states of Indiana, Illinois, and Missouri. Instruction began in 1830 with the appointment of John Matthews, a North Carolinian who had known Archibald Alexander in Virginia and who, like him, was field educated. By 1835 the " grammar school " had been chartered as Hanover College and had 235 students; the theological branch enrolled ten or twelve. The "Indiana Theological Seminary " owned no property and in 1839 it was separated from Hanover College and moved to New Albany, across the Ohio from Louisville. By the time of its relocation, the department at Hanover had graduated forty-six theological candidates.[3]

The New Albany establishment was the third spot where Presbyterian theological education implanted itself on its march down the Ohio Valley: Western at Pittsburgh, 1825; Lane at Cincinnati, 1829; and New Albany, 1839. At this date no one anticipated the concentration of land-borne population in the " northwest " with its hub at Chicago.

The constitution adopted at New Albany in 1840 was modeled on the Princeton plan, including the professors' subscription oath, the requirement that they submit teaching plans

---

[3] LeRoy J. Halsey, A History of McCormick Theological Seminary of the Presbyterian Church (Chicago, 1893), 17 f.

to the Board, and the curriculum. Working authority was vested in a Board of Trustees, ultimate control in "all the synods of the West in connection with the General Assembly of the Presbyterian Church in the United States that choose to cooperate in its management and support." With the adoption of a new name, "The Presbyterian Theological Seminary of the Northwest," in 1856, its patronage was redefined as the Synods of Cincinnati, Wisconsin, Iowa, Illinois, Northern Indiana, Chicago, and Indiana. The power of these synods was both large and direct, and at the transfer of the seminary to the General Assembly in 1859 these and other significant powers passed into the hands of the Assembly. Assembly's rights included "general supervision and control . . . of all its directors, professors, officers and agents, . . . power to direct as to . . . the disposition of its funds and property; to determine the number of its directors and professors and to appoint the same and to prescribe their term of office; to designate the branches of study to be pursued and the titles and departments of the respective professors and to suspend or remove from office any of the said professors at its discretion . . . and [it] shall have power of its own motion to review and to confirm, reverse or modify any decision of the Board of Directors." [4] Forty-seven years after Green composed the Princeton Plan, the tradition of close control of the seminaries remained unmodified in the Old School Assembly.

The reunion of Old and New Schools in 1869–1870 created a new climate. The Committee on Theological Seminaries of the Assembly of 1870 noted that historic differences of organization and control divided the schools between "Princeton Plan" seminaries — the parent school, Western, Danville, and Chicago — and those which were either wholly independent, such as Union of New York and Lane, or responsible to synods, as with Auburn. Differences notwithstanding, noted the committee, "it is obvious that a matter so important as the education of its ministry should in some way be under the

4 *Ibid.*, 526.

supervision and control of the Church." Yet it had become very difficult to operate a seminary too closely checked by the Assembly. The Princeton Directors, for example, had just laid a memorial before the Assembly "with the request that the Assembly would so far change its 'plan' of control over that Institution as to give the Board of Directors enlarged rights in several specified particulars, subject to the veto of the General Assembly." Right of veto over election of board and faculty members plus reversion of assets to the Assembly Committee was deemed to be a sound plan of control. Union of New York had never been subject to any judicatory but now voluntarily proposed "to invest the General Assembly with the right of veto in the election of Professors." The Assembly asked all Presbyterian seminaries to adopt the same plan.[5]

The following year the seminaries were all moving toward this adjustment. For example, the constitution of the "German Theological Seminary of the North West" (Dubuque) provided that "said election [to board membership] shall only be deemed valid . . . upon approval by the General Assembly. . . . The Board . . . shall establish the Professorships and appoint the Professors and Instructors . . . always subject to the approval and control of the General Assembly."[6] "The Presbyterian Theological Seminary of the Northwest" (McCormick) now dropped Article 2 from its Constitution of 1859, by which the Assembly exercised wide powers of control, and replaced it with articles conforming to the General Assembly's more flexible recommendations of 1870, granting also the Assembly's right to receive financial reports and to veto changes in the Constitution.[7] Princeton eliminated two comparable articles (Sec. 2 and 3, Article I, of the original plan of 1811) in favor of a single sentence affirming Assembly control. The original professors' subscription oath was retained unaltered at Princeton; a revision adopted at Chicago at this

---

[5] *MGA*, 1870, 62; 1871, 579 f.   [7] Halsey, *op. cit.*, 532–537.
[6] *Ibid.*, 1871, 581.

time exhibited slightly less fear of deviation by the church's educators. The phrase "I do solemnly promise and engage not to inculcate, teach or insinuate anything which shall appear to me to contradict or contravene, either directly or impliedly, anything taught in the said Confession of Faith or Catechism, nor to oppose any of the fundamentals of Presbyterian Church Government" was altered to read: "[I] do promise that I will not teach directly or indirectly anything contrary to or inconsistent with the said confession and catechisms of the fundamental principles of Presbyterian Church Government." [8] In 1958 the General Assembly recommended that the professors' oath be made uniform in all seminaries. The new wording almost exactly corresponds with the minister's ordination vows. [9]

The adjustments of 1870–1871 reflected both the need of effective local power in the greatly changed national situation and also something of the decentralist spirit of the New School. Seminaries founded after this date — San Francisco and Omaha — incorporated the simplified definition of Assembly control. [10]

San Francisco Theological Seminary was founded by the Synod of the Pacific in October, 1871, and instruction began immediately with a faculty of pastors unremunerated for their teaching, and four students. The plan of the seminary was modeled on Princeton's, even to the wording. The first building was constructed in 1877 and its first endowment obtained in 1880. Of the first seven professors, five were graduates of Princeton Seminary, one of Auburn, and the other had attended Andover for two years. By 1906 the seminary had graduated 149 students. [11]

[8] *Ibid.*, 528.

[9] *MGA*, 1958, Part I, 494.

[10] *MGA*, 1891, 151: " Resolved, that the General Assembly views with satisfaction the organization of the Theological Seminary at Omaha and orders that its relations to the General Assembly be those of the other theological seminaries as defined by the compact of 1870 and 1871."

[11] James Curry, *History of the San Francisco Theological Seminary of the Presbyterian Church* (Vacaville, Calif., 1907), 5.

Omaha Theological Seminary was proposed by a conference of ministers and elders from Nebraska, Kansas, and Iowa, and authorized by the General Assembly at Detroit in May, 1891. Like San Francisco, its faculty was first composed of volunteer pastors. Three professors were inaugurated in October, 1891, and classes began in the First Presbyterian Church with six students. The seminary listed neither property nor endowment for the first three years of its life but by 1901 these totaled $68,600.[12]

Neither San Francisco nor Omaha received substantial help from the General Assembly at the outset. Omaha was "most heartily commend[ed] to the benevolence of the Church" in 1899 and a committee appointed to raise an endowment of $100,000, but drought and recession brought this to very little. Omaha's ties were with Western Seminary at Pittsburgh and Union of New York. Western professors specially befriended Omaha in the General Assembly and Professors Harsha and Ridgley were alumni. John Gordon, professor of church history during the last decade of the century, was a graduate of Union. When Joseph J. Lampe accepted the Old Testament chair in 1895, Cornelius Van Alen Van Dyck, who had trained him at Union, was quoted by *The New York Tribune* as saying "that the Seminary at Omaha had been founded as a Seminary to be under direct control of the General Assembly, a plan which [we] did not approve. . . . We have not been particularly interested in the recent ecclesiastical agitation [the Briggs dispute]. We do not like heresy trials nor do we regard Assembly control as the only orthodox method of conducting a theological seminary. Our motto is 'live and let live.' "

Charles Herron, professor of church history at Omaha from 1904 until 1934, was a graduate of Western Seminary, and ties with Pittsburgh were confirmed by the liberality of Mrs. Mary

---

[12] Charles A. Hawley, *Fifty Years on the Nebraska Frontier: The History of the Presbyterian Theological Seminary at Omaha, Nebraska* (Presbyterian Theological Seminary at Omaha, 1941).

Copley Thaw of that city who assisted the school at a time when financial problems menaced its survival. Mrs. Thaw felt somewhat differently from Professor Van Dyck. "It has always been most gratifying to me," she wrote in 1901, "that through its charter, this institution is irrevocably safeguarded and under the control of the General Assembly of the Presbyterian Church and so may be regarded in a certain sense as one monument to the effort on the part of the church to protect its theological schools." [13]   In 1943 the General Assembly withdrew recognition of Omaha Seminary, and its academic program ended.

Shortly after the Civil War, acrimonious local schisms divided both Kentucky and Missouri into Northern and Southern synods. The Southern wings joined the Presbyterian Church in the United States (Southern) by 1874, and expanded the territory of that body far to the north and west of its original region. Central University of Richmond, Kentucky, sponsored by the Synod of Kentucky (South), opened a college of theology in 1889 on the pattern of regional sponsorship first proposed by Archibald Alexander. Other seminaries, its founding statement affirmed, "are too remote from us and from the institutions in which our young men are being educated. . . . There is constant danger . . . that our candidates for the ministry seek their theological training in seminaries which are not under our ecclesiastical control." The tide of heterodoxy and rationalism sweeping in upon the church demanded that the very best quality theological education be conducted within the Synod of Kentucky. Its memorial to the Southern General Assembly called for "supervision of the General Assembly . . . under the joint auspices and control of the covenanting synods . . . lying along the valley of the Mississippi and its tributaries." The Synods of Arkansas, Missouri, and Nashville responded, but Louisiana, Mississippi, and Tennessee preferred to support the theological department of Southwestern Presbyterian University at Clarks-

[13] *Ibid.*, 145.

ville, Tennessee, transferred to Memphis as Southwestern University in 1926. Its theological department was discontinued in 1918 and synodal support transferred to Louisville, Columbia, and Austin in Texas.

Louisville Theological Seminary opened in October, 1893, with six professors and thirty-one students and by its fourth year enrolled sixty-seven students, to the chagrin of its overworked treasurer. Two of its first six professors were field educated; three were graduates of Columbia Seminary and the last had taught there after graduating from Knox College, Toronto (Presbyterian).

Danville was moribund by 1883. Its directors proposed to the Southern Synod of Kentucky that it be made a joint responsibility, but the proposal failed in the General Assembly of the Southern Church. The success of Louisville opened the way to renewed overtures of merger and in 1901, Louisville absorbed Danville and became the joint project of both Kentucky synods and the Southern Synod of Missouri as well. The compact adopted by the reunited Northern Assembly in 1870 was applied, except that both Assemblies were to approve elections, appointments, and transfers of professors to other chairs. The Southern General Assembly approved the consolidation reluctantly but deferred to the wishes of its two member synods, who were responsible for the plan. The name borne by the Louisville Seminary until 1928 was the " Presbyterian Theological Seminary of Kentucky."

The Seminary of the Cumberland Church

One of the provocations that led the Cumberland Presbytery to cut its ties with the General Assembly in 1810 had been the need for clergymen on the Kentucky frontier. This distressed presbytery had insisted upon ordaining men who were neither trained to the standard of eastern Presbyterianism nor as unshakably Calvinist as the Princeton founders. The newly ordained ministers of the Cumberland Church, therefore, were scantily educated. In 1826 and 1843 two colleges were founded where theology was made collateral to the general courses, but neither of these included a professor of theology. Discussion of a theological seminary began in the Cumberland Church in 1830 but was consummated only in 1849, when its Assembly asked its two colleges to submit proposals. Cumberland University at Lebanon, Tennessee, acted, and there was immediate unanimity upon the plan proposed by its trustees. It corresponded with that devised at Princeton, New Jersey: clear control in principle by the General Assembly; control of the endowment and confirmation of all professors by the Assembly; and in case of separation of the seminary from the university, the yielding of all funds to the successor corporation.[14] This seminary was actually a department of theology of the Cumberland University. It opened in 1854 with one professor and two assistants. The school was wiped out by the Civil War but was reorganized after the war and gradually re-established.

In 1906 the majority of Cumberland Presbyterians rejoined their parent body, the Presbyterian Church in the United States of America. Litigation initiated by opponents of this union so handicapped the theological department at Lebanon, Tennessee, that both faculty and students were lacking. In 1909 the trustees of the university voted its discontinuance, leaving the Presbyterian Church without a seminary in the South to serve the former Cumberland constituents. The Assembly now authorized a successor school, "The Presbyterian Theological Seminary of the South," and this was chartered in 1910. While there was an adequate enrollment, failure to obtain housing and sufficient funds led to a proposal of union with Lane. This plan was consummated and the small faculty of the aborted seminary was added to the Lane faculty. In 1913 the consolidated school had a student body

[14] J. V. Stephens, *Lebanon Theological Seminary* (Cincinnati, 1934), 16. Cf. *MGA* of the Cumberland Presbyterian Church, 1852, 38; 1906, 76.

of seventy and very adequate support. The General Assembly brought the former Cumberland Church's program of theological education officially to a close by directing the Seminary of the South "to cease all activities in its official capacity and to take the necessary steps to dissolve the corporation and surrender its charter." During its career, this seminary, the theological department of Cumberland University and its successor, graduated 436 students and partly trained, in addition, 175 others.

THEOLOGICAL EDUCATION IN THE UNITED PRESBYTERIAN CHURCH

The United Presbyterian Church of North America, which united with mainstream American Presbyterianism in 1958, was born of the merging of two Scottish traditions of dissent: The " Covenanters " of 1638 and the " Seceders " of 1733. Each of these was exported to America and then partially united in the Associate Reformed Synod. A number of small beginnings in theological education followed.[15] Only foundations that proved to be tributary to a surviving seminary are discussed here.

The first program for the education of ministers that went materially beyond field education was undertaken by the Associate Synod ("Seceders") in Beaver County, Pennsylvania, in 1794. The Service " seminary," named for a lovely tree that shaded it, resembled William Tennent's effort earlier in the century: a two-story log building with a library, recitation room, and dormitory. John Anderson, a Scottish-trained adherent of the " anti-burgher " branch of the Associate Synod, served two frontier congregations and taught the entire curriculum, using Marck's *Compend of Theology* and *Medulla of Theology*, and the *Marrow of Modern Divinity*, by Edward Fisher, the second Bible of the Associate Church in Scotland.

---

[15] John McNaugher, *The History of Theological Education in the United Presbyterian Church and Its Ancestries* (United Presbyterian Board of Publication and Bible School Work, 1931).

The course included a general survey of church history, Biblical exegesis, and apologetic theology. Average enrollment was about six. Anderson worked uninterruptedly until 1819 and died in 1830, having trained about thirty students.

A seminary begun at Philadelphia in 1820 by the same synod was consolidated in 1828 with Service Seminary and the new program located at Canonsburg, Pennsylvania, in 1821. A second professor was added; the number of students increased and a substantial building was erected. By 1855 when the institution moved to Xenia, Ohio, 183 students had been instructed. Throughout its history to this point, theological education in the Associate Synod had been conducted part-time by scholarly pastors; only toward the end of the century was it manned by a proportion of full-time professors. Meanwhile, in 1858 the Associate Synod united with the Associate Reformed Synod to compose the United Presbyterian Church of North America. Xenia underwent two further migrations. It worked for a decade in St. Louis, but local response was disappointing and in 1930 it was consolidated with Pittsburgh Seminary and bore a double name until 1959. From 1930 until 1959, 783 students were graduated.

The origins of the Pittsburgh Seminary are scarcely less complex. Shortly after Dr. John Mitchell Mason's Seminary in New York closed in 1821, the Associate Reformed Synod dissolved into a number of independent regional synods. One of these, the Synod of New York, opened a seminary at Newburgh, New York, in 1829 with three students and a pastor-scholar as professor — virtually a program of field education. The library assembled by Dr. Mason was recovered from Princeton Seminary, to which it had been given at the unsuccessful " union " of 1821 between the Associate Reformed Synod and the Presbyterian Church. Newburgh advanced to the " log college " stage with the erection of a building in 1835. It resisted the vicissitudes of poverty and disorganization until 1878 when its assets were divided between the Xenia and Pittsburgh Seminaries of the new united denomination. During its lifetime, Newburgh trained about 130 students, manned most of this time by one professor.[16]

A second successor body to the original Associate Reformed Synod, the Associate Reformed Synod of the West, founded the Pittsburgh Seminary in 1825 with three students instructed by a pastor-scholar in the latter's church. The "seminary" migrated as its professor changed position until in 1833 its location was fixed at Allegheny, now Pittsburgh. Beginning in 1847, the faculty and student body grew until a seminary in the modern sense appeared, although most of its professors continued to hold pastorates well into the present century. To the date of the Pittsburgh-Xenia jointure (1930), this school educated 1700 ministers.

The Pittsburgh Theological Seminary, the second of that name, was formed in 1959 by the consolidation of the merged Scottish-branch institutions and Western Seminary. Western had produced 3,465 ministers since its founding. All the seminaries of the Scottish-American tradition had been controlled synodally. Even after the merger in 1858, the General Assembly of the United Presbyterian Church exercised only minimal control, approving professors elected by the synods and only very generally reviewing the curriculum. Professors in the Pittsburgh-Xenia Seminary, formed at Pittsburgh in 1930, were nominated by the Board of Directors, elected by the synods, and confirmed by the General Assembly. The present Pittsburgh Theological Seminary, formed at Pittsburgh in 1959 by the consolidation of Pittsburgh-Xenia and Western Seminaries, provides for "control of the Seminary through the Board of Directors"; Assembly's right to veto both the board's election of its own members and "elections, transfers, and removals" of faculty personnel; and for annual review of the seminary's financial records. The board holds "complete control" of all property: "the custody, management and disposal thereof and the investment of the funds of the Seminary." Reversion of property to the Assembly is not explicitly af-

[16] *Ibid.*, 27.

firmed.[17] The Plan of the Pittsburgh Seminary provides that every professor shall answer affirmatively six questions identical with the ordination vow except the last, a promise to perform the duties of the professorship. This oath replaced the subscription formula first drafted in 1812 for Princeton by Ashbel Green.[18]

We have noted the impact of Andover on theological education among New Englanders moving west and the influence of Princeton on church life and education in Pittsburgh, down the Ohio, and in the South. A third stream of influence flowed from the South directly west to Texas. In this new center of national development there arose Austin Theological Seminary of the Presbyterian Church in the United States.

Austin was founded in 1883 by Robert L. Dabney, for thirty years professor of theology at Union of Richmond. Dr. Dabney was a veteran of the slavery controversy and a contributor to *The Southern Presbyterian Review,* his church's most substantial journal. The Synod of Texas was equivocal about Austin Seminary and this, added to mismanagement of its limited resources, brought the school to a full halt in 1918. Dabney's view that Texas needed its own seminary proved to be right, however, and in 1921 the synod made up its mind to give full support and the school reopened with four professors and ten students. The Synod of Arkansas added its strength in 1923, and after that Austin's progress was steady. It achieved accreditation in 1941 and grew rapidly at the influx of students following World War II. In 1959 the General Assembly of the United Presbyterian Church approved a plan by which Austin would come under the " joint and equal control " of the United Presbyterian Church and the Presbyterian Church in the United States. The former church agreed to add three million dollars to the assets of Austin, joint management actually to begin when one million dollars had been paid, the charter to be altered when the full three million dollars had been received and at least three years after the

[17] *MGA*, 1959, I, 117–119.   [18] *MGA*, 1958, I, 494; 1959, I, 121 f.

beginning of joint operation. Both churches are now committed to this plan but at the present writing it has not yet been consummated.[19]

In keeping with the custom of Presbyterians in the South, Austin has thus far been under the "direction and control" of four synods: Texas, Arkansas, Louisiana, and Oklahoma, the Assembly having "the right of general supervision over the interests of the Seminary." The trustees report: "the Assembly can advise and recommend measures for its welfare."[20] The professors' inaugural oath reflects the confessional relationship to the Westminster Standards defined by the Adopting Act of 1729 rather than the legal subscriptionism of the Old School: "I do sincerely receive and adopt the Confession . . . as faithfully exhibiting the doctrine taught in the Holy Scriptures."[21]

SEMINARIES FOR AMERICAN MINORITIES

The close of the Civil War thrust upon Presbyterians a new obligation to the mass of emancipated Negroes, unready to earn their living and deprived by social upheaval of familiar patterns of conduct. The General Assembly of 1864 (North) established a Committee on Freedmen. Two members of the Southern branch of Presbyterianism, S. S. Murkland and S. C. Alexander, accepted commissions from the Northern Church to work among Negroes, but such was the inflamed state of mind at the time that they were forced by their presbytery to choose between service under Northern auspices and membership in the Southern Church.[22] They chose the former and with Willis L. Miller founded a presbytery affiliated

[19] *MGA*, 1959, I, 349 ff.; 1962, I, 392 f. Cf. Malcolm Bolin Durway, *The History of the Austin Presbyterian Theological Seminary* (M.A. thesis, University of Texas, 1955).

[20] *Constitution of Austin Seminary*, Article I, Sections 2 and 3.

[21] *Ibid.*, Article III, Section 2.

[22] The *Presbyterian Banner* reported January 10, 1866, that the Southern Church had ordered its congregations not to admit agents of schism — Northern missionaries, in effect.

with the Northern Church, a step essential to the conduct of their mission: the establishment of churches among Negroes and preparation of a ministry for them.

In 1867 this presbytery authorized Alexander and Miller to begin theological instruction at Charlotte, North Carolina, financed by a gift of Mary D. Biddle, of Philadelphia. Thus began the work of the " Henry J. Biddle Memorial Institute," renamed Johnson C. Smith University in 1923 in recognition of gifts made by Jane Berry Smith, of Pittsburgh, of such size as virtually to refound the school.

Biddle began with forty-three students and worked at a rudimentary level of instruction. From the outset it enjoyed the wholehearted approval of the General Assembly, yet received little financial support from it. In 1876, Biddle was incorporated as a university. Of its forty-five students at that time, thirty were candidates for the ministry and ten were enrolled in the theological department. In 1878 a new three-year course was required for the theological degree. It was manned by two professors and presupposed some preliminary arts education.

In 1891, Biddle elected its first Negro president, Samuel J. Saunders, and the next year three Negro theological professors were appointed to work with the one white faculty member.[23] The persistent and still largely unsolved problem of recruiting Negro youth for the Presbyterian ministry asserted itself during this period. It was felt that separate organization of the theological department as a seminary and the provision of buildings for its exclusive use would invigorate the program and in 1931 the " Johnson C. Smith Theological Seminary" came into existence. The depression notwithstanding, there were twenty-eight students enrolled in 1938, which marked a high tide in the history of the school. The total number of ministerial graduates of this seminary from its founding until 1959 is 412.[24]

[23] MGA, 1892, 292.

[24] Otha C. Harris, The History of Johnson C. Smith University Theological Seminary of Charlotte, N.C. (M.A. thesis, Presbyterian College of Christian Education, Chicago, 1946).

The Theological Seminary of Lincoln University, Pennsylvania, was founded under the control of the New Castle Presbytery of the Presbyterian Church in the U.S.A. John M. Dickey, pastor of the Presbyterian Church at Oxford, Pennsylvania, had long felt the need of a school for Negro youth. In behalf of James Amos, a promising ministerial candidate, he applied to several schools, but racial prejudice or advanced academic standards excluded Amos. Dickey undertook to train Amos himself and meanwhile purchased land, collected funds, and procured the support of Cortland Van Rensselaer, a former missionary to slaves in Virginia and General Secretary of the Board of Education. Dickey's proposal was conveyed to the General Assembly of 1853 in that Board's report, and the Assembly approved the " establishment of a high school for the use and benefit of the free colored population . . . with the understanding that it shall be wholly under the supervision and control of the presbytery or synod within whose bounds it may be located." [25] Opening as the Ashmun Institute in 1854, the school became " The Lincoln University " in 1866 and in 1869 the theological program was expanded to three full years and placed directly under the care of the General Assembly. In 1867 there were six theological students; in 1878, twenty-two; the total number of ministers produced by that date, fifty-five.

During its history, Lincoln has trained men of a great variety of nationalities and religious affiliations. Owing to persistent decrease of theological enrollment the trustees of Lincoln University closed the Theological Seminary in June, 1959. The ministerial graduates of Lincoln Seminary, 1868–1959, total 170.[26]

While Presbyterianism was acting in behalf of the free Negro, the problem of immigrant peoples, particularly Germans, was becoming ever more insistent. Two theological schools were established to provide ministers for rural and

---

[25] *MGA*, 1853, 454; 1871, 581.
[26] Statistical data procured from the university. Cf. George B. Carr, *John Miller Dickey, D.D., His Life and Times* (The Westminster Press, 1929), 161 ff.

urban concentrations of German populations.

The Dubuque Theological Seminary originated in the work of Jean Baptiste Madoulet, a German-born Congregationalist missionary of the American Home Mission Society, who in 1850 accepted one John Bantly for field education. He was succeeded as pastor of the German Evangelical Church at Dubuque in 1852 by Adrian Van Vliet, also an American Home Mission Society appointee. Van Vliet was licensed and ordained by a joint Presbyterian-Congregational Association and enrolled as a Congregational minister upon removing to Iowa. When his church became Presbyterian in 1854, he was enrolled as a member of the Presbytery of Cedar, Iowa. The distinction between these communions on the Iowa frontier was not theological but solely practical, interchange being common.

Van Vliet continued Madoulet's program of field education, using William A. Brakel's Dutch *Radlicher Godsdienst* catechetically. In 1864 the school passed into the hands of the Presbyteries of Dubuque, Iowa, and Dane, Wisconsin, both Old School, and received the name of "The German Theological School of the North West." Although Van Vliet was already suffering from tuberculosis, he continued to instruct until 1869. By 1871, the "seminary" had produced twenty-six graduates, some of them supported by Assembly's Board of Education. New School and Congregational work was much more strongly developed in Iowa in 1864 and the two Old School presbyteries welcomed an opportunity to strengthen themselves among the Germans.

In 1870, under the terms of the compact of that year, the seminary passed into the control of the General Assembly. In 1862 the Germans had organized a voluntary *Konvention*, and in 1912 this was reconstituted the German Synod of the West by the Assembly. This body, like its predecessor, gave special support to the seminary, which had always been the center of German Presbyterianism in the Midwest. After 1891 the Princeton subscription oath was required of professors, who at that date were being paid less than nine hundred dollars per year.

Dubuque Seminary did not achieve institutional form in the modern sense until 1905, when it moved into more adequate buildings, was effectively promoted, and started to grow. At this date the institution began to grant B.A. degrees, but the theological and liberal arts programs were not distinct from one another. In 1911 the theological program was denominated a "seminary" and the arts program a "college"; the name "University of Dubuque" dates from 1918.

Dubuque Seminary offered instruction in German until 1914, and many of its constituents expected graduates to preach in German as late as the 1930's. It remained small, its student body averaging about thirty-five, until in 1943 the General Assembly's Special Committee on Theological Education bade the university hasten its development or close the seminary division. Anticipating this, in 1942 the university had inaugurated a special program for training pastors of rural people. After 1943 the advancement of Dubuque was steady. In 1945 it was accredited by the American Association of Theological Schools;[27] by 1954 its student body had tripled; the curriculum was expanded, the faculty enlarged, salaries increased and new buildings, including a library, constructed. Dubuque is the only Presbyterian seminary which has proved able to advance despite the institutional hardship of association with a liberal arts college.

Bloomfield Seminary was founded April 22, 1868, by the Presbytery of Newark, New Jersey, bearing the name "The German Theological School of Newark." German immigration was concentrating so heavily in the seaboard cities that Presbyterianism had become wholly unable to supply German-speaking pastors. The seminary came into the standard

27 H. Clifford Fox, *German Presbyterianism in the Upper Mississippi Valley* (Ph.D. dissertation, University of Iowa, July, 1941, published by University Lithoprinters, Ypsilanti, Michigan, 1942), 43 ff. Also *The Presbyterian Constitution and Digest,* II (The Office of the General Assembly, Presbyterian Church, U.S.A., 1956), 1985.

relation with the General Assembly in 1870.

Recognizing that Americanization of German peoples was inevitable, the charter of the seminary provided that "whenever from a cessation of German immigration or from any other cause it may be deemed inexpedient longer to maintain said institution as a distinctive German theological school, it shall be lawful for the directors . . . to use the property and funds . . . for any other branch of theological education or transfer its property and funds . . . to any other theological seminary."[28] In 1909 the school sought the right to grant B.A. and B.D. degrees and in 1926 became the "Bloomfield College and Seminary." As the need for German-speaking ministers diminished, other language groups demanded attention. In 1890 an Italian department was established, and thereafter Bloomfield trained men for service with a number of Latin and Slavic minorities.

The Assembly's Special Committee report in 1943 recommended that Bloomfield Seminary be discontinued, but in 1944 the Assembly granted an extension for five years, urging the seminary to become accredited in that time. The energies for adequate development of the theological department not having been found, in 1961 the Bloomfield Board of Trustees took action to discontinue the use of the name "Bloomfield Seminary." The program at Bloomfield is now operated under the college and is no longer affiliated with the Council on Theological Education.[29]

All the permanent seminaries of American Presbyterianism originated in the single century between 1794 and 1893. The order of their founding traces the westward movement of the American people. Western lay at the head of the Ohio River as did Service and Canonsburg. Three lower in that watershed — Lane, New Albany, and Cumberland — united and moved to the crossroads of land-borne emigration, Chicago.

---

[28] Digest, II, 1999; also Frank Kovach, "Bloomfield College and Seminary." JPHS, XXIV, 1946, 113.

[29] MGA, 1961, I, 321.

Parallel movements to the West produced San Francisco on the Pacific and Austin in Texas. The seminary that now serves the Ohio Valley is a later foundation of Southern Presbyterianism, with support from the former Danville (Northern) constituency. Like Omaha, Austin was founded late in a region as yet only thinly populated. But the dynamic growth of Texas and present proposal for joint support by the two Presbyterianisms furnished an impulse that was lacking at Omaha in the depression that preceded its dissolution in 1942.

The impulse to merge its theological schools is of long standing in Presbyterianism. Financial problems first impelled the church to conjoin its too numerous seminaries. Improved transportation, concentration of population, and a heightened demand for high quality stimulated by America's universities have continued to make consolidation both convenient and imperative.

Some seminaries inaugurated by Presbyterians have expired; others have merged; a few have flourished on the basis of their original establishment. Among the present theological schools, all have maintained relationships with the General Assemblies of either the United Presbyterian Church of North America, the Presbyterian Church in the United State of America, or their recently united successor Presbyterianism, save one: Union Seminary of New York. The transfer of Prof. Charles A. Briggs to the chair of Biblical theology in 1891 was disapproved by the General Assembly and in October, 1892, the Board of Trustees of Union Seminary disavowed the compact of 1870, stating that they could not meet their chartered responsibilities if obliged to submit to the Assembly.[30] The subsequent merger of Auburn Seminary with Union established a limited new tie. Nevertheless, Union Seminary of New York remains independent of the General Assembly. In this relationship, it has rendered outstanding service to the Presbyterian Church.

[30] *Digest*, II, 1917.

208 THE PRESBYTERIAN MINISTRY IN AMERICAN CULTURE

SIGNIFICANCE FOR THE MINISTRY OF SEMINARY EDUCATION

The seminaries took the task of preparing clergymen out of the hands of scholar-pastors, but not as quickly as might be imagined. The earliest response of Presbyterianism to the acute shortage of clergy following the Revolution was not the founding of Princeton Seminary but a rise in the productivity of field education. Between 1800 and 1820 the number of Presbyterian ministers leaped from about 325 to a total of 849 ordained men and candidates. Yet only forty-seven men graduated from Princeton before 1820, although 116 others attended for periods of a few months to several years. By far the greater number of young men converted during the Second Awakening who offered themselves for the ministry continued to obtain their education in the homes of pastor-scholars. By 1830 the total number of clergymen listed in the Assembly *Minutes* had doubled again, yet Princeton still worked almost alone, scantily assisted by Andover, Auburn, and Western. As late as 1893, theological professors were still being drawn from the field-educated: two appointees to the Louisville faculty in that year had never graduated from a seminary.[31]

In their earlier years, most theological seminaries differed little from a scholarly pastor's home. Only as faculties were augmented, libraries established, curriculums organized, and student bodies increasingly composed of men with thorough liberal education did the modern seminary emerge as a principal supplier of clergy.

We may therefore discern three stages in the emergence of American theological education: the field school of the pastor-scholar; the collegiate program with liberal arts and professional studies intermixed; the independent, graduate-professional theological school whose applicants present substantial collegiate preparation. Four schools under Presby-

[31] Until late in the century the Western churches, pressed for pastors, continued to question the necessity of full collegiate and seminary courses. Cf. *New York Evangelist*, February 16, 1882.

terian sponsorship clung to the second plan, setting theological education apart from the collegiate course. Two of them have been terminated, Bloomfield and Lincoln; two are integral to small universities, Dubuque and Johnson C. Smith, and are the smallest of the Presbyterian seminaries. The history of Presbyterian theological education in success and failure suggests that seminaries first incubated as theological departments of colleges must eventually be reorganized and made responsible for their own progress in order to achieve major strength.

While the Cumberland schism stultified the growth of the Presbyterian Church on the southwestern frontier, it subtracted no substantial number of Presbyterians from the roster of 1810. That schism was the first of a series of breaks in the Presbyterian tradition that issued in a constellation of Presbyterian denominations. In 1836, there were 2,225 ministers and licentiates in a church facing imminent collapse of its unity. By 1840 the Old School Assembly listed 1,800 ministers and licentiates; the New School, 1,352. In 1862, a report of the Old School Assembly, which did not yet take cognizance of the sectional schism of 1861, listed 3,222 ministers and licentiates. The Presbyterian Church in the Confederate States took out forty-seven presbyteries and 729 ministers and licentiates, and in 1866, when the Southern Church had added the New School South ("The United Synod"), its ministers and licentiates numbered 850. The reunion of Old School and New School restored the total strength of the Northern branch to 4,576 ministers and licentiates.[32]

It is impossible to know how many Presbyterian ministers in 1870 were graduates of both a college and a three-year program of theological education, but it is certain that there were fewer graduates than men who had attended less than three years; and it is possible that in 1870 there were fewer seminary-trained ministers in the three Presbyterian Churches than field-educated.

[32] All figures are based on official General Assembly reports of the respective bodies at the dates indicated.

Despite periods of laxity or deliberate permissiveness, Presbyterianism in America has never lacked the means to control the education of its ministers. Before the founding of the seminaries, this was exercised exclusively through presbytery examination of candidates, which checked the effectiveness and orthodoxy of the pastor-scholars who opened their homes to young men. Presbytery control was highly functional throughout the nineteenth century.

At the founding of Princeton Seminary a second form of check was devised: the Old School imposed close Assembly supervision. While Assembly control of Princeton was considerably modified in 1870, the connection with the church's highest judicatory became almost uniform for all seminaries after that date, although the rein was lighter.[33]

A third form of church relation may be defined: regional control of a seminary by sponsoring synod or synods. Synodal control has always been preferred by Southern Presbyterianism; for example, the " Plan of Government " of the Columbia Seminary states that " this Seminary shall be owned and controlled by the Synods of South Carolina, Georgia, Alabama, Florida, and Mississippi . . . and such others as may be hereafter associated with them." Board members are chosen by the synods; right of review and approval of all board acts is " expressly defined as advisory jurisdiction . . . but no power of veto nor the right to originate measures for its conduct." [34]

Synodal control was also substantially the rule in both New School and Scottish-American Presbyterianism, occasionally modified by counsel or confirmation of decisions by the General Assembly. The simplified rule of Assembly control defined in the recommendations of 1870 was incorporated into the plans of seminaries founded after that date; earlier seminaries adapted or construed their governing documents to suit the

[33] Cf. *MGA*, 1894, 270.
[34] *Charter and Plan of Government of the Board of Directors,* revised May 13, 1947, Ch. I, Secs. 1 and 2.

new formula.[35] While Princeton conformed, it retained sections of its original plan calling for detailed Assembly supervision.[36]

Presbytery examination of candidates enshrines the historic principle, more highly valued by Americans than Scots, that it is the local judicatory that produces and qualifies the ministry. Before the founding of the seminaries it policed the otherwise unregulated programs of field education conducted by individual pastors. As seminaries improved their programs and related themselves to the church through the General Assembly, presbytery examining lost functional importance. Not only in examining ordinands but also in admitting younger men to the care of presbytery, presbyteries have sometimes been uncritical, with the effect that it is often left to the seminaries to determine whether local endorsement of a candidate is supported by a capacity to complete the theological course.

In present practice, the General Assembly is responsible for the control and review of the seminaries, and is steadily increasing its share of their financial support.[37] Except for the Southeast, Presbyterianism has effectively abandoned local control of theological education in favor of central guidance through the General Assembly. In recent years, General Assembly's agencies have called for the reinvigoration of the role of the presbyteries and there has been increasing alertness concerning the selection and counseling of ministerial candidates. In actuality, however, Presbyterianism still depends heavily upon the sound judgment of its seminary leadership for the quality and orthodoxy of its clergy.

[35] MGA, 1871, 578 ff.
[36] Charter and Plan . . . Somerville, N.J., 1927; Article I, Sec. 3.
[37] A full dossier of excerpts describing the evolving relations of seminaries to the General Assembly may be found in the Digest, II, 1766–1785.

XIV

THE MORALISTS AND THE CITIES

THE " American Revolution " ordinarily means the War of
Independence; it might better denominate the recurrent
waves of change that swept over the United States during the
century of the founding of theological seminaries. Both Andover and Princeton were designed in part to block the intrusion of humanism into the church, but such was the potency
of the cultural revolt that Protestants were to find little rest.
The age of Jackson pressed hard on the heels of Jeffersonian
democracy. The libertarian spirit, energized by economic conflict and complex moral impulses, kindled the Civil War. The
restlessness of the European masses overflowed in a series of
uncontrolled emigrations to the New World, and American
society was kept off balance for most of a century after 1830.

The reverberating social revolution fashioned a new kind of
American life increasingly dominated by its cities. City life
in turn created new problems or accentuated old ones in such
a high degree as to force American Christians first to redouble
their support of established solutions and then, as the century
waned, to doubt ever more seriously their usefulness in the
new era.[1]

A second reason for the decisiveness of the change in progress through the period of the mid-century lay in the religion

---

[1] Cf. *Princeton Review*, successor to *The Biblical Repertory and Princeton Review*, I (New Series), 246 ff.

of the immigrants. Before 1830 the nation had been reasonably homogeneous both religiously and politically. But massive Irish-Catholic immigration made it plain that American society could never again return to what it had been. With nonchurchmen, even antichurchmen, the clergy had learned how to deal. It was unimportant that Tom Paine, Ethan Allen, Thomas Jefferson, and Benjamin Franklin could not be converted, since revival shook the hold of their ideas on the American masses. So long as Americans remained accessible to Calvinism, separation of church and state was tolerable or even advantageous, as Lyman Beecher concluded shortly after 1820. But once there existed in the United States an enclave of citizens who could not be evangelized, a subsociety sealed off from both revival and the benevolent societies, separation of church and state became the charter of a pluralistic society. With some difficulty, the Protestantism of pre-Catholic America had been able to digest the dissent forced down its throat by Chauncy, Ware, and Jefferson, but the Roman Catholics were another thing altogether. As the Catholic community grew, America became irreversibly pluralistic, doubly afflicted with "warts and excrescences," as one baffled Protestant termed the Indians, Mormons, and Chinese.[2]

Calvinist clergymen of both schools believed they were responsible for the safety of the national society. At bottom the question was: What kind of country is it? " This is a Christian and Protestant country," answered Charles Hodge in 1859. " The people have not only the right but are bound in conscience to act on the principles of Protestant Christianity not only in their capacity of individuals but as a government. . . . In so acting, no violence is offered to any man's constitutional rights or natural liberty." [3] Again and again the more perspicacious Protestant leaders reproved the churches for their failure to convert or even materially leaven the Catholic communities. Since Catholics settled heavily in the cities and cities increasingly dominated the national life, the problem of Protes-

2 *Ibid.*, XXXI, 759.   3 *Ibid.*, XXXI, 757.

tantism in the new age was concentrated in the city.

The Congregational-Presbyterian clergy entered the urban era of American history equipped with the moral conviction and methods of its recent success in frontier expansion and revival. Preaching, whether revivalist or apologetic, was supreme. The benevolent societies had swept all before them. Presbyterians seldom questioned the fitness of the method of moral reform invented by the British, naturalized in New England, and transferred to a denominational setting by the Old School party. To be sure, there were differences on the question of revivalism. Old School men, ranging from the Hopkinsian Gardiner Spring of Brick Church, New York, to Ashbel Green, warned against undue emotionalism, especially when accompanied by the theological innovations of Charles G. Finney. But the Old School clergy never surrendered its claim on the tradition of Edwards, Tennent, and Whitefield, whose names they repeatedly invoked. It was well they did not, for at mid-century it was plain that once again the only really effective weapon in the church's arsenal for turning back the tide of uncouthness, materialism, and moral disintegration flowing so powerfully once again was revivalism.

From its very beginnings nineteenth-century revivalism slipped steadily toward the pervasive American preoccupation with human freedom. The ablest practitioners of revival were Methodists and Taylorites like N. S. S. Beman, the New School Presbyterian, and Finney himself, who was an outright perfectionist by 1830. Old School Presbyterians were horrified by this and professed great distress at being held in the denominational bond with Pelagianized Presbyterians. After the break of 1837–1838, however, they showed astonishing alacrity in accepting the methods and benefits of the revival. Even the hated Finney techniques — the anxious bench, protracted prayer, and sustained emotional preaching — excited far less animus than the rigid posture of 1837 would suggest. Old School men were soon arguing that revival belonged to them: for example, Lewis Cheeseman of Rochester, New York, claimed that the Old School church was a greater friend of true revival than Beman and Barnes.[4] James W. Alexander, articulate Old School pastor of New York, wrote in 1859 that in the revival of prayer excited by the economic reverses of 1857 "doctrines as held by believers of different persuasions have been set forth and inculcated in preaching and catechizing, but not we believe in the spirit of Shibboleth."[5] Prayer and thought on the gentle personality of Jesus stamped the character of this period of refreshing: it was pietistic and universally supported. Alexander referred with equal approval to the Calvinist and Arminian revivals of the past: "Accidents may vary but the essence is the same."[6]

NEW SCHOOL VOICES

Albert Barnes, the New School pastor and author around whom dispute had swirled so tumultuously, believed revival could solve the problem of the city. As early as 1841, Barnes published a series of sermons inquiring "whether it is to be expected that such scenes will be witnessed in large cities and towns or whether there are in the very nature of a city population insuperable obstacles to the existence of revivals of religion there."[7] He proceeded to prove that "the great and appalling evils which have threatened us as a people have been met and turned back by revivals."[8] Barnes shared the pride of the era in the swift advance of city life and recognized the shift of social power from the countryside. "Since the purposes of Christianity require that the wealth should be consecrated to the Redeemer," he argued, the church must master the city, where wealth is controlled.[9] If cities could become

---

[4] Lewis Cheeseman, *Differences Between Old and New School Presbyterians* (Rochester, 1848), 167.

[5] James W. Alexander, *The Revival and Its Lessons* (New York, 1859), 13.

[6] Cf. Lyman Atwater. *PR,* V (N.S.), 1876, 709.

[7] Albert Barnes, *Sermons on Revivals* (New York, 1841), 24.

[8] *Ibid.,* 82.

[9] *Ibid.,* 96.

centers of revival, strangers who pass through would carry its blessing far and wide; talent concentrated there would apply the Christian message to a myriad of occupations and profoundly influence public life. Barnes painted a glowing picture of a city fully revived: "Every family . . . would be a family of prayer . . . Each day they would go forth to its duties and trials consecrated by the morning offering of praises and prayer . . . Children would be taught . . . the Bible [and] the ways of virtue, religion, temperance, purity, and industry. . . . The Sabbath would return to bless each household. . . . The houses of pollution and infamy would no more open to allure and decoy the young to death and their inmates, made living and pure members of the body of Christ, would be preparing to walk before him in white robes in heaven." [10] Business would be regulated through elimination of dishonesty. Literature would encourage obedience to law and the press cease to be an instrument of mere incitement.

Barnes's optimism was typical of the spirit of the Presbyterian clergy. The *Princeton Review* stated flatly in 1853: "We regard the millennium as nothing more and nothing else than the increased expansion and power of our present Christianity" [11] and treated the premillenarian movement very severely, particularly its literalistic interpretation of the Bible. Irrespective of former party affiliations and consistent with their fundamental philosophical agreement, Hodge, Barnes, and the New Englanders regarded the millennium as the inevitable outcome of history, which everywhere exhibited to them the irresistible advance of Christian civilization.

This did not mean that the optimists were unaware of poverty. Barnes's protrayal of life in the " lower stratum " was as apocalyptic as his vision of the New Jerusalem about to arise in Philadelphia and New York was roseate. The city harbors " that dense and dark mass, the population of alleys, and cellars, and garrets — the ignorant, the degraded, the grossly sensual, the idle, the worthless — the refuse of society, and ' the

[10] *Ibid.*, 122 f.   [11] *PR*, XXV, 69.

offscouring of the world.' " Would " that numerous banditti
of thieves, robbers, swindlers, pilferers, incendiaries, burglars,
and ruffians " come to hear the preachers of revival? And what
of the classes drunk with luxuries — " the bed of down . . .
the robes of adorning . . . the joyousness of the mazy
dance "? [12] They are as far from the sanctuary of God as the
" wretches burrowed in foul recesses." Barnes understood that
the city could not be treated simply as an agglomeration of individuals but that its inhabitants were caught up in something
larger than themselves. For all their propinquity, for example,
city dwellers were strangers to one another. When one
stratum of city society was affected by revival, the awakening
was prevented from spreading to the whole. Sin in cities " is
not dissocial and solitary. It is united and interlocked and in-
terwoven with numerous customs of society." There are " vor-
tices of business and of pleasure that engulf all." The solidarity as well as the complexity of the city was clear to Barnes.

Converted laymen must carry the church's message through
all the tangled avenues of urban life. They would do so simply as Christians living in continuous encounter with the city.[13]
Barnes made no general accusation that the church lacked concern for workers and he did not even mention the Catholic
masses. But he saw that a new era impended. James Alexander's analysis of the city and his call for evangelism among the
poor paralleled Barnes's.[14]

But it was not the New School Presbyterian clergy alone
who rested secure in the moralism that underlay the revival.
Gardiner Spring was one of a handful of prominent Presbyterians influenced by New England who did not join the New
School in the division of 1838; indeed, Ashbel Green argued
that it was radical Hopkinsians, not " Old Hopkinsians " like
Spring, who were objectionable — an exception which he did

[12] Barnes, *op. cit.*, 158.
[13] *Ibid.*, 190.
[14] James W. Alexander, " The Harvest of New York," *op. cit.;* cf.
Presbyterian Banner, June 20, 1877; *New York Evangelist,* May 23,
1878, " The Temptations of City Life."

not choose to apply to a Congregationalist like Prof. Leonard Wood of Andover Seminary, who perfectly fitted the description. Pointing out that " political society ' moved on the axis of religion ' " in the eighteenth century, Spring argued that the pulpit should always remain a powerful voice in public affairs. Preaching was the best avenue to the minds of the middle and lower classes, while the upper classes, a category of wealth and moral elevation, were to learn "truths and obligations, benevolence and . . . morality" from the preacher, who not only summons sinners to repent but assures the stability of the national society. " Let infidelity ever become so rife among us and so rampant as to disrobe our ministry . . . and proof would not be wanting that moral power had been withdrawn from the land. . . . Law would vanish with religion." But in a land where the pulpit remains free, "men must exile themselves . . . if they would avoid its influence." [15]

For all their separation in a divided church, Barnes and Spring bespoke the common mind of the Presbyterian clergy. The venerable Puritan ideal of a society devoted to the laws of God persisted; the gospel was to them primarily a power of general moral renewal. It worked first in the individual, softening him if he were rich and powerful, rebuking and rehabilitating him if he were a pauper, and strengthening the worker for perseverance in honest, if unrewarding, labor.

The Old School Presbyterians, of course, vehemently rejected the theology of Hopkins, Beecher, Taylor, and Barnes and in 1837 refused to co-operate with the great independent societies. Did they, therefore, analyze the problems of the national life differently and propose another solution? When Old School men looked at cities, they saw the specter of Rome. This was the era of the publication of Maria Monk's *Awful Disclosures* of the goings-on in a convent; of *Six Months in a Convent*; and of *Rosamund's Narrative* of Roman scandals.[16] In January, 1835, at the invitation of the Union Literary and

[15] Gardiner Spring, *The Power of the Pulpit* (New York, 1848), 66 ff.
[16] Cf. Ray A. Billington, *The Protestant Crusade: A Study of the Origins of American Nativism* (The Macmillan Company, 1938).

Debating Institute of New York, John Hughes, a rising Catholic controversialist, and John Breckinridge debated the question: Is the Presbyterian Religion, in any or in all its Principles or Doctrines, opposed to Civil or Religious Liberty? [17] Breckinridge was primarily concerned for the integrity of the American system of government. To him, Protestantism was the necessary foundation of the national constitution, civil freedom, and morality itself. All this was threatened by the subjection of the citizenry to moral domination by an ecclesiastical machine and a political theory alien to the American system. The controversy was embellished by charges exhibiting Breckinridge's profound agitation. Beyond that, it set forth a problem that deeply troubled a Protestant mind steeped in the Puritan ideal of a Christian state: Considering the Catholic conception of moral authority and the historic homogeneity of the Roman Church, what is the relevance of the historic position of Rome on church-state relations to American Catholic political action?

The new Catholic community was obviously hostile to the notion of an America that granted tacit if not formal and legal recognition to Protestant Christianity. Would it prove hostile to separation of church and state — now at last accepted in principle by Protestants? Samuel Loomis wrote: "Considering the fact she has been compelled to push her system amid the full blaze of the light of modern times in an atmosphere permeated with that spirit of freedom whose pure breath is her poison, the success of Rome in the United States appears amazing. There are at the present time [1887] about 7,000,000 Roman Catholics in the land. In 1800 there were but 100,000." [18] Adna Weber, as scientific a student of the American city as appeared in the nineteenth century, referred to the

[17] *A Discussion of the Question is the Roman Catholic Religion . . . Inimical to Civil or Religious Liberty?* (Philadelphia, 1836). Cf. *Controversy Between Rev. Messrs. Hughes and Breckinridge . . .* (Philadelphia, 1833). Also Robert Breckinridge, *Papism in the XIX Century in the United States* (Baltimore, 1841).

[18] Samuel Loomis, *Modern Cities and Their Religious Problems* (New York, 1887), 87 ff.

recently arrived immigrants — southern European Catholics — as "the least desirable class of immigrants" and argued that the city problem was compounded by their consistent settlement there.[19]

John Breckinridge and his heirs in the tradition of anti-Catholic controversy were as deeply concerned for the social fabric as any disciple of Beecher. Citing the principle "that no human authority can in any case whatever control or INTERFERE with the rights of conscience," Breckinridge trumpeted that "this is an American, Protestant, Bible principle."[20] Ecclesiastical and theological differences between Congregationalists and Presbyterians did not keep them from agreeing that the moral and political welfare of the nation could be guaranteed only by the Protestant gospel.

THE THEOLOGICAL CAPITULATION
OF THE OLD SCHOOL CLERGY

How could the Old School tradition, which had historically contended that a perversion of evangelical Christianity would inevitably result from the surrender of the Augustinian estimate of the human predicament, so change its ground as to fall in step with the moralism that had swept the field by 1850? Orthodox Presbyterians had emphatically disputed the doctrine of "natural ability" in 1830. Logically this should have produced a vigorous new statement of the implications of the doctrine of grace anything but moralistic in thrust as in New England, and a ministry with an entirely different orientation.

[19] Adna Weber, *The Growth of Cities* (New York, 1899), 308. There were very different judgments on the strategic question of how to cope with Catholicism among Presbyterians fully persuaded that it was an abomination. Alexander McGill of Princeton Seminary, for example, refused to lecture on Catholicism, wondering in 1834 whether "there not be danger of producing reaction of the masses by the appearance of becoming the priests of Americanism . . . in bringing the pulpit to bear too much on the ballot box?" Letter of McGill to Robert Baird, December 11, 1834. HSP, Gratz, Case 8, box 38.

[20] John Breckinridge, *A Discussion of the Question,* 62.

The hinge of this astonishing transmutation was the dispute over the doctrine of imputation.[21] This refers to the sharing of natural man in Adam's sin and the sharing of spiritual man in Christ's righteousness and purports to explain precisely why man is born to condemnation, unless converted, and how man is saved. In the 1830's Old School controversialists claimed that the orthodox doctrine of redemption would eventually be eaten away by Edwards' distinction between natural ability and moral ability. Edwards had argued that the Fall left the former unaffected while wholly destroying man's power so to choose as to actually perform the good. The Old School suspected that the doctrine of natural ability nevertheless suggested that something remained of man's ability to save himself. Long before the partisan dispute arose, certain applications of the doctrine of natural ability were repudiated by the General Assembly, which in 1798 criticized Hezekiah Balch, of Tennessee, an enthusiastic Hopkinsian, for alleging that man's salvation was a consequence of the " fruits and effects " of the divine righteousness imputed to man, rather than a direct and immediate gift of Christ.

Charles Hodge was the artisan of the theory that quietly reversed the basic commitment of Old School Presbyterianism. "When it is said that the sin of Adam is imputed to his posterity," he wrote, " it is not meant that they committed his sin or were the agents of his act, nor is it meant that they are morally criminal for his transgression . . . but simply that in virtue of the union between him and his descendants, his sin is the judicial ground of the condemnation of his race, precisely as the righteousness of Christ is the judicial ground of the justification of his people." [22] Radical Old School men

---

[21] For the background of this problem in early Christian history, see *Augustine: Later Works*, Library of Christian Classics (The Westminster Press, 1955), VIII, 184 ff. For discussion of the point in American Calvinism in the eighteenth century, see " The Doctrine of Imputation and the Presbyterian Schism of 1837–1838." *JPHS*, September, 1960.

[22] Charles Hodge, *ST*, II, 195.

insisted that the sinfulness brought upon man by Adam penetrated to the farthest recesses of the physical nature of man. Hodge limited this to the incurring of a legal liability. Against Samuel J. Baird, a radical Old School apologist, he remarked: "The ground of the imputation of Adam's sin is the federal union between him and his posterity in such sense that it would not have been imputed had he not been constituted their representative. It is imputed to them not because it was antecedently to that imputation and irrespective of the covenant on which the imputation is founded already theirs; but because they were appointed to stand their probation in him. Moreover, the corruption of nature derived from Adam is not, as Dr. Baird, with strange confusion of thought persists in regarding it, a physiological fact, but a fact in the moral government of God."[23] Does sin then cripple man's capacity to choose all good, "natural" good as well as the primary spiritual good, salvation in Jesus Christ? Hodge insisted that sinful man is morally crippled only with regard to "the things of the Spirit." The Fall did not deprive man of liberty of choice as such, nor the power of self-determination, nor the capacity to perform moral acts in conformity with the natural law.

In limiting inability to "things connected with salvation,"[24] Hodge followed the New England theology into vindication of the moral freedom of man. Edwards himself had denied that fallen man possessed competence to choose and do *any* good, his will being dominated by motives that uniformly impelled him toward evil. Notwithstanding his continued denial of any sympathy with the New School theory of natural ability,[25] Hodge actually added to his large conception of the natural knowledge of God a generous area of ineradicable moral ability. His position was friendly to revival and equally

[23] PR, XXXII, 340.

[24] Hodge's argument against the distinction between natural and moral ability, the division of the soul into the "cognitive" and the "optative," is expanded in PR, XXVI, 28 ff. Cf. also *ibid.*, XXIX, 117 f., 121 ff.

[25] PR, XXVIII, 649.

removed from Edwards and the radical Old School.

By vindicating the moral ability of man, both fallen and saved, and defining the Bible as a text for piety and moral education, Hodge created for nineteenth-century Presbyterianism a novel new orthodoxy congenial to the revivalist climate that dominated the American church scene until the Civil War. Robert Baird testified that at mid-century it was essential to all progressive American churches "to preach to sinners as if they believed them to be possessed of all the powers of moral agency, capable of turning to God, and on this account, and no other, inexcusable for not doing so. . . . There has always been substantial agreement in their mode of preaching among those who have been blessed in turning sinners to righteousness." [26] "Even those Christian communions whose theory and practice are adverse to revivals often owe much of their growth to the direct or indirect influence of revivals," wrote Lyman Atwater, successor to Hodge in the editorship of the *Princeton Review*, in 1876.[27]

Despite the torrent of dogmatic literature poured out by critics of New England theology, the great majority of Presbyterians had always been sympathetic to revival and honored its practitioners. Very few laymen fathomed the Old School uneasiness over the distinction between natural and moral ability. Hodge minimized it and used the term "natural and moral inability" as a composite. Discussing the history of revival, Lyman Atwater threw the warm light of the era of church reunion on his interpretation of the problem here under discussion. He pointed out that although the respected Professor Nettleton of East Windsor, Connecticut, was a "strenuous Calvinist after the strictest New England type of those days," he nevertheless preached to sinners that "the reason why God will punish you for not obeying him is not because you cannot but because you will not." Atwater termed Nettleton's revivalist theology no more than "what all the Old Cal-

---

[26] Robert Baird, *PR*, XXII, 204.   [27] *PR*, V (N.S.), 1876, 691.

vinists, but exceptional extremists, admit and insist on." [28]
Even Finney was defended, it being alleged that Princeton
had never opposed him. By 1870, the *Princeton Review* was
arguing the case of Barnes and Beecher.

The substantive fact is that Congregational–New School revivalism and theology mastered Presbyterianism, while Old
School denominationalism dominated its institutional development. In the earlier revival, doctrine was not at stake; there
was little sympathy on either side of the eighteenth-century
schism for the Arminian movement in English Presbyterianism.
But in the nineteenth century, revival was accompanied by a
hotly disputed theological revision and when the urban challenge excited the revival once more, the Old School was confronted not only by its manners but by its supporting theories
as well and fell in step.

[28] *Ibid.*, 699. Cf. Letter of Samuel Blatchford to James Richards, professor at Auburn Seminary, January 29, 1827, recording Nettleton's
opposition to Finney's measures. Nettleton and Beecher at this date
agreed sternly against Finney despite fundamental theological kinships. HSP, Gratz, Case 8, box 36.

XV

INDUSTRIAL SOCIETY
AND THE OLD SCHOOL MIND

AFTER the Civil War, the American city underwent a drastic change of character. First an enlarged agricultural service center, it became an extravagant producer of manufactured goods. As an industrial phenomenon, it was different from its predecessor in organization and called for different forms of ministry. If the Hodgean synthesis laid to rest the theological quarrel over natural ability, its healing effect had no bearing on the rising division among Presbyterians on the relation of church and ministry to culture.

The heart of urban change lay in the economic reorganization of the people. Industry — the steam engine and the endless variety of machines it powered — was the restructuring principle. Rural population was falling proportionately by the time the second census (1800) could be compared with the first; after the western lands were occupied, it began to drop numerically as well. By contrast, industry made possible the absorption of both immigrants and American rural emigrants in the cities. There workers gathered around the factories and discovered that bonds of common economic interest united them without respect to religious identity. A second pluralism, the economic, was added to the religious pluralism of the nation, and the second was scarcely less distressing or dangerous to the Protestant churches than the first. Charles Hodge voiced the deep distress of the Calvinist conscience when he wrote in 1862: " Our system which requires the minister to rely for his support on the people to whom he preaches has had the following inevitable results: In our cities we have no churches to which the poor can freely go and feel themselves at home. . . . The churches are private property. They belong to those who build them . . . they are intended and adapted for the cultivated and thriving classes of the community . . . the mass of the poor in our cities are excluded from our churches. The Presbyterian Church is practically . . . the church for the upper classes." [1]

In 1877, Samuel Loomis spoke not only of wealth and cultivation but understood the issue as one of relative economic power. The *Iron Moulder's Journal* in 1885 asked: " Who is it that takes the [reward of their labor] from them and grudgingly gives back to them just sufficient to keep body and soul together? " Not just owners, replied Loomis; Protestants. Does the faith of the Protestant justify exploitation, tolerate poverty, and close its eyes to the onrushing social conflict? " City churches of the Protestant order are usually attended and sustained by persons of means and intelligence," answered Loomis. " The Protestant city churches are, therefore, to the laborer, the churches of the capitalist. He will have nothing to do with them. . . . This, after all, is the chief of the reasons why working men so rarely enter the door of a Protestant city church. They identify the churches with the capitalists and the capitalists they count their enemies." [2] Loomis feared the Roman Catholic masses as much as the frenetic controversialists earlier in the century but he was nonetheless able to recognize that the economic schism, the alienation of the laboring class by a largely Protestant ownership, was the characteristic mark of the new American city.

The attention of Old School intellectuals was attracted to the rise of scientific naturalism rather than to the national social reorganization. While Americans were inventing mechanical

[1] *PR*, XXXIV, 143.
[2] Samuel Loomis, *Modern Cities and Their Religious Problems*, 87 ff.

marvels, all but unaware of their social potential, Europeans like Charles Darwin, Herbert Spencer, and the German historical critics were directly challenging established values. Calvinists might share the excitement of the conquest of the West and the rising production of consumer goods, but Europe was calling into question their beliefs that God had created the world in six days and made man in a moment from a trifle of dust, and that he had sanctioned private property with his blessing and confirmed the fundamental institutions of post-Puritan society in an infallible Book.

During the era of the schism, the two schools of Presbyterians steadily moved toward harmony around revivalism and semi-Pelagian theology; after 1870, the pressure of industrial society created in Presbyterianism theories of ministry so divergent that they are not yet reconciled within the church.

Neither the separate organizations nor the distinctive doctrinal positions of the Old and New Schools survived the reunion of 1870, but a continuing difference of basic mentality was ineradicable. The difference was not, on its face, theological. The two schools had conflicted on public issues — most conspicuously, slavery; yet the new divergence was not a simple reassertion of the earlier dispute on social questions. It was rather that in two post-Calvinist climates of opinion, different decisions were made about what was significant to religion in the age of science and industry. The continuing Old and New School groups made fundamentally different analyses of the new environment, and these issued in conceptions of ministry that were not specifically opposed in theory — most Presbyterian social preachers adhered nominally to the inherited theology of the evangelical revival — but worked at odds with one another as the church attempted to decide where its energies should be directed.

The heirs of the New School believed that the basic challenge to church ministry lay in the disorder and injustice that afflicted the new economic relations among Americans; the latter-day Old School attempted to discredit the new science, judging its fecklessness with regard to traditional religious values the principal danger. The Old School redoubled its effort to vindicate the authority of the Bible, refute modern value theory, and to control by disciplinary measures any clergymen who might adopt mistaken ideas or argue that the social crisis was the overarching question.

APOLOGETIC MINISTRY FORTIFIED

The Old School response to events after 1870 did not, therefore, define a new conservatism. Rather, it enlarged and fortified its conception of the ministry as defense of the faith; it increasingly returned to the earlier Old School theme of withdrawal into cultivation of a churchly piety; and it grew increasingly suspicious of social concern among clergymen.

Prof. Lefferts Loetscher has recounted and analyzed the debates that broke out in Presbyterianism after 1870: the Briggs dispute; the trial of David Swing; the attack on Henry Preserved Smith; the expulsion of Harry Emerson Fosdick from a Presbyterian pulpit; and the Princeton controversy of the 1920's.[3] Each of these was initiated by a conservative group bent on defending the faith by imposing the new precisions of Biblical veracity devised at Princeton after 1880, most notably by Benjamin B. Warfield. Nevertheless, this movement represented no fresh form of defense by conservatives against the intrusions of science and social theory, but simply an intensification of the previously established apologetic response. The Old School knew that poverty and depressions menaced the American social system, but these did not suggest to them that any general re-examination of the work of ministry should be undertaken or that traditional pastoral occupations were insufficient to the times.

Since the Old School program of defense included discipline,

[3] Lefferts A. Loetscher, *The Broadening Church* (University of Pennsylvania Press, 1954), Chs. 6, 12 to 15.

the General Assembly was frequently occupied with contests that stultified the growth of concern for the social crisis.

The Presbyterian Church had experienced three schisms, all unhealed in 1865: the Cumberland dispute of 1810, the Old School–New School break of 1837–1838, and the secession of the Presbyterians of the Confederacy in 1861. The reunion of Old and New Schools in 1870 was built on tacit agreement that neither party would permit a fresh outbreak of divisive theological discussion.[4] Both New School men, who aimed to protect the union by repressing debate, and Old School men, who wanted to renew it, concentrated their attention upon the state of the church. Meanwhile, the social movement pondered the urban economic crisis and the problem of the church's new duty. It deplored the failure of Protestantism to win Roman Catholics and the de-Christianized urban masses, weighed the social theories arising in Europe, and inquired as to the justice of the demands of labor. Social Christianity simply lost interest in ante bellum church problems. Congregational clergymen were deeply involved in social issues, but Presbyterians were trying to engraft their Southern branch and were bemused by novel theories of Biblical authority, so they did not join Washington Gladden and Josiah Strong in discussion of principles. Although far from callous to the harsh realities of city and countryside, the Presbyterian clergy did not share materially in the creating of a new theory of church and in-

---

[4] In the harmonistic spirit of the Centennial Assembly of 1888, Theodore L. Cuyler stated: " After the disruption in 1838 the ' New ' and ' Old ' school wings of the Presbyterian Church pursued their respective ways — not in a spirit of mutual hostility but of generous rivalry. For with the organic separation controversy ceased. . . . As disruption had been inevitable, so reunion became still more inevitable. Each side had conquered the other. The Old School, who were the special representatives of Orthodoxy and Order, had established the wisdom of Ecclesiastical Boards and of conducting the affairs of the church without incongruous alliances. The New School, who were the special representatives of Liberty and Progress, had vindicated the right of fraternal toleration within the bounds of loyalty to the common standards of faith and Church Government." *New York Evangelist,* June 7, 1888.

dustrial society.[5] Contrary to general assumption, this is not
to be explained by the persistence of a morally crippling predestinarianism — Hodge's natural theology had long since
driven any functioning predestinarianism from the Presbyterian
mind — nor by any lack of New School clergymen in the Presbyterian Church. The largest reason was that Presbyterian
leaders were immersed in problems internal to the church
itself.

Early impulses toward ecclesiastical introversion have been
described in Chapters VII and X. The slavery debate gave
basic form to Presbyterianism's relation to public life as such
for most of a century.[6] Because sectional schism impended in
the 1830's, Northern and Southern churchmen were hopelessly
divided on the moral aspect of slavery. Theologians on both
sides first appealed unctiously to the universal testimony of
moral conscience, but this field of debate was gradually va-
cated by Southern apologists in favor of the unassailable if
limited position that the Bible nowhere forbids slavery. This
line of defense called for a strong assertion of a purely revela-
tional theology. For such bizarre reasons, therefore, Scripture
drove " natural theology " from the field in Southern Presbyterian thought and literal exegesis alone was admitted as the
basis of debate.

Defender of natural moral intuition though he was, Charles
Hodge granted to the Southerners that the Bible said nothing
against slavery and supported their urgent wish to protect the
church from the damage it would surely suffer if it became
embroiled in the slavery issue. The result was the disengagement of " reformed " religion from public life, a doctrine subsequently buttressed by theological articles and broad application to other social problems.

[5] Cf. Henry F. May, *Protestant Churches and Industrial America* (Harper & Brothers, 1949), 192.
[6] C. Bruce Staiger, " Abolition and the Presbyterian Church Schism,
1837–1838." *Mississippi Valley Historical Review*, XXXVI, 391 ff.
Also, the article of the present writer, in *CH*, XXXIX, 44 ff.

THE THEOLOGY OF DISENGAGEMENT

In his three systematic volumes, the "patriarch of American theology" [7] worked out the full theoretical ground of Old School disengagement from culture. It hinged on his interpretation of piety as a way of life for the justified man: a morality of salvation to be distinguished from the natural moral requirement of civil and legal goodness.

Hodge sharply marked off the sphere of life actuated by the Holy Spirit from that other world of decisions determined by the general conscience of mankind. While a Christian lives in that world too, he is related to its laws and customs as natural man, not in his peculiar character as a Christian and spiritual man. The fruits of the Spirit and piety do not therefore bear upon public questions. This does not mean that the Bible never mentions civil issues; slavery, for example, is referred to repeatedly. It does mean that revealed knowledge has to do with the inward life of attitude and feeling, the sphere of religion proper, as distinct from public life, which lies in the field of natural morals. Hodge argued that the prophets, even when condemning public scandals in Israel, said no more than any man without the help of revelation and the Spirit could have observed and condemned. These Biblical passages contain "revealed" or "spiritual" truth in so far as God's people are urged to adopt attitudinal changes, not as they relate to social reform. By grounding civil law and moral custom in natural law and distinguishing them from revelation, Hodge effected a coup of definition that enabled him to justify the exclusion of the mooted social questions of his era from church discussion. To him they belonged to the civil sphere alone, where natural law rules. The church is "spiritual," which is to say that it has no business pronouncing on matters social and civil. The prophets notwithstanding, these are not really broached in the Bible.

[7] *New York Evangelist*, June 27, 1878, in an article paying tribute to him at the time of his death.

While this position had its earliest use as a justification for excluding discussion of slavery from a sectionally divided Old School Presbyterianism, it enunciated a principle that broadly divorced the " spiritual " life of Christians from social and civil responsibility. To Hodge, social action as such could have nothing to do with the church in its distinctive character as an institution of revelation and the Spirit. While Christians were churchmen, they were also citizens, and it was in the latter role, exclusive of the former, that they related themselves to public problems. Hodge's treatment of property, a problem central to both the slavery debate and the industrial era, was a highly significant application of the principle.

Hodge hung his discussion of property on the Eighth Commandment. The Decalogue as a whole he held to be an enunciation of natural law, not an exposition of the duties of the justified alone. The Decalogue deals with fundamental social institutions, which are grounded in natural law. Among these are the civil state, monogamous marriage, and property. The Eighth Commandment " forbids all violations of the rights of property. The right of property in an object is the right to its exclusive possession and use. The foundation of the right of property is the will of God." Property rests on " an implanted . . . sense of justice in the nature of man which condemns as morally wrong everything inconsistent with it." Property is held by divine right. " Only by making property sacred, guarded by the fiery sword of divine justice, . . . can it be safe from the dangers to which it is everywhere and always exposed." Property is the material upon which moral imperatives act. Since the law of nature is its true foundation, the primary fault of communism and cognate social systems is that they are unnatural.[8]

---

[8] ST, III, 421, 426, 430. In 1852 the PR published an article, " The True Progress of Society," that discussed point-blank the problem of progress and defined conservatism as the attitude that " proceed[s] upon the presumption that the whole body of such [previously established] principles are true, so far, at least, that they are to be regarded and treated as true until their falsity is shown and so far also,

Hodge clearly saw that misery among the masses had to be dealt with. " It was minds burdened with the consciousness of misery and the sense of injustice which were inflamed by the new doctrines and which burst forth in a fire that for a time set all Europe in a blaze. . . . Had it not been for the preceding centuries of cruelty and oppression, France had not furnished such a bloody page to the history of modern Europe." The cure lies in " bringing the people to know and believe that there is a God on whom they are dependent and to whom they are responsible; in teaching them that this is not the only life, that the soul is immortal, . . . that it is not the rich and noble but the poor and lowly that are his special favourites; and that the right of property, the right of marriage, the rights of parents and magistrates are all ordained by God and cannot be violated without incurring his displeasure. But religious training is only half the task. The great body of the people must be rendered comfortable, or least have the means of becoming so; and they must be treated with justice. Misery and a sense of wrong are the two great disturbing elements in the minds of the people. They are the slumbering fires which are ever ready to break out into destructive conflagration." [9] The solution, in short, was revival and moral reform.

The weight of Hodge's sense of church responsibility to the poor fell on the preaching of the gospel. A scruple for relief of hunger did appear — these were the duties of the diaconate [10] — but the heart of the matter lay in preaching. Food and healing prepare the pauper to hear the gospel and must therefore be understood as instruments of the spiritual. Jesus' association with outcasts was intended, Hodge argued, to re-

---

as to throw the burden of proof upon all who call them into question."
Yet progress is essential to the health of proved truth. In the right adjustment between change and conservatism of established values lies the true course. Among other practical implications of this position is the principle that " the Bible contemplates the perpetual existence of these two classes [holders of property and the poor] and prescribes their respective duties," XXIV, 19, 35.

[9] ST, III, 433 f.   This position is expanded in PR, XXIV, 35.
[10] ST, III, 626 ff.

buke the Jewish authorities who had forgotten the poor. It is axiomatic that "where the church fails to reach the poor with her gospel, she ceases to demonstrate her Divine mission." [11] The possibility that an alteration of the social structure might virtually wipe out poverty not only was abhorrent to the conservative economic instincts of Princeton-taught Presbyterians but could not stand in any relation to the ministry of the Christian as a spiritual man or of the church as a spiritual body.

[11] *Ibid.*, 619.   Cf. *PR*, XLIII, 1871, 83 ff.

XVI

BREAKTHROUGH
TO SOCIAL MINISTRY

ALTHOUGH preoccupation with ecclesiastical politics kept the New School clergy from participating in the fashioning of a theory of the social gospel, Presbyterianism produced a remarkable lay mind fully twenty years before the first generation of social seers emerged among the Congregationalist clergy. What Albert Barnes perceived in dim outline was prophetically clear to Stephen Colwell, of Philadelphia. Colwell's significance lies in the fact that beyond his anticipation of the opinions of the social gospel, he was thinking in the basically different way that made possible the development of a Christian social ethic.

Colwell was outraged at the failure of the church and the clergy to take seriously the plight of the poor.[1] He had thoroughly studied the literature available on the problem, largely English and French, and reacted against the preoccupation of the churches with doctrine and priestcraft, against clerical thought control and love of power, against the divisiveness of denominations and sects, against the lecturing and finger-pointing of the reform societies. He explicitly announced a new controlling principle for the church: the Fatherhood of God and the brotherhood of men. Colwell demanded that the church repudiate theology and give itself to ethics. "The Christians may be right and the reformers [such as

[1] Horrifying descriptions of the slums of New York appeared in the public press during this period. Cf. PR, III (N.S.), 217.

Paine] wrong . . . but what is chiefly to be lamented is that Christians suffer these controversies to assume a shape and aspect which have the appearance of infidelity being on the side of human well-being while Christianity stands upon defense of ancient abuses, oppressive legislation, and social enormities." [2] In the church it was the missionaries and ministers living among the poor — the doers, not the thinkers and managers — that he admired and he derided the ornate sanctuary and the exclusive congregation financed by pew rentals. The question of the direct dependence of the founders of the social gospel after 1870 upon Colwell does not fall within the bounds of this study, but the close correspondence of view invites investigation. [3]

Fifteen years earlier Calvin Colton, a Presbyterian clergyman en route to Episcopal orders, had blazed a narrow path of Presbyterian dissent by condemning the all-powerful reform societies as intruders into the business that Christ had delegated to his church. [4] Although his churchmanship paralleled Old School sentiment, Colton was striking at the entire Protestant system of ecclesiastical power. He was rather a church reformer than a social analyst, but he was as keenly aware as Colwell that the public image of the church was not an attractive one. [5]

Colwell perceived that society was unitive, not simply an assemblage of individual parts, but he never grasped the revolutionary effect of this insight on ethics. Thus his specific proposals for action were innocent of realism. He advocated reform through bringing " brotherly kindness " to bear on economic life. Government might be instrumental, to be sure, but revolutionary force was inconsistent with Christian

---

[2] Stephen Colwell, *New Themes for the Protestant Clergy* (Philadelphia, 1851), 267 f.

[3] Cf. Henry F. May, *Protestant Churches and Industrial America*, 15–20; Charles Howard Hopkins, *The Rise of the Social Gospel in American Protestantism, 1865–1915* (Yale University Press, 1940), 6.

[4] Calvin Colton, *Protestant Jesuitism* (New York, 1836).

[5] Colwell, *op. cit.*, 265.

ethics. Colwell was erudite and uninhibited, but he had everything to learn about the hardships of social revolution. His proposal for cutting down the sword of slavery, then hanging over
the head of the nation, was typical. The Scriptures speak
not a word against slavery, he pointed out, but obedience to
Biblical precept, nevertheless, would lead inevitably to its
abolition. "The Christian process will be to incite masters
to love and cherish their slaves. . . . A patriarchal relation
will arise between the master and his slave; the fetters will
drop off . . . and finally, when the master is brought to the
point of emancipation, the servants are brought to that preparation for liberty which enables them to accept the boon
with advantage." [6]   Christian goodness could be trusted to
loosen the grasp of authority and lift the burdens of all the
oppressed. Colwell's ethical idealism prefigured the simplicity
of heart that distinguished the early development of the social
ministry of the church.

Old School Reaction After Hodge

Against the layman Colwell, whose "New Themes for the
Protestant Clergy" were not often preached on, was the
Presbyterian phalanx, anchored in Princeton and extending its
wings to pulpit, classroom, and newspaper. A fair view of the
response of Presbyterians to the accumulating social crisis is
found in the quarterlies and religious papers they read.

Soon after assuming principal editorial responsibility for
the *Princeton Review*, Lyman Atwater wrote that the quarterlies should help the more serious readership to reach "right
conclusions on momentous or controverted subjects; to aid the
thinkers of society in gaining the truth for themselves and for
the guidance of their fellowmen." [7]   He gave much more space
to discussion of contemporary problems such as monetary
policy, foreign affairs, and the economic crises.

In 1872, Atwater himself published a virtual charter of

[6] *Ibid.*, 257.   [7] *PR*, XLIII, 1871, 3.

Christian opinion on the vexing problem of labor relations. His theological and ethical presuppositions corresponded with those of Hodge but he spelled out the "Christian" attitude in detail. Atwater argued that the deepest truth of labor and capital was their interdependence. If unrecognized, the destruction of both must follow, but if grasped and acted on through profit-sharing and sale of stock to workers accompanied by attitudes of forbearance and charity, interdependence could lead to affluence for both worker and owner.

The methods then being proposed by social radicals were wholly destructive, believed Atwater, because of their hostility to the "law of liberty" in economic life. "All restrictions upon the use of capital or labor by monopolies, strikes, trade-unions, or other artificial obstructions, impair the united product of both. . . . Let capital be at liberty to enter that field of honest employment in which its owners see their way to the largest profits without legislative, trade-unions or other artificial obstacles. . . . Then let labor be perfectly free to follow its chosen occupation, . . . to fix its own terms, prices, hours, and other conditions without let or hindrance from legal obstructions or illegal violence from individuals or combinations."[8] Laws restricting the working day to eight hours as well as strikes, picket lines, and trade-unionism were all improper impediments. Strikers should simply be fired.[9]

"Demagogic agitators" like Wendell Phillips were irreligious in their attitude toward property, stated Atwater. Besides discouraging investment, such sentiment struck at the very root of Christian civilization. Distribution of capital among workers must end in the destruction of all property, the dissolution of the family, free love, and "unbridled licentiousness and the abomination of desolation."[10] The critical flaw of socialism was that it attempted to furnish idlers with goods by the "unfair seizure and consumption of the earnings and savings of others."[11] Is it consistent with the Christian principle that

[8] *Ibid.*, XLIV, 1872, 477.   [10] Cf. *ibid.*, IV (N.S.), 518.
[9] *Ibid.*, III (N.S.), 105, 123.   [11] *Ibid.*, 521.

"the laborer is worthy of his hire" to seek ten hours' pay for eight hours' work? he asked. The truth is that "the law of free competition will inevitably bring all industries, quantity and quality considered, upon a virtual level of uniform compensation, that are not kept at an unequal height by special gratuities."

Trade-unions are "conspiracies against the laws of God, the rights of man, and the welfare of society." Their success would destroy the market, debase the quality of work, multiply "vagabonds, desperadoes, thieves, and robbers. . . . We do not hesitate to say that society should put forth its extremest power to repress those dangerous movements that thrive only by forcibly preventing men from using or developing their gifts or faculties."[12] Atwater nevertheless regarded tariff protection, limitation of child-labor, interstate commerce law, and banking laws as practical and moral necessities. Although he condemned speculation, his reading of the panic of 1873 bore principally on labor, which should have learned the futility of strikes from it.[13]

The church's peculiar duty in the industrial crisis was to "christianize the laboring masses" and to teach employers so to "let their Christian love radiate in kindly and blessed ministries to their employees and their families . . . as to disarm hostility, extinguish jealousy and provoke not to envying and malice."[14] The traditional Calvinist virtues of "industry, temperance, frugality, fidelity and reasonable self-denial" constituted the "sovereign remedy." Only if the struggling parties acknowledged the supremacy of Jesus Christ could these remedies work, and here above all lay the duty of the church in the social crisis.

The violence and destructiveness of the railroad strikes of 1877 staggered the churches. "It partially uncapped the crater of a social volcano over which we have been sleeping, nearly

[12] *PR*, XLIV, 486.
[13] *Ibid.*, III (N.S.), 123. Cf. " The Currency Question," VI (N.S.), 732.
[14] *Ibid.*, XLIV, 492.

all of us without suspicion or alarm," wrote Atwater.[15] For two generations their confidence in the effectiveness of moral teaching had never swerved. Clergymen of all schools of thought had steadily saluted the approach of the millennium, a period when Christ's authority would be vindicated by the victory of his gospel over the sinful condition of society through the agency of the church. But now the new wealth that had seemed to promise so much was being destroyed by the very men who had created it. It was not just a case of vandalism; the strike was wrong in principle. Justified though the workingman's resentment of the wage cut that triggered the strike, " by their own illegal act they opened the gate for the basest element of society and practically invited the work of destruction."[16] Picketing was wrong. "If any class of men can be permitted to possess themselves of the property of others by violence and breach of trust and hold that property in defiance of all legal authority until their demands are complied with, there is an end of all civil government." The editors of the *Presbyterian Banner* of Pittsburgh roundly blamed management and government for ineptness and negligence; but their moral censure was reserved for labor.

The depression of 1877 came under examination in the religious press. "Indirectly sin lies at the base of our troubles," wrote the *New York Evangelist*.[17] "There has been widespread violation of the laws of God. The Sabbath has been broken by our great corporations, our legislatures, our Houses of Congress, and our chief officers. The Press with few excep-

---

[15] *Ibid.*, VI (N.S.), 719.

[16] *Presbyterian Banner*, August 1, 1877. The *PR* called resentment " no mere selfish principle " but a " social sentiment " requiring due regulation. XLIII, 738. It will be observed that the inauguration of Atwater's editorship was marked by the introduction of articles on a wider spectrum of interests and less rigid methods of discussion than under Hodge's regime. For example, in discussing the purpose of punishment, vindication of divine justice is qualified by saying " the divine purpose or natural law of punishment . . . is that punishment shall be reformatory." *PR*, XLIII, 77. Cf. " Professional Ethics and Their Application to the Legal Profession," *PR*, XLIII, 286 ff.

[17] *New York Evangelist*, August 1, 1878.

tions has fed the passions of men." The *Banner* dipped somewhat helplessly into economics. "Consumers have increased
out of all due proportion over producers," it declared in a
period of agricultural surpluses. "The country needs young
men; the city does not. . . . All the poetry of rural life remains while the irksomeness is in a great measure removed." [18]

Long before the crisis of 1877, the *Princeton Review* had
said in a hundred ways that "we can conceive of nothing that
would be more fatal to all industry and thrift, that would more
completely blight and paralyze society (the extinction of religion alone excepted) than insecurity in the tenure of property." [19] It was the threat to property that was most ominous.
"Capital is absolutely necessary to great undertakings but
capital will stand aloof when its proceeds may be swept away
in a moment at the bidding of a mob," declared the *Banner*.
"Financial credit should be considered sacred." [20] This journal estimated that there were not more than a half million unemployed who wanted to work and called for the most rigorous
repression of tramps, bums, and dead-beats — terms chosen
by the editors. Agrarian reformers, "tramps with ideas," were
threatening farmers with destruction of crops and machinery.[21]
Communists had wrecked Pittsburgh on one unhappy Sabbath
morn in 1877. Idlers were a seedbed of socialism and communism. "Everyone capable of labor must be made to know
and feel that he must earn his daily bread and that not to do
so is an offense, probably we ought to say a crime," declared
the *Banner* shortly after the railroad riots. "Religion, sound
political economy and the public safety alike require stringent
measures against able-bodied pauperism." [22] While neither
Charles Hodge, Lyman Atwater, nor the papers lacked the

[18] *Presbyterian Banner,* August 8, 1877.
[19] *PR,* XXIV, 35.
[20] *Presbyterian Banner,* December 5, 1877. Cf. *PR,* XXXIV, 310, " The
Nature and Effect of Money and of Credit as its Substitute."
[21] *PR,* V (N.S.), 430 f.
[22] *Presbyterian Banner,* December 12, 1877. " Able-bodied pauperism "
was a phrase used by Atwater two years earlier arguing against a dole
for the unemployed. *PR,* IV (N.S.), 520.

courage to criticize the public leadership, the analysis did not
go beyond the familiar demand for a revival of personal integrity. "All possible means must be taken to awaken and
maintain a spirit of independence, a determination to help
oneself." [23]

Social utopianism was at this time creating its own experimental communities. The scandalous morals of the Oneida
community appealed to traditional Calvinists no more than in-
cendiary communism.[24] Labor organizations, while supported
by many honest workers, were furnishing ready-made audiences to communists and anarchists. Its Philadelphia correspondent reported to the *Evangelist* that "there is no doubt
that there is plenty of this element lying around loose in this
city, but whether there is an 'organized' movement secretly
preparing for violence and revolution (as is confidently asserted) is not so sure. . . . The alarm . . . is kept excited by
the boldness with which capital is assailed by threats in the
meetings of certain workingmen's Associations." The situation
of the majority of workers was described as adequate, if not
generous. "These men must know that . . . a rapacious seizure upon property for pretended equal division means the
robbery of their own little all. Still there are here, perhaps by
the thousands, men who really feel the pinch of hunger. . . .
Talk violence and force long enough to men whose reason is
almost dethroned by the agony of intense want and who can
tell to what desperate measures they may not be incited?" [25]
Americans would have nothing to fear from "crude theories
and visionary projects" were it not for "a vast deal of real poverty and distress among wage-earning people and distrust of
existing political organizations." The danger was heightened
by the irresponsibility of social leaders like the jurist who advocated "prevention of crime by the least possible amount of
force or suffering." Cried the *Evangelist:* "Is there no sacred

[23] This position was endlessly fortified by books and articles. Cf. *PR*,
228; XXV, 1853, " Mercentile Morals "; " The Bible in the Counting
House," 390.

[24] *New York Evangelist*, August 15, 1878. Cf. *PR*, V (N.S.), 435 f.

[25] *New York Evangelist*, May 30, 1878.

majesty of law to be vindicated? Is sin not to be punished because it is sin . . . ? The moral restraints upon crime have almost all passed away." [26]

Fear of socialism produced some softening toward Roman Catholicism. "The late President Hitchcock said to us when we discussed the dangers to society from Socialists and Communists that we might yet come to look upon the Roman Catholic Church as the most conservative power in this country if, by its influence over the Irish, it should keep them from running into the excesses by which so many of the French and Germans were carried away," remarked the *Evangelist*.[27]

Although the religious journals of this numbing period of American history could not yet grasp its full dimensions, the social upheaval had shaken them. The confidence of the moralists was scandalized by premillennialism, which was vastly less optimistic. "They sneer contemptuously at the Church's professed hope of converting the world by the agency of Bible and missionary societies," noted the *Princeton Review*.[28] It was increasingly admitted as the '70's and '80's advanced that the churches alone — their wealthy congregations, revivals, and moral societies — could not cope with the crisis.[29] Conservative editors began to call for united action by managers of the nation's wealth; for stronger assertions of will by conservative laboring men; even for social legislation such as regulation of child labor, application of bankruptcy laws to debt-ridden workers; and tariffs, although there was continued opposition to regulation of freight rates and other internal economic measures.[30] Presbyterians felt that the situation increasingly

---

[26] *Ibid.*, June 6, 1878. Cf. *ibid.*, 239 ff. Cf. *PR*, XXIX, 345–375, "Moral Insecurity." An important spokesman who strengthened the conservative mood of Presbyterians was Robert E. Thompson, author of *A History of the Presbyterian Church in the United States*. American Church History Series, Vol. VI (New York, 1895).

[27] *New York Evangelist*, February 23, 1888.

[28] *PR*, XXV, 71. Cf. XXVIII, 524 ff. Also March, 1879, "Pre-millennialism," 415 ff.

[29] *PR*, III (N.S.), 224 f., 230.

[30] *Ibid.*, VI (N.S.), 734. "The Great Railroad Strike." Also, *ibid.*, July, 1882, 1–15.

called for an alliance of all right-minded social forces in defense of property and righteousness.

The corporate mentality of the social gospel appeared in the conservative journals only in the '80's. Charles H. Parkhurst, a New York pastor, wrote: "Christianity . . . regularly puts society before the individual and never the individual before society. . . . It is certainly clear that the proprietary rights of the individual are to be arbitrated from the standpoint of the State and not the rights of the State from the standpoint of the individual. . . . The individual is to be thankful for whatever concessions the State in wise pursuance of its own weal may see fit to allow him. . . . There is no disguising the fact that there is in this an approach to the fundamental doctrine of communism. . . . All that is argued for here is contained in the expression . . . that we *belong* to society. And that is exactly it: we do *belong* to society." [31] This expression stood absolutely alone in the Princeton organ from 1850 to its terminus in 1888.

By 1880, Presbyterian conservatism admitted that new social problems existed but it did not grant that any real corner had been turned. In 1886, Henry W. Farnam wrote: "We must not consider ourselves on the brink of a new era nor talk as if the present difficulties [the recession of that year] indicated a decided change in the relations of labor and capital." But a sense of the inherent difficulty of the ministry in industrial society was beginning to replace the moralism that had prevailed so long. Farnam felt that clergymen ought to be cautious in suggesting that Christian principle will solve economic problems. "The fact is that Christian churches are guided in their business transactions by the same law of supply and demand that guides the most soulless corporations. . . . What we need is not sympathy but knowledge. . . . The world must be improved, but it cannot be improved very rapidly, nor is there

---

[31] *New Princeton Review*, I (January, 1886), 33–45. "The Christian Conception of Property." Cf. C. H. Parkhurst, *My Forty Years in New York* (New York, 1923).

any short cut to the economic millennium." [32] These were the years in which Josiah Strong, a Congregationalist, was writing *Our Country and the New Era* and *The Twentieth Century City;* when Samuel Loomis was writing *Modern Cities and Their Religious Problems;* when Washington Gladden was reflecting: " One could not help wondering whether in liberating the force which gathers men into cities and equipping it with steam and electricity, a power had not been created which was stronger than the intelligence which seeks to control it; whether such aggregations of humanity, with wills no better socialized than those of the average nineteenth-century American, are not by their own action self-destructive." [33] While the Presbyterian Church was agitated throughout this period by the troubled industrial and economic situation, such reputable scholars as Robert E. Thompson continued to deprecate the social critics and to commend their church for its power "to counteract the sudden breaks with history which each new tendency has threatened to accomplish." [34]

THE COMING OF A SOCIAL GOSPEL

Presbyterian doctrinal history in the nineteenth century had all but negatived any breakthrough to social Christianity from the side of theology, and the theorists who anticipated it were economists and sociologists, not theologians. But Presbyterianism was not insensitive to the rising level of social suffering and from an early period acted to meet manifest need. Social reform had been a pervasive concern of Calvinism from early in the century, but on the basis of an individualistic moral theory. [35] The " social gospel " represented a particular view of the character of man as a member of society; it argued that

[32] *New Princeton Review,* July, 1886, 60 ff.
[33] Quoted from *Recollections* (Boston, 1909), by H. F. May, *op. cit.,* 124.
[34] Thompson, *op. cit.,* 303.
[35] This is the subject of Timothy L. Smith, *Revivalism and Social Reform* (Abingdon Press, 1957).

society was different in kind from the individual and considered it an object of ministry; and it proposed radical new courses of action in discharge of ethical duties. The Presbyterian Church did not cease to act on conventional moral theory at a specific moment and commence to act on new assumptions; the flow of action was never broken by a revolution. Yet changes in the manner of its acting preceded its acceptance of new theory and implicitly conceded that changed social conditions demanded new ways of thinking. The official emergence of the "social gospel" in Presbyterianism was delayed until 1910 when the General Assembly issued its historic declarations on social problems and reorganized its early experimental approaches to them. But the way was paved much earlier by a change in the Presbyterian Church's sense of responsibility to the culture. First came scattered social pronouncements, then the reorganization of the Board of Home Missions, and finally a social theory of ministry.

In 1891 the General Assembly noted: "The city presents a most serious problem to our Christian thought because of the abandonment of our churches in downtown districts, thickly populated not only with foreigners but with native Americans, the great working class as we call it. . . . This field demands organized work, calling for the outlay of much money and the employment of many consecrated workers. It seems to your Committee a great evil that any church site should be abandoned while thousands of souls are clustered about it." [36]   In 1894 the Board of Home Missions reported to the Assembly: "The cities dominate the nation. They are the centers of thought, the sources of enterprise and the originators of great popular movements for good or evil. . . . What the cities are the country will be." [37]

By 1896, Board reports were speaking of "social conditions," even though their description was still in the style of Albert Barnes and James Alexander. In 1898 the Board of Home Missions focused authority in a single executive and appointed

[36] *MGA*, 1891, 60.   [37] *MGA*, 1894, 270.

Charles L. Thompson of New York its General Secretary. Thompson soon recognized that the traditional preoccupation of the Board with western expansion through evangelism must be broadened to allow for an attack on the pressing urban problem. Although retarded by the economic reverses of 1896–1900, by 1903 Board expenditures had risen $90,000 (to $812,668) and the expansion of the Board staff had begun.

Thompson took the first step toward a departmentalized system of work with the appointment of Charles L. Stelzle " to special mission for workingmen." This soon became the Department for Workingmen and was followed by others for School Work, Immigration, and Country Life. By 1912 the system included four Field Secretaries and five departments and annual expenditure had risen to one and a half million dollars. Thompson recognized the need of co-ordination of local effort with that of the church's central agencies. " The cramping effects of extreme independency in Synods or Presbyteries is apparent from experience. . . . Larger plans, conceived in a moral liberal statesmanship, will alone develop these resources [for giving]. No Synod should rob the national enterprise of its cooperation; no Synod should rob itself of the tonic of a large task. The time is past when the fear of centralized power can properly deter intimate cooperation." [38]

The time of such fears had, however, not quite passed. The expansion of the Board staff, increased cost, and the social orientation implicit in its organization and explicit in many of the utterances of its secretaries, especially Stelzle, resulted in the appointment of an Executive Commission to investigate and recommend reorganization. Reporting in 1913, the Commission found no fault with the internal administration of the Board, recognizing that departmentalized work was indispensable in the new circumstances. It yielded to the tradition of local authority, however, by recommending an early end to supervision of mission appointees by field secretaries in favor of local supervision and administration, but vindicated the

[38] MGA, 1912, 138.

"Bureau of Social Service" which now embraced Stelzle's earlier departments of "Workingmen" and "Church and Labor." The major points of the social declarations of 1910 were accepted. "The work of this department embraces a study of moral and social problems, such as 'labor and capital,' 'child welfare,' 'charities,' 'women's work,' 'public health and housing,' 'recreation.' Original research is conducted, such as 'workingmen's leisure time,' 'economic aspects of the liquor problem,' 'attitude of organized labor toward the saloon,' 'the labor press,' 'surveys in cities,' 'efficiency methods for the church.' The Executive Commission has heard considerable criticism of this department but is inclined to the opinion that the criticisms relate to methods rather than to functions; that a Bureau of Social Service 'to study social conditions, etc.,' is needed and should be continued but with such modifications of *methods* as will more fully exalt and magnify the Church as the Body of Christ." [39]

THE ACCEPTANCE OF SOCIAL MINISTRY: CHARLES STELZLE

With the adoption of this report by the General Assembly, the social understanding of the gospel had withstood counter-attack from Presbyterian conservatives. The long-established pietism whose history we have traced in this study is reflected in the admonition to Stelzle, in effect, to pay more attention to evangelism and less to social surveys. Stelzle construed the reorganization recommended by the report as an attack upon himself and resigned in 1913 to work interdenominationally.

Stelzle's career in Presbyterianism was made possible by the leadership of Charles L. Thompson, who created his position and supported him consistently. Until the founding of the Workingmen's Department of the Board, no American denomination had actually changed its organization to meet the problems of industrial urban society. With the appointment of Stelzle, himself one of the prophets, the social gospel for the

[39] *MGA*, 1913, 186.

first time became an affair of the priests of Protestantism.

Stelzle's leadership was significant for two reasons: with Thompson, his work marked the re-entry into organized Presbyterianism of a conception of ministry whose norm was cultural confrontation, not the apologetic and pietistic mood which had seized so many clergymen since the Old School first thrust its concerns to the center of Presbyterianism. Second, wherever the highly ramified American society was accepted as itself a proper object of Christian ministry, specialism in the professional work of the clergy became inevitable. So long as the ministry was confined by traditional conceptions of duty — preaching, pastoral calling, educational and organizational work — the established specialties satisfied its need. But Stelzle called for a thorough knowledge of society and for the use of scientific methods of social research.

A number of new forms of ministry now emerged. Institutionalized centers of social service embracing health education, home visitation, relief, instruction in infant care, consultative services, athletic and other activity programs had already been inaugurated by the Episcopal Church. To this Stelzle added co-operation with trade-unionism and uninhibited debate with the peddlers of the going social panaceas, publication of popular literature on a larger scale, and even arbitration of industrial disputes. Stelzle argued that these were duties of a church authentically concerned with the will of God.

Stelzle was one of the few protagonists of social Christianity to take seriously the ethnic and racial minorities, and published well-supported criticism of Negro public education, health care, and other evidences of social inequities.[40] Ministries to economic, national, and racial minorities required special training and experience. The problem Stelzle dramatized for the ministry was almost limitless. How large a variety of preparatory courses could seminaries afford or even justify as proper to their function? Were not these specialized ministries really

[40] Charles Stelzle, *American Social and Religious Conditions* (New York, 1912), 123 ff.

nonministerial; or if ministerial, actually lay offices? What kind of conception of the ministry did this sudden broadening of the field of church duty imply?

To traditional specialisms, Thompson and Stelzle had added novel ministries whose common denominator was involvement with the American culture. This clearly violated the " spiritual" frontier of the church drawn by Charles Hodge. The vexing modern question of the relative responsibility of clergymen to church and culture, and the problem of the church as itself a minister to culture had been implicitly raised.

Stelzle himself was unconventional, half layman, half clergyman. He never graduated from a college or seminary but was ordained after private study and proof of his pastoral capacity in a St. Louis parish. His early life was dominated not by the spiritual climate of a middle-class congregation but by the struggle of his mother, a widow, to prevent poverty from breaking up her family and by his experience as a child laborer in a tobacco-stripping room, later as a machinist and an amateur student of sociology. Stelzle never disputed the evangelical beliefs mediated by the revival tradition but his operative personal conviction was that the reproduction of Christ's character in men would transform them inwardly and induce them to accept social responsibility. Stelzle's adherence to the familiar ideal of social Christianity — the Fatherhood of God, the brotherhood of man, and the prospect of " bringing in the Kingdom " — was practical. He did not press it to the point of a fresh theology; that remained to Walter Rauschenbusch.

Stelzle's social faith is succinctly captured in the pledge card distributed in the Labor Temple of New York: " I accept the purpose of Jesus — I will help bring in the Kingdom of God." [41] This was the thrust of his religion: to convert the society. He was a millenarian in the optimistic spirit of the sons of both New England and Princeton. But Stelzle's fellowship was not with Princeton and only distantly with New Haven,

---

[41] Stelzle, *A Son of the Bowery* (New York, 1926), 130.

for both of these were committed to the social *status quo.* He shared the mind of Gladden, Strong, Loomis, and Rauschenbusch. He demanded that the church change its theory and attitude concerning poverty and make a fresh approach to the helpless poor, the self-respecting but marginal worker, and the city's focuses of social infection: street corner, saloon, and brothel. He advocated neighborhood surveys and with Thompson sired the sociological services of the Presbyterian Church. He argued that the church should leave its quiet houses and go into the street, theater, lecture hall, and home. He addressed audiences assembled for secular business more often than those convened to worship. In founding the Labor Temple, Stelzle changed a declining Presbyterian Church into a forum for discussion of the issues that troubled anarchists, socialists, paupers, and union members rather than topics favored by clergymen and elders involved in management and finance.

It need not have happened so, but in actual fact the invitation to the world to bring its concerns into the church for decision was attended by a loss of interest in traditional theology and churchmanship amounting almost to a deliberate cutoff. The debate of the 1830's had already been neutralized theologically by the Hodgean truce with the New School and ecclesiastically by the reunion of Presbyterianism in 1870, itself part of a comprehensive movement of Protestant Church cooperation. Stelzle's principal opponents came from a sector of church opinion determined to renew older traditions of piety and apologetics. He blamed Pittsburgh conservatives for their hostility to his work. To them he was simply a socialist; he believed that they represented everything retrograde in the church. He condemned them for refusing to recognize their share in social evil and held them responsible for the widespread rejection of the church among workers. This was not the theological division of the nineteenth century: it was a profound spiritual division around the problem of the church and culture. Stelzle did not hold a new theological position;

the ethical ideal of brotherhood may be treated theologically but in 1900 it had not yet produced a systematic theological affirmation. Stelzle was among the first Presbyterian clergymen to demand that the church be oriented upon ethics and guided by the limpid light of brotherhood.

What did Stelzle owe the tradition of Beecher? Unlike Barnes, Stelzle doubted the utility of revival in the city. The laborer simply would not come to formal church meetings. Revival could purge the heart but it did little to solve the problems that engrossed Stelzle: relief of poverty, reform of labor laws, and the progress of the unions. These were the concerns of workers, not revivalists. Unless the subject under discussion were chosen by the worker, he would not enter the church. To workers Stelzle argued that the personality of Jesus and a society motivated by his ideals would resolve their problems. He was profoundly suspect to a majority of Presbyterians, not least because he described himself as a sociologist.[42]

As for moral societies, Stelzle believed that they often misunderstood the problems they were trying to solve. He opposed the unrestricted use of alcohol but was not prepared to close every saloon and convict every bartender. Bartenders, he argued pleasantly, often understood their customers better than ministers knew their own members; and in any case, barkeepers did more for workers than clergymen did. If saloons were frequented at the expense of family life — to Stelzle this was the real problem — Presbyterian owners of virtually uninhabitable tenements and Presbyterian businessmen who depressed wages were responsible. Overwork caused excessive drinking, he wrote; what man, exhausted to the point of pain, would prefer his wretched and overcrowded tenement home to the good fellowship of a well-polished saloon? Stelzle was impatient at the confusion of poverty with sin, of recreation with degeneracy, and of middle-class morals with religion. He rejected the misunderstanding that underlay the prohibitionist movement. The familiar gospel mission in the slums he held

[42] *Ibid.*, 96 ff.

to be useless for anything but relief of the down-and-outer; its patronizing spirit guaranteed its repudiation by self-respecting workmen. Stelzle was as thoroughgoing a moralist as any member of the New England reform movement but he had grasped the economic and social complexity of the industrial city and demanded a church ministry suited to the new conditions.

Conclusion: The Inner Spiritual Meaning of Ministry

The ministry that American Presbyterians have known has made sense to them when they have understood it as a commission to the church to bring home to the will of man the Word of the sovereign God. Understanding of the "Word of God" among Presbyterians has ranged from restrictive Biblical literalism to the most diffuse moralism; nevertheless, wherever the supremacy of Word in ministry has been acknowledged, the churches have not doubted the authenticity of the work of their clergymen.

The American Calvinist tradition has not been content, however, simply to declare the Word; it has insisted that its ministers effectuate the Word in the minds and motives of its hearers. Revivalism doubted the sufficiency of doctrinal preaching that did not produce actual faith; moralism and pietism represented a determination to enforce God's law on human life. Even when the Word amounted to little more than new law and all but lost sight of the gospel of forgiveness, it lent a certain coherence to the ministry and enabled clergymen to recognize an inner spiritual meaning in their vocation.

The schism that in varying forms afflicted American Presbyterianism from its founding until well into the twentieth century may be described as a dogged quarrel concerning the relation of Word and ministry to the world. The eighteenth-century Awakeners were not content to defend the church as it then existed; they demanded an attack on the world that had penetrated the church and profaned its singleness of mind. Except toward its close, the eighteenth century produced al-

most no theological novelties; Edwards himself, its most crea-
tive mind, was completely loyal to the basic Calvinist theological structure.   Its liveliest spirits were persuaded that the
law kills and the Spirit makes alive, and they called for practical evidences of faith.

The cultural onslaught of the post-Revolutionary period
evoked the schism afresh.   Should the church counterattack,
as Beecher and the New School argued, proposing their peculiar moralism as the fitting form of the Word; or should
Christians withdraw into defense of doctrine and manners?
Throughout the nineteenth century the power of culture steadily increased: the slavery dispute intruded on church life; parishes were engulfed in growing cities; social pluralism made
new demands; the intellectual attack by a scientifically sophisticated humanism had to be met.   By 1910 it was clear to
most Presbyterians that there was no longer any possibility of
withdrawal from culture.   Skepticism concerning ministry to
culture began to disappear from the official policies of the
church and from the minds of an increasing number of Presbyterian ministers.

This did not mean, however, that the Presbyterian clergy
was able to formulate an integral conception of ministry in its
complex new relations to culture.   On the contrary, culture
thrust itself ever more insistently into every archaism of church
belief, custom, and organization.   The most obvious problem
of the minister now is how to do well all that he is expected to
do; but beneath that problem is the unanswered question as
to whether even when he meets these demands successfully he
is a minister of the Word, for he does not yet know the Word
as a Word that strides out to minister concretely to the particular issues of modern times.   Most Protestant ministers are
serving denominational bodies whose vision of ministry is so
blocked by institutional necessities as to be blinded to the
power and right of the Word of God to restore direction and
integrity to the ministry.

If the emerging view of the minister as a " pastoral director " is to do more than democratize the clergyman's relations with the laity, it must be informed by a fresh understanding of the Word in its relations to all that he is required to be, think, say, and do. The Word is the heart not only of worship; the Word gives culture its meaning and it thus saves the world as well as the church that abides in the world.

The Presbyterian clergy is already benefiting from a better grasp of the modern mind. Yet the numerous professional services offered by clergymen are not yet the ministry of Christ's Word by his church. It needs to be understood afresh that the ministry belongs to the church, not the clergy; and that the clergy ministers only on behalf of the church. Improved ministerial training, increasing involvement of laymen in serious forms of ministry, ecumenical advances, and a host of other contemporary church movements furnish vehicles for a critical question that modern Reformed churchmen have not yet answered clearly: What does it mean to regulate every ministerial act of the church completely by the authority of the Word of God?

BIBLIOGRAPHICAL COMMENT

BIBLIOGRAPHY

For the eighteenth century, the *American Bibliography* of Charles Evans furnishes not only a chronological listing of many published treatises but also constitutes an index to the microtext edition of its titles produced by the American Antiquarian Society. Evans' numbers are included in the notes to this study when the document is most readily available in microtext.

Leonard J. Trinterud has assembled a "trial bibliography" of Presbyterian source material to 1788, which exists at Mc-Cormick Theological Seminary, Chicago, Illinois, in typescript. His own use of documents in *The Forming of an American Tradition* (The Westminster Press, 1949) is included in the bibliography to that work.

The mutual involvement of American Presbyterianism and Congregationalism has been noted in this study as elsewhere: for example, Trinterud's "The New England Contribution to Colonial American Presbyterianism" (*CH*, XVII [March, 1948], 1). This requires examination of the New England heritage. Perry Miller indicates in the Foreword to *The New England Mind: The Seventeenth Century* (The Macmillan Company, 1939) that he has deposited a bound set of complete notes to his volume in the Harvard College Library. His

256

"Bibliographical Notes" in *The New England Mind: From Colony to Province* (Harvard University Press, 1953) contain limited comment on his materials, arranged by chapter.

The bibliography included by Prof. William Warren Sweet in *Religion on the American Frontier: 1783–1840,* Vol. II, *The Presbyterians* (Harper & Brothers, 1936), lists a large number of specific sources as well as secondary materials. His catalog of periodicals is especially useful. As yet there is no comprehensive listing of the sources of American church history in the eighteenth and nineteenth centuries.

A complete catalog of periodicals and religious newspapers published in the first part of the nineteenth century has been assembled by Henry Smith Stroupe: *The Religious Press in the South Atlantic States, 1802–1865,* in the Historical Papers of the Trinity College Historical Society, Series XXXII (Durham, N. C., 1956). This bibliography includes historical introductions and critical notes.

The most comprehensive recent bibliography of religion in America is contained in *A Critical Bibliography of Religion in America,* by Nelson R. Burr, Vol. IV (in five parts, bound in two volumes) of *Religion in American Life,* James Ward Smith and A. Leland Jamison, editors (Princeton University Press, 1961). While this work deals less with the vast range of sources than with precritical and critical historical works, it is valuable both for the methodological principles suggested by its manner of organization and its wide reference to recent historiography, both articles and monographs.

Critical studies published between 1953 and 1958 have been reviewed by Robert T. Handy in "Survey of Recent Literature: American Church History," appearing in *CH,* XXVII (June, 1958), 2.

Several recent studies of American benevolent activity include bibliographical essays. *Their Brothers' Keepers,* by Clifford S. Griffin (Rutgers University Press, 1960), dealing with "moral stewardship in the United States, 1800–1865" (the subtitle), reviews both manuscripts and published materials relating to conceptions of morals and ministry by churchmen in New England and the middle states. *Revivalism and Social Reform,* by Timothy L. Smith (Abingdon Press, 1957), furnishes a critical bibliography of both modern historical works and a substantial range of sources, classified under subject-matter heads. A list of reports and other papers published by independent societies and denominational agencies is included by Charles I. Foster in *An Errand of Mercy* (University of North Carolina Press, 1960).

SOURCES

Manuscript materials figuring in this study consist of letters and journals, some personal, others concerned with the official business of independent societies, church boards, educational enterprises, and church judicatories. Manuscript copies of sermons and lecture notes have also been used. The notes contain full titles (or descriptions) of each of these, with information as to their location. Of particular importance are the following classes of manuscript materials.

Correspondence between eighteenth- and nineteenth-century persons such as Joseph Bellamy, Samuel Davies, Samuel Finley, Gilbert Tennent, Benjamin Rush, Charles Nisbet, Jedediah Morse, Alexander McWhorter, Ashbel Green, John Rodgers, Samuel Miller, and others plays a major role in study of this period. The principal collection of Rush's letters is deposited in the Library Company of Philadelphia; the library of the Presbyterian Historical Society in Philadelphia includes many holograph documents of the Tennent brothers, Charles Nisbet, and others; the Kollock Papers are of special significance. The Dreer Collection and the Simon Gratz Papers in the library of the Historical Society of Pennsylvania, also in Philadelphia, are invaluable. *The Journal of the Presbyterian Historical Society* (March and June, 1961; XXXIX, 1 and 2) has published correspondence of Nisbet with William Marshall deposited in its collection. The papers of Charles Hodge await thorough appraisal in the library of Princeton University.

Periodicals, both weekly religious newspapers and quarterlies, come into the foreground early in the nineteenth century.

Religious weeklies followed one another in a confusing succession of failures, mergers, and fresh beginnings. In the South, these are helpfully traced by Stroupe. John H. Rice's *Literary and Evangelical Magazine* was among the earliest; it furnished devotional and instructional readings and carried news of religious affairs. While the weeklies contained considerable material designed to fix the image of the minister as a man of learning and devotion, the substantive issues of church and ministry were hammered out in the quarterlies. Conspicuous among these are: *The Christian Advocate,* edited by Ashbel Green, whose role as a literary figure is rivaled only by his importance as an activist; *The Biblical Repertory and Princeton Review,* the voice of Princeton; and in New England, the *Panoplist,* edited by the group around Jedediah Morse and expressing the thought of the Andover Seminary faculty. A considerable quantity of controversial literature first published in the weeklies and quarterlies was reprinted for general distribution, both bound and in paper: for example, Samuel Miller's famous *Letters to Presbyterians* appeared first in the *Presbyterian,* an Old School weekly published in Philadelphia.

Biographies and autobiographies from the early nineteenth century on demand attention. One full-length manuscript of an unpublished book is deposited in the library of the New Jersey Historical Society: Ashbel Green's *The Life of the Reverend John Witherspoon. . . .* Green composed his own life story, subsequently edited by Joseph H. Jones and published as *The Life of Ashbel Green V.D.M.* (New York, 1849). The lives of Samuel Miller, Charles Hodge, and Archibald Alexander were written by their sons; and Samuel Miller wrote a *Memoir of the Reverend John Rodgers* (New York, 1813). All of these must be used critically, but they contain extensive quotation from letters and other materials of historical value, some of which can be compared with extant manuscripts. An early twentieth-century figure, Charles Stelzle, left an autobiography, *A Son of the Bowery* (New York, 1926), which, like much of Stelzle's writing, was also a tract and for that reason an important document of the period of social ministry.

Certain collections, documentary and historical, may be listed among primary sources. The work of T. C. Pears, Jr., and Guy S. Klett in assembling their *Documentary History of William Tennent and the Log College* (Presbyterian Historical Society, 1940, in mimeograph) brings important sources into a single compass. F. B. Dexter's *Documentary History of Yale University* (New Haven, 1916) illuminates the relations of New England education to the development of the Presbyterian ministry. William B. Sprague's nine-volume *Annals of the American Pulpit* (New York, 1858) furnishes primary materials through extensive quotation from letters and other documents. Sprague's assiduous search for fugitive materials has supplied the historian of eighteenth- and nineteenth-century America with a massive collection of pamphlets on every conceivable subject. Princeton Theological Seminary's Speer Library contains almost one thousand bound volumes of such material; Union Seminary of New York has a smaller quantity of equal significance; and the Andover Library at Harvard concentrates its range of Sprague material in the eighteenth century. Individual references to pamphlet titles are made throughout the notes to this study; their presence in the Sprague Collection is indicated in each case.

Formal literary compositions, published either in collections or by separate title, are indispensable to any grasp of the intellectual history of the eighteenth and nineteenth centuries. The *Works* of John Witherspoon (Edinburgh, 1804–1805) in nine volumes; the first Worcester Edition of the *Works* of Jonathan Edwards (1808–1809) in eight volumes; and the *Lectures on Moral and Political Philosophy* of Samuel Stanhope Smith (Trenton, N. J., 1812) in two volumes; and a number of others are named in notes to this study. Only rarely are these publications available in critical editions; where new issues are available, as with Edwards' *Freedom of the Will*, edited by Paul Ramsey (Yale University Press, 1957), they have been used.

Addresses and books of edification for clergymen and candidates for the ministry furnish information about the mentality and idealism of churchmen in the eighteenth and nineteenth centuries. Among these are Gardiner Spring's *Power of the Pulpit* (New York, 1848); John Breckinridge's *The Christian Pastor* (Baltimore, 1845); Albert Barnes's *The Revival and Its Lessons* (New York, 1859); and Ichabod Spencer's *A Pastor's Sketches or Conversations with Anxious Inquirers . . .* (New York, 1853) in two volumes, and numerous others. This abundant literature opens the mind of the opinion-makers to the historian.

EARLY SECONDARY WRITINGS

For the purposes of this survey, we distinguish between recent critical work and earlier noncritical histories, many of them partisan. These latter hold interest also as sources, since they spell out the lines of controversy and policy advocated by participants in debates in progress at the times of their composition. The Old School apologists figure strongly here: Samuel J. Baird's *History of the New School* (Philadelphia, 1868); Richard Webster's *A History of the Presbyterian Church in America . . . until 1760* (Philadelphia, 1857); Charles Hodge's two-volume *Constitutional History of the Presbyterian Church in the United States of America* (Philadelphia, 1851). On the New School side should be noted William Hill's *History of the Rise, Progress, Genius, and Character of American Presbyterianism . . .* (Washington, 1839), and after the reunion, Charles A. Briggs's *American Presbyterianism* (New York, 1885).

While few Presbyterian writers were untouched by the contest over revival and doctrine, several produced works relatively free of bias. The most complete of these is the two-volume *History of the Presbyterian Church in the United*

States of America, by Ezra H. Gillett (Philadelphia, 1854). More detailed than Baird's *History of the New School,* Gillett recounts the advance of Presbyterianism region by region, period by period. W. H. Foote's two volumes of *Sketches of Virginia* (Philadelphia, 1850 and 1855) are generally accurate and always winsome and astute. Robert Ellis Thompson's *History of the Presbyterian Churches in the United States,* Vol. VI in the American Church History series (New York, 1895), remains standard, although an up-to-date general history of Presbyterianism, written from the point of view of its manifold kinships with other religious and cultural movements, is greatly needed.

Seminary histories figure prominently in Chapters XI and XIII of this study. They vary widely in quality. A few are critical: for example, William Child Robinson's *Columbia Theological Seminary and the Southern Presbyterian Church* . . . (Decatur, Ga., 1931). A number of dissertations in this area have been used to complete the account of the seminaries.

RECENT CRITICAL HISTORIOGRAPHY

In reaction against denominational history that at its best was chronological description and at its worst ranged from polemic to myth, recent critical historians have preferred to treat "the movements of the common Christian mind, the issues which drive planes of cleavage through all denominations . . ." (W. E. Garrison, *The March of Faith: The Story of Religion in America* [Harper & Brothers, 1933], p. 171). While this has produced a rich harvest of understanding, it has often ignored authentic longitudinal traditions in American Christianity. At some points these major traditions correlate with denominational history but they do not often correspond with them. The Calvinist tradition, for example, is shared by Congregationalists and Presbyterians and enters deeply into the fabric of the Protestant Episcopal, Baptist, Disciple, and other denominational groupings; nevertheless, it is distinguishable for historical purposes from the Arminian-Wesleyan tradition. It is a paradox of recent historiography that while proposing to treat the great general movements in American religion largely apart from denominational categories, some authors have inevitably imposed their own identity on their work.

Timothy L. Smith's study of *Revivalism and Social Reform* (Abingdon Press, 1957) is a case in point. "What is proposed is that insofar as equalitarian, perfectionist optimism is a *spiritual* inheritance in America," he states of his book, "John Wesley, George Whitefield, and Samuel Hopkins more than Benjamin Franklin or Jean Jacques Rousseau were its progenitors." (Pp. 8 f.) Smith also writes: "It happens that I hold deep affection for the faith of the revivalists whose labors this book recounts." (P. 10.) His excellent critical study is the product of his commitment both to an American tradition and to scientific historical method.

William Warren Sweet's work is similarly stamped by his identity as a Methodist. Prof. Sidney Mead has written: "Consideration of the total range of [Sweet's] work has led more than one serious student to the conclusion that all his history is shaped to the perspective of a great Methodist circuit." (*CH,* XXII, 1, 42; March, 1953.) Is this altogether a failing? Perhaps it proves that it is impossible for "the historian of Christianity in America . . . to escape entanglement in the subtle relativities of his own denominational heritage." On the other hand, notes Professor Mead, historians "cannot too easily dismiss the possibility that the Methodist is in fact the most influential and most typical American denomination." (P. 43.) The "subjectivity" of Professor Sweet's work makes as substantial a contribution to his writings as his redoubtable care for "objectivity."

Critical readers of recent studies in American church history, including the one here presented on the Presbyterian ministry, do well to listen closely to the counterpoint between an author's identity and his methodology, not only to be warned of his bias but also to profit from his recognition of the participative nature of historiography of the recent past.

Studies by Leonard J. Trinterud, *The Forming of an Ameri-can Tradition* (The Westminster Press, 1949); Lefferts A. Loetscher, *The Broadening Church* (University of Penn-sylvania Press, 1954); and by two older authors, Robert E. Thompson and Charles A. Briggs (both noted above), must be understood in this dual perspective. Open controversy in Pres-byterianism between the historic disputants (Old Side–Old School–Fundamentalist on the one hand; New Side–New School–Broad Churchmanship on the other hand) was quelled in the wake of the Machen dispute; but the interpretation of the history of American Calvinism remains open to scholarly debate. Briggs and Trinterud argue the originality in Presby-terianism of Westminster Calvinism modified by the Great Awakening; Thompson's work is conservative and unitive, hav-ing been written in a period of danger of new schism. With the advantage of nearly a generation's perspective, Loetscher recounts the development of broad churchmanship as a work-ing solution to the persistent threat of schism.

A variety of other recent critical writings, both books and articles, deal with particular questions among Presbyterians or major movements which affected them. In the former group, for example, is the effect of the slavery question on the clergy: the article by C. Bruce Staiger, "Abolitionism and the Presby-terian Church Schism, 1837–1838" (*Mississippi Valley Histori-cal Review*, XXXVI, 391 f.), and my own article on "The Role of the South in the Presbyterian Schism of 1837–1838" (*CH*, XXIX, 1, 44 f.; see bibliography in note 49, p. 63); also Lewis G. Van der Velde's *The Presbyterian Churches and the Federal Union, 1861–1869* (Harvard University Press, 1932). In the section "Bibliography" above have been mentioned examples of the latter class of works, analyses of major move-ments that affected the Presbyterian clergy: Foster's *An Er-rand of Mercy* and Griffin's *Their Brothers' Keepers*. In this group should be included John Bodo's *The Protestant Clergy and Public Issues, 1812–1848* (Princeton University Press, 1954).

INDEX

DATE DUE